"Looking back, the writing was pretty damn good at times. Remember, there were no laugh tracks. There were no retakes. It was on the air live, and damn it, you had to get your laughs, or you could get fired. The comics would throw fits if they weren't getting laughs."

— Charles Isaacs

"I miss some of the excitement. I miss the thing that I imagine an explorer on a safari down the Amazon would miss, with all the danger and the mosquitoes and the crocodiles and the heat. When he comes back years later, it was *an adventure*. Which it isn't today. You didn't know what you were going to get. It was closer to a World Series ballgame; you didn't always know what you had."

— Sol Saks

Norman Panama and Melvin Frank, 1942

The Laugh Crafters

Comedy Writing in Radio and TV's Golden Age

by Jordan R. Young

Vintage Comedy Series

Past Times Publishing Co.

for John and Larry Gassman

THE LAUGH CRAFTERS
Comedy Writing in Radio and TV's Golden Age

FIRST EDITION
Published by Past Times Publishing Co.,
P.O. Box 142, Beverly Hills CA 90213

1 3 5 7 9 8 6 4 2

Printed in the United States of America on acid-free paper ∞

Table of Contents

Preface

I live in the past, and I readily admit it. In fact, I've made a career out of it. I would love to have written comedy for radio in its heyday. Having grown up during the television era — Jack Benny made his TV debut the week I was born — I did not have this opportunity. As a show business historian, however, I have been able to live this dream vicariously, interviewing many of those who did.

For an oral history of radio drama (a work-in-progress at this time) I have interrogated a number of comedy writers about their work in radio and early television. And while I have sat at the feet of countless actors, comedians, musicians, announcers, producers and other industry veterans, the writers were a revelation. They proved, invariably, to be the best raconteurs and the most articulate interview subjects.

While screenwriters have finally won a measure of recognition in recent years, far less attention has been paid the writers of radio and television's Golden Age. Several of the writers featured in this book have been celebrated for their creative efforts of the 1960s and '70s, but most have seldom, if ever, talked about their work in the early days of broadcasting — the '30s, '40s and '50s — a decidedly different era of popular culture that has been largely forgotten.

I have been a lover of comedy and comedians all my life. This book may present a somewhat unflattering portrait of some of my favorite entertainers. But as we know, there are at least two sides to every story. Behind every successful radio and TV comic was a hard-working writer — or a platoon of them — who toiled in virtual anonymity. It is high time these invisible comedians took a bow.

These interviews were conducted between 1990 and 1995. Many of the subjects required little or no prodding, and since my philosophy as an interviewer is simply, "shut up and listen," I let them go right on talking. I have edited the interview transcripts only slightly and rephrased next to nothing.

The delay in completing this volume is due to various factors. My previous book, *Spike Jones Off the Record,* required a lengthy hiatus. I also felt a need to experience this book on a deeper level. Having written and staged a number of plays in recent years — and adapted one for a Hollywood radio production performed by veteran actors — I now feel a little less like an outsider than I did when I began this project. Making an audience laugh is one of the hardest writing tasks there is — and one of the most gratifying.

Special thanks to Randy Skretvedt, my collaborator on the aforementioned oral history, for joining me on the Hal Kanter interview and posing some of the questions asked in others; John and Larry Gassman, the twin encyclopedias of old-time radio, upon whose computerized brains I often rely; and Kathy O'Connell, my eagle-eyed editor, for advice, corrections and other favors.

Thanks are due also to Jeff Abraham, Joe Adamson, Norman Corwin, Jessica Curry, John Dunning, Parker Fennelly, Mike Hamilburg, Ruth Henning, Ronnie James, Mitch Kaplan, Frances Langford, Bob Levy, Dennis McLellan, Gregg Oppenheimer, Phil Rapp, Keith Scott, Lionel Stander, Pam Young; ABC; Academy of Motion Picture Arts and Sciences, Margaret Herrick Library; CBS Entertainment; Friends of Old-Time Radio; Hope Enterprises Inc.; *The Los Angeles Times;* NBC Inc.; New York Public Library at Lincoln Center; Pacific Pioneer Broadcasters; Paramount Pictures; SPERDVAC (Society to Preserve and Encourage Radio Drama, Variety and Comedy); Universal Pictures; University of Wyoming, William Robertson Coe Library; Warner Bros. Inc.; Writers Guild of America, West.

Finally, I owe a debt of gratitude to the subjects, without whose enthusiastic cooperation there would be no book.

Jordan R. Young
September 1998

About the Author

Jordan R. Young is a show business historian whose work has appeared in *The New York Times, The Washington Post, The Los Angeles Times, The Christian Science Monitor* and other publications. He has written 12 books, including *Spike Jones Off the Record, Acting Solo, The Beckett Actor, Reel Characters* and *The Nostalgia Entertainment Sourcebook*. His original plays include *Hollywood Is a State of Mind*, a trilogy of one-acts produced by California Artists Radio Theatre. He has worked as a writer or consultant on documentary films, radio and TV shows, stage productions, compact discs, websites and online publications.

PARKE LEVY

"Every joke is like a new-born baby. You never know how it's going to turn out."

For Parke Levy, who failed to graduate college because he was too busy writing professionally, it turned out spectacularly well. Three decades of writing for radio and television — beginning with *The Jack Pearl Show*, and culminating in the long-running *December Bride* — made him a millionaire, and enabled him to retire in his mid-fifties.

Levy, who was born in Philadelphia July 15, 1908, earned a scholarship to Temple University. In addition to writing campus publications and stage productions, he spent much of his time grinding out pulp fiction under pseudonyms. "I was making so much money writing detective stories that after five and one-half years at Temple, I quit school," he recalled.

Before long he discovered a penchant for comedy. "I think I inherited a sense of humor from my father, who was a shoemaker. He used to tell jokes to his customers while they were waiting," said Levy. "You are born with the ability to be a comedy writer. It's almost like being a computer; you associate thoughts and words, and that's what makes jokes." He never laughed at his own jokes, however: "I would go see a show, and sit there terrified. The only reason I ever went was to see if the people would laugh."

Levy's computerized brain made him much in demand in the early days of radio — beginning when the medium was virtually in its infancy — writing for Al Jolson, Joe Penner, Bert Lahr, Abbott and Costello, Ed Gardner and others. It also brought him to the attention of Broadway producers, who hired him as a script doctor, and Hollywood studios, which imported him to the movie capital on several occasions. Asked for his advice to aspiring writers in later years, he warned, "Whatever they do, beware of California. It's a deadly place. You mustn't go there. You must be sent for."

After reaping the hard-earned reward of his labors, by creating three television series, Levy decided it was time to quit the rat race. He bowed out in 1965 after a running battle with CBS over creative control of his show, *Many Happy Returns,* which he refused to relin-

Jack Pearl, aka Baron von Münchhausen, is remembered for the catch phrase, "Vas you dere, Sharlie?"

quish. "Three out of every five people I know in this business either have nervous tics, bad stomachs or they drink like fish," he noted. "There's a great deal of tension in this kind of work. I got out before it got to me."

Levy busied himself with investments, travel, gardening and painting in later years. ("I've been asked to write my own book 100 times, but I'm just lazy," he asserted.) He died March 8, 1993 in Los Angeles, at 84, after a long illness. Despite his failing health, he never lost his sense of humor. At the conclusion of our first interview session, he quipped, "That's about as much time as I can give you, 'cause I'm very old and very sick, and I have to cater to four women tonight yet... would you believe three?"

You began in radio in 1932. How did you get your start?

Luck is as important in life as talent and other things. Timing and luck. I was at Temple University in Philadelphia. I was a big shot — I started their magazine, *The Owl,* and I wrote their first four musical comedies, one of which was sold to Broadway. And Jack Pearl was appearing at the Ritz Theater in a show called *Pardon My English,* a George and Ira Gershwin show. I had heard Pearl on the air [as Baron von Münchhausen] two or three times, and I said to myself, "I can write funnier jokes than that." I was at the university; I sat down at the typewriter and I typed out six jokes that I made up.

How did you get the material to Pearl?

I called the Ritz Carlton where Pearl was staying. I said, "My name is Parke Levy." He said, "I never heard of you." Which made me feel good right away. He said, "What do you want with me?" I said, "I wrote some jokes, and I think they're good for your program." He said, "I'll tell you what — I'm so busy right now, this is the matinee — why don't you come down tonight and read your jokes to me?" I had to take the Elevated [train] from where I lived; they had advertisers over the seats of the subway cars. There was one called Cook's Tour, a travel agency. "Take a Cook's Tour." So I made up a joke: "Baron, I was on this ship, and it sank, and I saved 600 chefs." He said, "You saved 600 chefs? How could 600 chefs be on one ship?" "It was a Cook's Tour." So I wrote that down.

Very clever.

I went down to the theater later that day, as Jack had instructed me, and I sat in his dressing room. When he came to Cook's Tour, he just broke up. He said, "Oh, this is funny. I'll be in touch with you." I got a call three or four days later from the J. Walter Thompson Agency, would I please come down. They wanted to use the material. I went to the theater that night, to the broadcast, and when Jack Pearl said, "How could 600 chefs be on one ship?"— "It was a Cook's Tour" — the whole fuckin' audience fell down. And I was signed up. The jokes I had at the matinee were nothing compared to the Cook's Tour.

You found gold on the subway that day.

This is why I say timing and luck are such an important part of your success — if I hadn't taken the Elevated back to my house and seen that sign — and if Pearl hadn't been busy, and had listened to my earlier jokes — I would never be here, in Beverly Hills.

Pearl's radio show was a big success, wasn't it?

Oh, sure. He had a pretty good ear for what was funny. He was getting $5,000 a week — which would be like $50,000 now — when nobody else was anywhere near that. He lived at the St. Moritz Hotel on Central Park West, and I had gone up to his apartment to bring a script to him. As we get outside it's snowing like a sonuvabitch. I said to Jack, "Why don't we take a cab to the studio?" What the hell, it was like a dollar a ride. He says, "Oh, no, this is air is so good, so invigorating..." In the meantime, the snow is falling all over, and I'm absolutely miserable 'cause it's going right through my bones. We walked about a half a block, and as we do a bus pulls up to the curb. And Jack says, "You know, Parke, maybe you're right. Maybe we should get out of the snow." And we jumped on the bus. This is for a guy who's making $5,000 a week.

How much did you get paid for writing The Jack Pearl Show?

I started at $50 a week. In those days, they didn't pay a lot of money. I took Joe Penner from nowhere to number one on the air, and he raised my salary from $150 a week to $200 a week. I think Jack Benny set a world's record when he paid Harry Conn $750 a week — all of Broadway gasped. That was a stupendous salary. The thing I remember about Jack Pearl, he was incredibly tight, almost worse than Dennis Day, who was the king of all cheapskates. Dennis was so cheap — one time when we started his TV show out here, we went out to lunch. And it was just a plain lunch, I guess six or seven writers and producers — and we're sitting there 'til my ass gets paralyzed. I couldn't understand the star not saying to the waiter...

"Bring me the check."

Finally I thought, this must be a real cheapie, so I said with all enthusiasm, "Look, I know we're going to be together for a long, long time, so why don't we set a precedent and we all go Dutch? With that, the color came back into Dennis' face, and we all went Dutch, and we did from then on. He had a reputation for being cheap.

Jack Benny had the facade, but the cheapskate was really Dennis Day.

Al Jolson was also one of the cheap men. I put Jolson on radio. He would pay me in those days, I think $150 a week, and we would go walking — we'd go for a stroll, and I'd say, "Al, you haven't paid me for four weeks now." He'd say, "Parke, it's a beautiful day... the sun is shining, people are smiling, and you want to talk about money? You ought to be ashamed of yourself." I finally got my money; I had to threaten to sue him.

How did you make the move from Jack Pearl to Joe Penner?

I wrote for Pearl with Billy K. Wells, and Billy's son George, who was sort of an apprentice. Billy called me one night when we were doing the Baron and said, "Parke, you've got to do a favor for me." He said, "I've signed to write a program for a burlesque comedian named Joe Penner." He was very sick; I don't know whether it was alcohol, but he was so sick. He said, "Parke, you've got to do this..." I said, "But I don't know the man." Billy said, "Well, he talks about a duck — he's a burlesque comic. I promised J. Walter Thompson I'd get the script to them." I said, "When?" He said, "Tomorrow

Joe Penner's trademark line — "Wanna buy a duck?" — made him rich overnight, but his success was short-lived.

morning." This was eight o'clock at night.

So you burned the midnight oil...

I said, "Billy, I don't know what the hell to do. I'll write it, but it's very hard to write for a man you've never seen, never heard." I had a little room on West Third Street — so I sat down at my typewriter, and I wrote a half-hour script and took it to J. Walter Thompson.

Was Joe Penner appreciative of your efforts?

The night of the first Joe Penner broadcast we were at the St. Moritz. I was a young boy, in my early twenties; here I had written what was to be the number one show on radio. There were a number of celebrities there. Joe was sitting very close to me — he leaned over and said, "That was a wonderful script you wrote for me tonight,

Parke, and I don't know how to thank you." And I said, "Oh, this is nothing. Wait 'til you see the one I'll have coming up for you." And his wife, Eleanor, happened to be sitting next to me in a gold brocaded evening gown, trimmed in mink or something. I was half looped by this time, and as I said to Joe, "You don't know what I have planned for you in the future" — I made a sweeping gesture with my arm, and I knocked a tumbler of champagne right into her new gown. I wanted to cry, and Joe put his arm around me and said, "Parke, you write scripts like this for me every week and you can dump champagne on Eleanor every week."

Did Penner decide what worked for him and what didn't, in terms of material?

To a point. He addressed it to his straightmen, Monk Purcell and Dick Ryan. He would look at them, and if they nodded, he would buy it. He let them serve as his advisers. There was an attorney who would sit in and give his opinions.

What do you think made Joe Penner such a huge success?

The children. Then along came a guy with a new brand of comedy, and his name was Jack Benny. He became kind of the new *in* guy, and Joe resented this. And he said to me, "Maybe you can get me a little more sophisticated, like this fellow Jack Benny." And I said, "Joe, when you lose the kids, you lose everybody. You're the kid's comic." He didn't like that too much.

His primary appeal was to children, then. Did he understand what made him successful?

I think he understood it, but I don't think he thought that they were indispensable, let me put it that way. He thought he could still be a big star without the children. And he was wrong in that respect.

I wondered what caused his popularity to fall off so quickly.

So abruptly. I stayed with him for two years. I came out to Hollywood to do pictures, and Joe would come out here to eventually do his pictures. He was basically a very sweet man. He'd look at me as if he was dying to ask me to come back and write for him, because he tried all these Jack Benny writers, Harry Conn and others, and they couldn't write for him. They couldn't sell him — he was a kid's comic. And I would look at Joe as if I knew he wanted to ask me to come back and do his writing, but our pride kept us apart.

Over the years you worked in radio, how did the medium change?

More important sponsors came in, I guess. And they found out that radio was such a big draw, they combined radio with personal appearances. Like with Joe Penner. We traveled all over, playing vaudeville, and did the broadcast from the cities where we were playing. Whatever studio was available. We toured around the country, certainly through the Midwest — all the big cities where they had these vaudeville houses.

This was all just to plug the radio show?

No, it was to cash in. The radio show didn't pay him any money. You can tell how much money Penner was making — he paid me $150 a week to write his program. But he made $100,000 a week maybe, playing the theaters. The line extended like you can't believe —they had policemen keeping the people in line for maybe two blocks.

The radio show sold the tickets.

That's right. It just mushroomed. Wherever we went, we were invited to the swankiest restaurants — and the owners always thought they had a novel publicity idea when they would have Joe Penner hold a live duck, 'cause his slogan was, "Wanna buy a duck?" They gave him a live duck for the photographers to snap, and the ducks always shit all over him - - all over his pretty white suit. The suit would be immaculate, and he would have that smile, and the duck would be shitting all over him. He tried to get me to hold 'em, and I being a gentleman said, "Fuck off." I wouldn't hold the duck.

You also wrote for Ben Bernie in the early days of radio. How did his "feud" with Walter Winchell develop?

They were the best of friends. That was a put-on. I was with Bernie at that time — three years writing for Ben. I did a great deal of writing for Winchell too.

Bernie had a flowery delivery...

I wouldn't say flowery. In what respect do you mean?

Sort of effeminate. How would you describe it?

It's hard to describe Ben. He had a very appealing personality, especially through the Midwest, Chicago. He was a sportsman — he lived for the horses. Ben Bernie was a guy who went to the racetrack. He never would read the script for the broadcast. He would come tearing in from the track and come right into the rehearsal booth where the sponsor was sitting — and he would read the script — and read so poorly that we would grit our teeth. We'd say, "Fer Chrissake, why doesn't he read sometime — look at the script *once?*" And we — my collaborator, Alan Lipscott, and I — decided to fix him.

How did you accomplish this?

We used to write the introduction to all the musical numbers. Let's say the song was "I Love You, Susie." Ben would say, "Now, me and the Half and Half Lads are gonna play 'I Love You, Susie.' This is for all guys who like girls named Susie." Then they would go into the number. His favorite at that time was making jokes about Myrna Loy.

As sort of a running gag...

We decided this time to fix him. The song that was to be played was "Song of India." And we wrote a little thing, in conspiracy, my collaborator and I: "Now me and the Half and Half Lads are going to play 'Song of India'. Ahhh, Myrna, if I could only get India." We spelled it I-n-d-i-a. Now, when you read it, it looks like a geographical joke. Well, the sponsors were in the booth, Ben comes rushing in from the track and picks up the script — we know he hasn't looked at the goddamn thing — and he gets up there and says, "Ahhh, Myrna, if I could only get India."

Great. I'll bet Bernie never did that again.

You should have seen the pandemonium in the sponsor's booth. The buzzer's goin', the fuckin' orchestra fell right down — they fell down on the floor, they didn't know anything about this. Bernie comes over, he says, "What is all this *gelachter*?" — the Jewish word for laughter is gelachter. He says, "What is it, a travel joke? I don't get it. What's so funny about India?" We said, "Ben, read it out loud, and read it slowly. He says, "Now, me and the Half and Half Lads are gonna play 'Song of India'... Ahhh, Myrna, if I could only get... you sons of bitches." From that day on, he read the script.

This didn't go out over the air...

No, no, in the booth. The sponsors always came down to every rehearsal.

Didn't you rehearse at Bernie's hotel sometimes?

We used to rehearse in his beautiful living room, I think at the Sherry Netherland Hotel. And his wife, Wes, had two little dogs she was crazy about. But they used to come running in and out during rehearsal, and we would be annoyed. Ben used to say, "Wes, will you keep the goddamn dogs outta here?" And one day he decided to fix *her*. He went to a confectionery shop, and he had a replica of a dog's stool made out of the best chocolate in the world. Ben had a beautiful sofa. Right at the beginning of the rehearsal, he put this chocolate thing which looked like a dog's doo on the sofa, and he yelled, "Wes, will you come in here! Wes!" She says, "What is it, dear?" Ben says, "Look what those goddamn dogs did! I told you to keep 'em out of here." She said, "Oh, my God. I'll pick it up..." He says, "Don't bother." And with that, he puts it in his mouth and eats the whole goddamn thing. Wes almost fainted. She took the dogs out from that time on.

Ben Bernie was quite a character.

Yeah. Nothing compared to some of the others...

Like Al Jolson?

Oh, he was a crazy man. To tell you what kind of a guy Jolson was, he got a request from the head of NBC at that time, John Reynolds. The wire said, "Dear Al, You've sung 'Toot, Toot, Tootsie' on the first three shows, and I think you ought to give it a rest now, until later in the series." The following week — Jolson gets on the air, he says, "By special request of my dear friend John Reynolds, I'm now going to do 'Toot, Toot, Tootsie.' " Can you believe that, after that wire? May he rest in peace, that prick.

I gather Jolson was a difficult man to work with.

Very difficult. I can only tell you, one night I got a call: "Parke, how're you coming along with the script?" It was about midnight. I said, "All right. I've got some good California jokes." Al says, "Change 'em all." I'm going to Florida instead." I said, "Okay, I'll have 'em in the morning." So I get to work. I get a call about three hours later: "Parke, did you change it from California to Florida?" I said, "Yeah." Jolson says, "Well, change it again." I said, "What do you mean, change it again?" He says, "Make it I'm going off the air." I said, "*What?*" He said, "Yeah, I'm going off the air. I've got $2 million in Warner Bros. stock. My little Ruby's out there, I don't know what the hell she's doing out there, and I don't like it." Al says, "I don't need this fuckin' money, and I'm gettin' off." And he did.

How long did you write for Jolson?

I wasn't with him too long, several months I guess. I didn't like him 'cause he didn't pay me the money. I had to beg him for the money. He was a cheap bastard. We became friends later on. He came out to California — I found out Al was related on my wife's side, and we became very friendly. But I always liked Harry, his brother, much better as a person.

It was impossible to be friends with Jolson while you were working with him?

You just couldn't, no. He was so arrogant. His conceit was enough to kill you. He used to like to take walks with me around Times Square, so the people could see him, and all that. While I worked for him he was mind-boggling; you didn't know what the hell he was thinking. But I survived.

You worked on Bert Lahr's radio show, along with Harry Tugend. Did you have a rough time writing for him?

Bert Lahr was very difficult. He would ask people in elevators if a joke was funny. That's how nervous he would be about his material. I'm not exaggerating. He would take a total stranger: "Is this funny, Miss? 'A white horse bites a black dog...' " And if she didn't laugh, he'd ask us to change the joke.

Did Lahr have any feeling for the material himself, whether it was funny or not?

Once in a while he would give out with that laugh. But he was the most nervous man — the most insecure man I ever worked for. And yet his son, John Lahr, in his book calls me and Herman Wouk [two of] the best comedy writers in America at the time.

Carroll Carroll said Lahr couldn't resist making a funny face — the studio audience would laugh like crazy at a straight line, because he was mugging.

Oh, yeah, we had that problem with him. We'd tell him not to mug, because the audiences at home didn't know what the hell was so funny.

You also wrote for Ed Wynn in the '30s, not on radio but on Broadway.

I doctored shows, some alone, some with Alan Lipscott. Alan and I took a flop called *Hooray for What?* with Ed Wynn, written by Howard Lindsay and Russell Crouse, two fine writers. When we got to Boston, the theater had two rows sold out on Saturday night — the front two rows, nothing else. And in two weeks, the theater filled because we wrote wonderful, hilarious material. I say this with all modesty. And then it came to New York and the critics raved. And Wynn took credit for the material. He said he wrote it all.

Most of the comedians did that then, didn't they? They took the credit.

Oh, sure. A lot of those guys like people to think they write their own material. So we had to take ads in *Variety* saying *"Hooray for What?* Hooray for Parke Levy and Alan Lipscott, who made *Hooray for What?* what it is today."* Ed Wynn finally acknowledged it, years later.

I understand you were one of the original writers on Duffy's Tavern.

It's a long story. When I was writing the Joe Penner series, we had a director from J. Walter Thompson who got $50 a week. His name was Ed Gardner. He'd just sit around with a stopwatch in his hand — nobody paid any attention to this guy. But I did; I befriended him. We became lifelong friends.

He had greater ambitions than holding a stopwatch...

Yes, he did. He was a bright guy. Next thing I knew, he was directing a program called *This is New York* with Deems Taylor. He asked me if I wanted to do some writing with him, and I did that. After that I didn't hear anything from Ed for some time. Then he got with a guy named Abe Burrows, and they had an idea for a show called *Duffy's Tavern.* They came East, and Ed wanted to know if I would write for him, and I did, for two or three years. There was another writer, a fine writer named Mac Benoff.

Ed Gardner originally created the character of Archie, the bartender, on This is New York.

Yes, that's right. He couldn't find an actor, and he finally said he was going to try it himself. He auditioned a few guys, real New York *dese* and *dose* guys. But he settled for himself and it was a wise choice.

Do you think Gardner had ambitions as an actor when you first met him?

Yes, certainly. He wanted to be an actor very much; I think he'd like to have been a star in any sense of the word. Incidentally, on *Duffy's Tavern,* Ed would do the broadcast from the stage of one of the studios, and he would work behind what looked like a little counter. This was most unusual, but we soon found out the reason. His knees were shaking so — this is the truth — he didn't want the studio audience to see it. He was so nervous, my chore, and sometimes Abe Burrows', was to go into the men's room and take him off the john because he'd get diarrhea five minutes before he was to go on the air. That's a fact. In the early weeks of the show he was in the john right up until the gong.

I understand Ed Gardner was a tough taskmaster.

Duffy's Tavern was a helluva show, a well-written show. It was, I would say, the best written radio show ever. But we used to curse Ed Gardner under our breath because that son of a bitch was so meticulous. We would have a line that would go, "I love you darling, so please kiss me." This is 4 o'clock in the morning — we'd work all night, at the Hotel Royalton. About four hours after we wrote the line, Ed would say, "Wait a minute. I was just thinking about that line. Archie wouldn't say 'darling,' he would say 'sweetheart.' So we had to go back and change it. Then about an hour later, he'd say, "Wait a minute. You know that line we changed? He wouldn't say 'Kiss me,' he'd say 'Give me some lip'." This went on and on. I had a daughter about a year old, I was anxious to get home — and that son of a bitch made us write — but we were so proud of it, we never openly rebelled.

Not openly.

However, he would call me sometimes, say five o'clock in the morning, and he would say, "Parke, I'm going out of my mind." In absolute panic. His father, I believe, spent some time in an insane asylum, and Ed was always obsessed with the fact that he too would get wacky. I used to say to him, "Listen, you dumb bastard, you've been taking Benzedrine, and then you've been taking downers. You're taking uppers and downers — you've got a civil war going on in your head. " I'd calm him down and console him, and we'd go to work again the next day.

Abe Burrows said in his autobiography that Benzedrine really kept the writers awake.

Abe used to sit there with the Benzedrine in his nose. Ed and Abe had it in their nose all the time. I smoked cigarettes then, but I just wouldn't take the Benzedrine.

You wrote the show with Burrows and Mac Benoff, and Gardner would function primarily as the editor?

Yes. He was a very good editor. Between screwing and editing he kept pretty busy.

Between screwing and editing?

Screwing, yes. Anything that walked — if it breathed, he'd go for it. Gardner was a real cocksman. He was married at that time to Shirley Booth, a fine actress. Ed cheated like mad. But it never bothered him.

Did you have any problems on Duffy's Tavern *with interference from the ad agency?*

I know I didn't have — I wasn't that important on this thing. And Ed Gardner had a way of putting people down, especially agency people. He wouldn't have brooked any great interference. And the agency evidently sensed that the show was going to be a winner because they didn't do anything to interfere with what Ed was going to do or say. They thought it was going to be a hit, and they left him pretty much to himself.

You also wrote for Abbott and Costello's radio show.

I can't think of anything humorous. In fact, I found Costello to be...

Difficult to work with?

Not a nice guy. And Abbott wasn't much better. I wasn't with them very long. They settled my contract for a lot of money. I insisted on that, 'cause they refused to do new material.

They wanted to keep doing their old routines.

That's right. Monte Hackett, the very prominent agent who got me the assignment, came to me and said "The boys are afraid to do new material, Parke. I didn't know that." He said, "Do you want to get out?" I said, "Of course, I want to get out." So he gave me a few thousand dollars; that's what they did in those days.

Did Abbott and Costello participate at all in the writing of the show, or the editing?

No, no. I got a script together. I was head writer. Whoever the writers were, I would compile a script, and put my own material in — after all, I was getting top money, so I had to have something by way of a contribution — and then I would give it to Costello. I think I was only two weeks with them. They didn't like any of the material. And I finally said, "Look, if you're not going to take a chance with new material, you don't need me. Let me out." I was on a firm 13-week contract as I recall. I forget whether I was getting $1,000 or $1,250; I know it was up around $10,000 when they settled with me.

You worked on My Friend Irma *for a long time.*

Seven years, I think. I was writing some show and I got a call from a guy named Cy Howard. I went over to talk to him; this frenetic guy Howard was dancing around. He says, "Here's a script, will you read it?" When I finished reading, he said, "Well, do you think you could write this show?" I said, "I don't see why not, it's already been written. This is *My Sister Eileen*." He says, "Shhh. Don't say that. They're talking about suing us." I said, "Look. You indemnify me and I'll write it. But I'm telling you right now, I don't want to be any part of this thing, because you're going to be sued some day."

Cy Howard is supposedly the "creator" of that show.

Yes. He didn't create it. The guy that created *My Sister Eileen* created it. Cy Howard couldn't write his name.

So Howard took Eileen *and just reworked it a little bit?*

Yep. There was a big lawsuit. And of course CBS did pay off in the end; it cost them a lot of money. And I'll tell you something else. Howard would never let the writers come down to the show. I

Lou Costello, singer Marilyn Maxwell, Parke Levy, bandleader Skinnay Ennis, Bud Abbott and producer Nat Wolff, 1946.

would get a phone call: "We need a joke, Parke..." In all modesty I was very fast in those days — and he couldn't get over it. "Parke, you're wonderful, I don't know what I'd do without you." But he never — he had a secretary — her instructions were to see that the writers never came down to the broadcast.

You didn't write Irma *when it went to television, did you?*

No. I was pissed off that Harry Ackerman didn't ask me to come on the television show. About the second week, they got in trouble, and he said, "Parke, would you like to come on, 'cause you know the show so well, and do the TV program?" And I, in so many words, said, "Harry, go fuck yourself. You can only finger me once." I said, "You had no business not including me as the head writer, all the time I spent making this show a hit."

You did work on the film version of My Friend Irma, *however.*

Hal Wallis didn't know what to do with Martin and Lewis, and neither did Cy Howard. They didn't call me in until they were desperate. And then I wrote one or two outstanding sequences. One was
in the parking lot where Jerry Lewis runs over all the cars, that was
mine. Then they invited me to work on the second picture, which
was not so good.

Was there a problem in adapting the show from radio to film?

No. I was fixing Broadway shows in the meantime. Radio was not
the only medium, as far as my writing was concerned. Once you've
had theatrical writing, you can go into the other mediums. The
switch from legitimate theater to motion pictures is not so great.

Was it easier or more difficult to write for radio than other media?

It was easier to write for radio because your imagination has no
limits. You have to be specific in the theater and in film.

Which was more nerve-wracking, radio or television?

TV. Because I think looking at something — if there was any kind of
error, besides hearing it you saw it — so it was double the crime.
On radio, you could say something that wasn't the most logical
thing in the world, and it could get by, because nobody's sitting on
it. So we had to be more particular in television, much more.

So television was the more stressful medium?

Oh, yes. I would say so. We did 39 shows every year in radio; we
always took the summer off, 13 weeks. Television, I don't think you
could do 39 shows; I never did. Even *December Bride* when it was
going well, we never did 39. Maybe 26.

What were some of the special challenges in writing for radio?

I did it so long and so easily, that I never regarded it as much of a challenge, radio. The main thing was to keep it clean, because censors were a pain in the ass in those days.

Did you experience any trouble with the censors?

Yes. But not too much. When I was doing *December Bride* on TV — to show you what's happened with obscenity — we had a joke in there about a girdle. The sponsor said if we didn't take out the word "girdle," which they considered shocking, they would not pay for the entire show, which was $30,000 in those days. Today the word "girdle" would not even be looked at — I tune in, I can't believe my ears.

Where did you get the idea for December Bride?

I'm the only guy who's made a fortune off his mother-in-law. I wrote *December Bride* first as a book. The publisher liked it; he thought the middle of it was a little repetitious, and wanted to know if I could add to it. I said "Sure," but then I was offered the *My Friend Irma* contract; that kept me tied up for seven years. But *December Bride* was based upon my mother-in-law. She was a widow, very attractive — not the stereotype. She was quite a gal. And being attractive and not too old, she attracted a great many men. One guy was captain of a fishing boat. Instead of bringing her a bouquet of roses when he came to see her, he would have a large newspaper-wrapped package — he would come courting her with his fish offerings.

Harry Morgan made his television debut on that show.

I gave Harry his start as a comedian; he was always a fine dramatic actor. Harry was the neighbor on *December Bride*. Dean Miller played the son-in-law on the show; he used to come to rehearsal always with a black luncheon box, in which he always had a hard-boiled egg and some bread. Harry Morgan has a great sense of humor. I'll never forget the day he sneaked into the dressing room and took out the hard-boiled egg and put a raw egg in. Dean always used to crack the egg on the edge of the luncheon box...

I'm beginning to get the picture.

Dean Miller chased Harry Morgan around the entire lot. He was livid, because naturally when he hit the egg it splattered all over him.

CREDITS

Radio: *The Jack Pearl Show, The Rudy Vallee Show, The Joe Penner Show, The Chase and Sanborn Hour (The Bert Lahr Show); Ben Bernie, The Old Maestro; Presenting Al Jolson, This is New York, Duffy's Tavern, The Abbott and Costello Show, Listen America, My Friend Irma, December Bride* (creator-director).

TV: *The RCA Victor Show, December Bride* (creator), *Pete and Gladys* (creator), *Many Happy Returns* (creator).

Film: Paramount educational shorts, *Higher and Higher* (dialogue), *George White's Scandals, Having Wonderful Crime, Earl Carroll Sketchbook, Hit Parade of 1947, My Friend Irma, My Friend Irma Goes West.*

Theater (in collaboration with Alan Lipscott): *Hooray for What?, Right This Way* (lyrics only), *Three After Three, Streets of Paris, Keep Off the Grass, Walk With Music, Off the Record, Johnny On the Spot.*

PAUL HENNING

"There are writers people don't really know who contributed a great deal to comedy," asserted veteran comedy writer Hal Kanter. "A highly-overlooked folklorist is Paul Henning. A helluva comedy writer."

Henning was born on a hog farm near Independence, Missouri, on September 16, 1911. His first exposure to radio was listening to a homemade crystal set his brother crafted from an oatmeal box. He still recalls the excitement: "At night — that's when you got the best reception — you'd take the cat's whisker [a piece of wire] and touch various facets of this crystal — and you'd hear voices!"

Before the Missouri farm boy discovered his true calling — and long before Dennis Potter created *The Singing Detective* for British television — Henning threatened to become the singing attorney, simultaneously working toward two disparate professions. While appearing on radio as a singer in the early '30s, "I was going to law school at night and jerking sodas during the day," he recalled. "I did everything; I was the youngest of eleven children, and we were a little bit strapped for money. So we all pitched in and contributed to the family."

Henning was pressed into service as an actor at Kansas City station KMBC — opposite his future wife, Ruth Barth, as "a pair of star-crossed lovers on a program about a little country town and its characters." He also found himself filling in as disk jockey, news announcer, movie editor and janitor. "If you wanted to get into radio — the new, glamorous thing — you did whatever you could do, whatever they'd let you do," he observed.

Eventually he turned to writing out of desperation, scripting his own show on KMBC before moving to Chicago to work on NBC's top-rated *Fibber McGee and Molly*. His mother, however, was unimpressed. (When she first heard her son's literary efforts on radio, she reportedly said, "From that you make a *living*?")

After relocating to the West Coast, Henning conceived and co-wrote singer Rudy Vallee's show for Sealtest; he wrote songs for the show as well. In 1942 he joined George Burns and Gracie Allen's writing staff, supplying laughs for the couple's radio and television shows for ten years. He also penned some of Gracie's "campaign speeches" when she ran for President (following the lead of fellow comedians Eddie Cantor and W.C. Fields) against FDR.

Henning made his debut as a producer in TV with *The Dennis Day Show*. In 1955, he created *The Bob Cummings Show* (syndicated as *Love That Bob*), a popular sitcom about a swinging bachelor photographer that enjoyed a four-year run. He followed it up with a pair of film comedies — in collaboration with *Burns and Allen* co-writer Stanley Shapiro — the Oscar-nominated *Lover Come Back,* and *Bedtime Story.*

When *The Beverly Hillbillies* tapped a vein of rural humor in the fall of 1962 and struck it rich, he found himself in great demand. The show recalled the residents of the Ozarks Henning first met and fell in love with as a youth. The creator-producer initially hesitated when approached about doing "another hillbilly show," but was prompted to devise *Petticoat Junction,* which co-starred his daughter, Linda Kaye Henning.

Although Henning's wife, Ruth, was once quoted as saying she preferred "something a little more sophisticated," *Hillbillies* — the top-rated show on television during its first two seasons — remained on CBS for nine years. The show's popularity was no mystery to its creator: "Maybe it's because these people aren't just funny," he asserted. "Underneath, Jed Clampett has a certain dignity. You might even say all the virtues. I'd be proud to have him in my house."

Despite his success as a producer, Henning kept his hand in as a writer, working 12 to 14 hours a day. "I believe in the country-store concept of TV. It means you gotta watch the store yourself," he explained at the time. "I don't believe in genius," he told another reporter. "Working hard and minding the store is the answer. Anyway, most writers are city people, and they'd injure the characters, so I'll keep writing." He cited a line of Granny's as an example of his corn-bred way with words: "That's harder than sneaking daylight past a rooster."

For all his success, Paul Henning proved a modest, affable and charming host, as folksy and as homespun the *Hillbillies* of his creation. Our interview took place in the warmth of his equally down-to-earth Toluca Lake home near North Hollywood, a masterpiece of design and decor which he credited largely to his wife of over 50 years.

You started out to be a lawyer.

I went to law school. I wanted to be a lawyer, before I actually had a little run-in — I worked in a law office in Independence, Missouri, and that's when I found out I didn't really want to be a lawyer.

How did you move from law to writing comedy?

It was sort of a gradual transition. I started out in radio actually as a singer. My idol was Gene Austin, so my idea of being in radio was to be a singer. I would go around and sing on any station that would let me, 'cause I just loved to sing, and I wanted to be heard and hopefully get a job. There was a radio station in Kansas City [Missouri] owned by the *Kansas City Star*; it was affiliated with NBC. *The Nighthawk Frolic* went on around midnight — if you wanted to be on the program, you went to the newspaper building, and the radio station was upstairs on the top floor. There would be someone there who played the piano, and if you wanted to sing, they'd listen to you and say, "Okay, you're on." It was really that informal.

This would have been about 1929 or '30?

Yeah. The rival station was KMBC, which was the Columbia Broadcasting System. Ted Malone, the fellow who became program director there, was a graduate of the high school I went to in Independence, and I knew him. When he became program director, I thought, "Gee, I've got to sing..." In the meantime I was going to night school at Kansas City School of Law to learn to be a lawyer.

But then you decided you wanted to be a writer.

I didn't really decide. What happened was that — in those days, it was really the depth of the Depression — I worked at the radio station for nothing, for the sheer pleasure. One day I went to the program director, who was a good friend, and I said, "I want to make some money." He said, "Well, the only way to make money is to get a sponsor. Talk to our time salesman." I talked to him; he told me that the Independent Grocers of Greater Kansas City were forming an organization called the Associated Grocers, to combat the first of the chain grocers, I think it was Piggly Wiggly. He said, "Think of an idea for them."

They indicated that they wanted to sponsor a show?

Yeah. So I dreamed up this idea and took it into the program director, and he said, "Sounds good. Write it." I said, "I'm a singer, I can't write." He said, "Well, we don't have any writers. If you want to sing it, you'll have to write it." So that's how I became a writer. I didn't become a *writer*, but I at least took a stab at it, just self-preservation — it was the only way you could get a program. And it sold. Another fellow who sang — we worked together at the station, his name was Gomer Cool — we became "Al and George, the Musical Grocers." And we had a mythical grocery store; we would sing about the various products. A customer would come in and say, "Do you have so-and-so?" and we'd sing about it. What I did was write parodies to popular songs; I didn't know you couldn't do that.

You couldn't do parodies?

In Kansas City you could — it was just a local show. The publishers fortunately were all in New York. So I blithely and innocently wrote parodies to all the popular songs. We were on six mornings a week. I found out then that singing was easier than writing.

You gravitated toward writing, though?

It turned out to be more in demand. Everybody who heard themselves in the shower thought they were singers.

It's a long way to Hollywood from Independence...

That again is a torturous trail. But in an effort to make a living, I went in to my friend, Ted Malone, the program director, and said, "I would like to be the movie editor." Of course, the real reason was 'cause I could get passes, to take my wife Ruth — who was then my girlfriend — to the movies for free. Anyway, he wrote letters to the studios here in Hollywood. I worked a pass on TWA, the only airline in Kansas City that flew to the West Coast. And for zero outlay of money, I was on my way to Hollywood. And I fell in love in

Southern California; I just thought it was paradise after shoveling snow in Missouri.

How did you start writing for shows in Hollywood?

Ruth was on a radio program in Kansas City called *Red Horse Ranch,* and they went to Chicago to make rural transcriptions. And she found out that the casual extra actors who would come in to do voices made more money in one session than she made in a week back in Kansas City. She said, "I'm going to go to Chicago and try my luck." So she did, and she wrote to me and said that Hugh Studebaker, a friend of ours who had worked at KMBC in Kansas City, was doing very well in Chicago. She said, "He's on a program called *Fibber McGee and Molly* and the writer of the program, Don Quinn, is looking for someone to help him, 'cause he's doin' it all alone. So I quickly listened to *Fibber McGee and Molly,* and I said, "I can write that."

You didn't need an engraved invitation.

I wrote a whole script on speculation and mailed it to Chicago, and a few days later I got a call from Don Quinn. He said, "We like your script." He said, "Can we meet with you? Can you come to Chicago?" So my little pass on TWA took me to Chicago, no problem — that was a one-hop. Coming out to Los Angeles was five stops that I could get kicked off on any one, 'cause I was on a pass.

This would have been when?

1937. I went to Chicago and I got a job with *Fibber McGee and Molly* — after a bit of trouble getting out of my contract in Kansas City. This contract was voluminous; it was a frightening thing. When I said to my boss, the owner of the station, "I have an opportunity to go to Chicago and write for *Fibber McGee and Molly,*" he said, "Well, gee, that's a shame. At the end of your contract in five years, you're free to go." There was one professor at night school who lectured on contracts — he was a prominent attorney, so I took the contract to him. He gave me a call at the radio station; he was laughing uncontrollably. He said, "I have never read anything this funny." I said, "Well then, I can give my two weeks' notice?" He says, "You can give two minutes' notice. You can leave *now.* Today."

Did they change their tune?

I asked Mr. Arthur Church, the owner of the station, to meet with me and talk about the contract. He had his attorney in his office. I said, "I took the contract to my attorney," and he said, "Who's your attorney?" And I named this professor. He said, "Arthur, I think this young man should have a chance to spread his wings..." What a phony. But it was an interesting experience, and it reinforced my desire not to be an attorney. That's how I got to Chicago. But Chicago was just as bad as Kansas City, worse in many ways in the winter, horrible. You really had to fight to walk. All the time that I was in Chicago working for *Fibber McGee and Molly* I loved it, and I worshipped Don Quinn — he was the most brilliant man I've ever met — but all the time I kept thinking, "California. I want to get back to California."

Did you work independently of Don Quinn? Did you write your scripts at home and bring them in?

Yes. Don was used to working alone. I would make contributions, and Don would put my name on the script. Then when I took the script down to be — whatever they did in those days, it wasn't mimeograph but some process — I'd scratch my name off, because I felt like I shouldn't have it on the script. Later I wished I'd left my name on a few scripts.

How long would it take to knock out a script for Fibber McGee and Molly ?

Don's method of working is what killed him. A wonderful man — but he believed in waiting until the last minute, and then staying up all night. I used to go over and see him, and he'd have a carton of cigarettes, a Thermos jug of coffee and his portable typewriter — he irreparably damaged his heart with this self-punishment.

He'd turn the script out in one night?

Yeah. And I, being very impressionable, I thought, "Well, gee, that's

Marian and Jim Jordan performed *Fibber McGee and Molly* in full costume and make-up the first two years.

the thing." So I got a carton of cigarettes, a pot of coffee and I tried it — I fell asleep, and my head — when I woke up, it was imprinted with the keyboard. I thought that was not good, I couldn't handle it. But I did find out that I was the most productive person in the morning. If I got up and sat down at the typewriter I could write something.

How did it work exactly? Did Don Quinn say, "Here's the idea for this week's show?"

Yeah. We'd have a meeting at the account executive's home in Evanston, Illinois. His name was Jack Lewis. They [his agency] had the Johnson's Wax account, I think by virtue of the fact that Mr. Lewis was married to S.C. Johnson's daughter. We'd go out on a Sunday and meet, and Don would read a kind of synopsis of what he hoped to do, and then he'd say to me, "Pick a scene..."

The sponsor in those days had a great deal of control.

He had all the control. But he had as much regard for Don Quinn as I did, and usually — whatever Don wanted to do — and Jim Jordan [Fibber McGee] ...

Would Jim Jordan be at the weekly meeting on Sunday?

Yeah. His wife Marian [Molly] was quite ill at that time. He was a helluva nice guy, but he didn't really contribute too much. He depended completely on the script. But anyway — Don would leave it up to me, whatever I wanted to do. These various characters like The Old Timer, Nick the Greek, would be regulars. He'd say, "Do whatever you like on this particular scene." It was fun; I enjoyed it. And I learned a lot from Don. And some of it was good and some of it was bad. Staying up all night with the cigarettes and coffee was bad — but he had an absolutely fabulous sense of humor. His favorite expression was, "Idiots delete." I thought he was absolutely brilliant, and so inventive. I would say that Don and Fred Allen were the two quickest wits that I've ever been around.

You would put Don Quinn in the same class with Fred Allen as a comedy writer?

Yeah. I would have to do that. They were both wonderful guys, and both died much too young. Fred never quite successfully made the transition from radio to television.

Don Quinn would stay up all night with the script, then the next day was the rehearsal?

Yeah. And then whatever was left to be done, he'd stay up the next night. Then after the program, he would just collapse for about two days — sleep. But it was a terribly punishing way to conduct your life. And of course it eventually took its toll. They were a wonderful bunch of people. I enjoyed that year...

But then you decided to come out to Hollywood.

Southern California was heaven in those days. Ruth and I were married in 1939 — we had an apartment that was $35 a month. Hollywood was like a little town. We had no compunction walking down to the boulevard at night. By nine o'clock, it was dead.

Did you have a commitment for another show when you gave up Fibber McGee and Molly?

I had the name of an agent at the William Morris Agency. I remember one of my last talks with Don Quinn; he said, "I don't like agents as a class, but I met one I think is really a nice human being. George Gruskin." He said, "When you get to Hollywood, call him up." Gruskin was a wonderful man — still my favorite agent. He got me a job on *The Joe E. Brown Show.* He said "Call so-and-so, he's the head writer." I called and he said, "Go to your file and get out all the fortune-telling jokes. And then call me back." I had never even heard of a file. Here I was in Hollywood, I figured I'd better do what — anyway, I worked for a few weeks or months, whatever it was — I still didn't succeed.

So much depended on Brown's personality, his great rubber face and his big mouth — I can't quite see him as a radio comedian.

Joe E. Brown was really out of place, as were other comedians. Visually he was wonderful; his warm-up with the audience got roars. And he'd do bits from his baseball routine. But when it came time to read the words — he'd read the script and nothing would happen.

The funny thing is, the best radio jokes were visual.

That was true of many — for example, *The Eddie Cantor Show* with the Mad Russian [Bert Gordon]. The Mad Russian had some way of tucking his ears in, and then when he was introduced he would let his ears pop out, and of course that got a tremendous laugh. There were things like that.

Did you write for the Cantor show?

Well, when I first came to California, among other things George Gruskin said, "If you have an idea for Eddie Cantor, he's always looking for writers. I heard that he was going to have a famous animal trainer on the show, a lion tamer, and I wrote a script with this guy in mind — and Cantor liked it. But I didn't like Cantor.

Did you find him difficult to get along with?

I took the script over to him and he said, "Oh, that's good." He said, "It just happens that my writers wrote exactly the same thing." Which is bull. He said, "But I'm going to pay you. I'm going to give you $75." So I said, "That's fine. $75 then." It took me, I would say conservatively, two or three months to collect that $75. I'd go up to the studio and see him, and he'd say, "Didn't my business manager pay you?" I even went out to his house in Beverly Hills on the bus, because we needed the money. He was — after the people I had known in Chicago, by contrast...

Were there any radio writers whom you admired, other than Don Quinn?

I worked with Abe Burrows when *The Rudy Vallee Show* was in its early years. He was one of the most brilliant writers I ever worked with. Abe and I got along very well. We were opposites. He was a kind of a bear of a man — loud — and I was kind of quiet and timid. We got along just so great. Ruth and I had a little apartment on West End Avenue in New York, and Abe would come over, and we'd work together. Abe would come on so strong, he'd practically scare Ruth — she said the only place she felt she wasn't in the way was in the bathroom. Abe and I had a lot of fun. He was wonderful, a constant joy. A great mind. When I heard [in later years] he had Alzheimer's disease, I thought, "My God." Such a tragedy, a mind like that.

How did you come to work for Rudy Vallee?

At that time, he'd come to the West Coast and was looking for a format. I heard that through the Morris office. I found out who the producer was going to be, a fellow by the name of Vick Knight; he had been with Eddie Cantor. I walked over to his house and knocked on the door, and I told him that I was anxious to be a writer, and I heard Rudy Vallee was looking for a show. He said, "That's right." He said, "We haven't come up with the right idea yet." I said, "Oh. I'd like to try." He said, "Fine." So I went home and dreamed up some kind of idea I then went back and told him about it. He said, "That sounds good to me."

This was a variety show, wasn't it?

Actually my idea was that Rudy through one pretext or another dreamed the program. How it ever got on, I don't know. Those were the days of stealing the money. We used to meet at one of the writer's apartments — it could've been Jess Oppenheimer, he had an apartment — two or three writers were in the same vicinity. We'd get together — everybody loved to go to the beach. The apartment building had a switchboard. We would say to the switchboard operator, "If the producer calls, we're out having coffee. Then you call us and tell us, and we'll call back and say, 'Yeah, we just got back.'" That's what I mean by stealing money.

How did you get the show on the air?

We would spend the entire day at the beach — come home very tired, after surfing and volleyball and the whole thing and say, "Well, we'll get together in the morning." If the weather was right, we might do that for four days. Not even discuss the show. Then, on about the fifth day when the producer said, "I want to see some pages," we'd all [come up with] a script and work like crazy.

Did Vallee have much participation in the writing of the show?

No. He couldn't care less. Rudy Vallee's great claim to fame was that these stars were on his show. That was none of his doing — they were all chosen for him — he just fronted the band. Rudy lacked judgement. I guess he walked into what success he had. He really needed guidance every step of the way. One week we gave him a line — it got a great laugh. The following week he used it again, apropos of nothing. Silence. He couldn't figure it out. We had to explain that it was out of context.

What was Vallee like off the air?

He was kind of a Jekyll and Hyde; he could be a wonderful host or a real pain in the ass. Rudy's dates had to sign a form his lawyer drew up, saying they realized they were going to get screwed by a famous man. They had to agree not to make anything out of it. I must say, he was extremely nice to me and my family; he would invite us over and put out a big spread.

John Barrymore was a regular on the Vallee show.

We loved to write scenes for John Barrymore. Because they were cheap laughs. All you had to do — for example, he was telling about when he was a boy, and how he always studied late at night, and the illumination was very poor — he had to study by the light of an alcohol lamp. And he said, "Often there wouldn't be enough money for the lamp *and* for me, in which case I had to study in the dark." All you had to do was mention marriage, or drinking, and it was a cheap laugh.

It wasn't all for laughs. He also did dramatic readings of Shakespeare.

We had Orson Welles on. Orson and John were gonna to do a scene — I can't recall what it was — Orson of course was at the peak of his powers then, and John was very much in decline. So during the rehearsal Orson just overpowered John. Everybody was saying, "We shouldn't have done this." And "Poor John..." It was so embarrassing. Came the show, Orson more than met his match. John, where he got the strength and the power — but he came on like — it was thrilling.

Maybe Welles inspired him.

There'd be a reading [of the script], and then there'd be a dinner break. And one time we had Lionel Barrymore as a guest. They had a bridge table with a hole cut in the middle, and the microphone was level with the table. John was on one side of the table and Lionel on the other. Manny Mannheim was one of the writers — not having anything to do, Manny and I went in the control room — we were just sitting there, and the guy was fooling with the mike controls. He turned on the mike. Lionel and John were reminiscing. If we'd only had the foresight to say, "Record this" — it'd be priceless. Lionel says, "John, do you remember that whorehouse in Buenos Aires..."

Did any of this go out over the air?

No, this was while everybody was out having dinner. They were reminiscing about their early days, and about their sister. We wanted to use her name, and the NBC attorney said, "You'll have to get permission from Ethel." We sent her a telegram, and a telegram came back: "Under no conditions can that foul-mouthed John even mention my name on the air." We said, "My God, how do we tell him? How do we tell him Ethel refused to let him even speak her name on radio?" Finally, I think it might have been Manny, who got to be kind of friendly with John — he said, "John, I'm sorry to say this, but your sister Ethel will not give us permission for you to talk about her on radio." John laughed. He said, "I don't blame her. I used to steal her blind; I hocked her jewelry."

Everyone in show business seems to have a Barrymore story.

He was quite a character. But it was sad, because he was in his declining years. The William Morris office paid a guy just to keep him away from the bottle. But he got a drink somehow, I don't know...

Did that ever present a problem as far as the show was concerned?

Not on the air. They really kept a close watch on him after the preview night. On preview night, he would quite often get big laughs. We had a starlet from MGM, cute as can be — a real Lana Turner type. John and this starlet were at the same mike, and Rudy was over at the other mike. All of the time this girl was reading her lines, John was tracing her anatomy with his hands on the downstage side, so the audience could see — he was patting her fanny, and he was giving her the feel of the world. She kind of slapped at his hand, and the audience burst out laughing. John looked out at the audience: "What the hell are you laughing at?" This was a preview — had it been on the air...

The audience could see...

Oh, yeah. Lecherous son of a bitch. She was a very curvaceous starlet. We had as a guest Billie Burke. We said, "They haven't seen each other for such a long time, and isn't this going to be a tender moment, to see Billie Burke and John Barrymore after all these years." So Billie walked in — John looked at her, he says, "Billie! Are you still the same great lay you used to be?!"

You left Rudy Vallee to write for George Burns and Gracie Allen.

I was with Vallee for a couple of years. A couple of fellows that I had known — Frank Galen and Keith Fowler — were writing for George Burns. We had known one another, and they put in a good word for me with George. My first meeting with George was in 1942, and I was with him for ten years. We made the transition to television together. That was a very happy decade. I had one funny experience — I wrote to my mother and told her I was now writing for George. Mother wrote back and she said, "Congratulations. But who writes for Gracie? She's the one who says the funny things." Mother never quite understood what it was I did and why I got paid for it. I was the eleventh child, and by that time...

You wrote for Gracie as well as George, of course.

Sure. Now we didn't see much of Gracie, because George had the contact with the writers. My wife Ruth saw her more than I did. Gracie loved to play cards — we made many trips back and forth across the country on trains, and Ruth played cards with Gracie and the other actresses.

Can you describe how Burns worked with the writers?

Well, there was a vast difference in radio. He absolutely left the writing of the radio show to his writers. He used to tell us — he'd

Paul Henning and Gracie Allen take a break during the comedienne's presidential campaign.

go out to the golf course, and somebody, some friend who also had a radio show, would be saying they were working so hard — and George would say, "Why don't you leave it to your writers, like I do?" He was very good about that.

How did you put the show together?

My job, initially, was to come up with concepts, with ideas — what do we do, what's the theme? Then Frank and Keith would divide up the first couple of scenes; they'd come in and I'd read the script to George, he'd approve or disapprove, and say, "Okay, see you fellows tomorrow." But I gradually became more active in writing scenes, and not just the story.

So with Burns and Allen *you didn't spend four days at the beach.*

Oh, no. That was different.

But it was easy money compared...

Ohhh, compared to television.

You really had to create the picture for the listener, though.

In words, dialogue — but it was fun. In radio, after the show had been on for a while, the locale was pretty much established, so you didn't have to worry about painting any kind of picture. And sound effects — a door would open and close, and Blanche [Bea Benaderet] was in the kitchen with Gracie. And on *The Rudy Vallee Show,* Rudy was not too concerned — he would be careful about what songs he sang — that was his concern.

Did you meet with Burns on a daily basis?

Oh, yeah. He had an office in the Hollywood Plaza Hotel, two adjoining rooms on the fifth floor. We'd meet there. Then of course when we made the transition to television, that took place in New York. Because in 1950 that's where television was, in New York. So we all lived at the Algonquin for six months. I remember, we were all hoping we could get back home by Christmas.

Did you have a producer or director on the radio program?

George thought a producer on a radio show a fifth wheel; there was no reason to have a producer. The radio director, all he needed was a quick thumb with the stopwatch — you had to have somebody time the show. Of course, in those days, when we originated out here, we'd do one show for the East, then do the same show again with another [studio] audience three hours later. It was amazing, the difference between audiences and their reaction to the same words. Either they'd had dinner, or the performers were not as sharp as they were on the first show — sometimes there would be an amazing difference. The audience laughter would spread one show, and then it wouldn't spread the next one, and you were stuck — you'd have to restore some of the stuff you cut out.

Would that catch the performers off guard, if they got a certain response the first time?

With the exception of a movie star who wasn't used to sight reading — people like Bea Benaderet and Hans Conried and those wonderful performers could sight-read my writing — amazing people, tremendously talented. These people were sort of a stock company. Occasionally some producer would say, "I don't think we should use these same performers all the time," from show to show to show. But then you'd try out someone new and it would be a disaster. Either they'd freeze or they'd have mike fright or misread or drop the pages or something.

Gracie had terrible mike fright, especially in the beginning.

George was actually uncomfortable doing radio, if you want to know the truth. His whole background was vaudeville, of course. Once we got into television, he was really deeply involved. He was then in his element. Radio was not his element; he was just a straightman for Gracie. And of course it was live, which made them both nervous. It would be 20 minutes before air time for the first show [broadcast] — George would say, "C'mon, Paul, walk with me." And we'd go to a bar, and he'd have either one or two quick jiggers of Scotch. This was to calm him down. But he never showed any ill effects.

Twenty minutes before air time?

Twenty minutes, or half an hour. Without fail. George was nervous on radio, he was nervous in front of the mike. I think the talent of the group [of supporting actors] kind of shamed him. I think he was uncomfortable — their ability to pick up a script and just give a flawless first reading threw him. And I think the drink tended to calm him down.

I knew Gracie was nervous, but...

This was only on radio. I don't recall George ever needing that kind of — whatever it was, sedation — on TV. That's why I say, on television he was in his element. He loved to work to an audience. It was like vaudeville; it brought it all back to him. But radio — I remember the jigger of Scotch...

Do you think television captured Burns and Allen better than radio?

Oh, yeah. Well, I don't know — they were very popular on radio. And of course, Gracie was Gracie. She was not happy about going on television. Those were the days of live television — there was a lot of memorizing to do, and God help you if you made a mistake — there was no going back. But they were just wonderful.

Gracie didn't want to work that hard, by then — she was ready to retire.

That's right. Every hiatus, she'd say, "George, I don't want to do this any more. I want to retire." He would do his best acting, talking Gracie into one more season. "Just one more season." He called her Googie. He'd say, "One more season, Googie. Just a couple of months."

I've heard Burns was a tough taskmaster.

I never found that. But then, we got along so well for ten years. I always found him to be fair, and generous — he was not beyond becoming upset about something. I never in ten years asked him for a raise, not once. Ruth and I saw a lot of them because we traveled across the country — when they went to the Palladium in London they took Ruth and I along as their guests.

Was Burns funny off the air, without a script?

After the rehearsal — during the war — we would all walk up to the theater. They'd have the newsreel. MacArthur was in Australia, and he was addressing Congress or something. When we got out of the theater, George said, "I guess MacArthur is a good general. But he combs his hair from his hip." Wonderfully succinct description. George always was a funny, funny man. He could describe people — as he did MacArthur — perfectly.

You just fell into writing. Did you ever have a hard time coming up with the ideas?

Always. *Always!* You just beat your brains against the wall...

Until the blood starts to flow.

Right. Like Ed Wynn said, "Television is the glass furnace." It burns up material, it burns up people...

Did you ever bring Burns anything where he said, "This wouldn't work for us"?

I don't think so. But to last ten years — and I left because I had — for the first time, I had an offer to do a show I could produce as well as write, with Dennis Day. It was great, even though we were opposite *I Love Lucy.* You can imagine what a horrible time slot that was.

Would you say the writer had more creative control in radio?

No. Depends who the boss was. And the producer. The only producers I knew were enthralled to the star, so the writers — one reason I wanted to become a producer — you could write a script, and it was a good script, but the producer could make any changes he wanted. He had the authority to do it.

Did that happen a lot? Were a lot of your shows rewritten by producers, or directors?

Not rewritten — although some producers imagined themselves to be writers. But they shall remain nameless. I thought that George's brother, Willy Burns, was the best director that we ever had in radio. He was very, very good at it, and a genius with a stopwatch. He would have a section of dialogue timed just to the second. I thought Willy was in a tough spot, being George's brother. But I liked him, and I thought he had a wonderful sense of humor. And he was cool under pressure. He had to prove himself over and over. George would let off steam to Willy. He'd accuse Willy of...

In other words, he was a scapegoat.

It was a tough job, being George's brother — it really was. And I thought Willy was great. For example, one day George and Willy

and I went across the street to the Brown Derby to have lunch. And
Eddie Cantor was sitting in a front booth, and he jumped up and he
said, "George! George, I'm in trouble. I've got to have you and
Gracie on my show — please, for me, do it..." George just hugged
Eddie and said, "Sure, Eddie, we'll be on, you can count on it." And
they embraced and so forth. And we walked back, and just out of
earshot, he says, "Willy, get me out of it."

It sounds like Willy Burns earned every dime in that job.

I never will forget one of the first days I was in George's office, he
was just furious about something — it didn't concern me — he was
giving Willy hell. And Willy says, "Listen, George, I don't have to
take this. I can go back to Brooklyn and do what I was doing when
you asked me to come out here." George says, "And what was
that?" Willy says, "I was sitting on my ass and you were sending me
$25 a week."

Did you have difficulty adapting to television?

Oh, sure it was difficult. You get so damn spoiled in radio.

And how did you make that transition?

Just — you make a lot of mistakes. We had a wonderful director —
Ralph Levy. He was really quite exceptional, I thought. Stanley
Shapiro and I worked together on *Burns and Allen*, and then Stan
went over to Universal, and he was quite successful in pictures. We
wrote a movie [*Bedtime Story*] for Cary Grant and Tony Curtis; they
were feuding and didn't want to work together. The studio finally
cast Marlon Brando and David Niven. Stan Shapiro and I thought
so highly of Ralph Levy as a director that Stan prevailed upon
Universal to hire him to direct it. He did a marvelous job, but he just
couldn't resist the martinis for lunch.

It must have been fun writing for Gracie Allen.

Oh, yeah. She was delightful. I'll tell you a funny thing about
George and Gracie. This was especially true in radio — we'd have a
reading, and Gracie would say, "Natty [George], I don't like that

joke about Pasadena" — or whatever — and George would just give her hell in front of everybody. "Googie, goddammit, that's the best joke in the whole script" — and so forth. Then we'd break up for that day. Next morning, George would come in and say, "You know, I was thinking about that joke about Pasadena — I kind of think we ought to lose that." Pillow talk.

And that was fairly common with them.

Oh, yeah. Keith Fowler and I would kid about that a lot. George would just scream and rave, "Goddammit, Googie, you don't really know comedy at all. Stick to reading the script. Leave it to me" — or "Leave it to the writers." The next morning — *invariably* — "I've been thinking about that..." But he would never say that Gracie was the one.

She had a better sense of comedy than he gave her credit for. She was nothing like the character she played...

In some ways she was. We used to go to the racetrack, and she'd pick a horse. And the horse would win. And everybody would say, "How'd you know? How'd you pick that horse?" And she would give you the most complex — the horse's name, let's say, was Sagamore. She says, "Well, I have a second cousin called Sag. Moore is the name of the fellow who..."

What kind of radio actress was Gracie? Was she a pretty quick study?

Not compared to Bea Benaderet. But she was fine. She had an absolute, divine sense of how to get the audience with her. It was God-given — she couldn't possibly have studied that much. But the audience was with Gracie all the time, very sympathetic. And that's why she would be especially sensitive about certain things. She had an innate sense of what the audience would like her to say, and would not like her to say. She was some kind of a genius. And that's why, when George would yell at her for being stupid, we — Keith and I particularly — would look at one another. "Come tomorrow morning, that's going to be out."

You had a number of guest stars on the show. Would some of them bring in their own writers?

No. We'd have Cary Grant, Clark Gable, all the stars. We used to book a long time ahead. Bing Crosby was on, and he was doing *A Connecticut Yankee in King Arthur's Court* or something. And he came in his makeup — you still had to write him a script. Radio was stealing the money, I'll tell you. I remember Cary Grant had such a good time, he said, "When can I be on again?" He said, "You don't have to pay me, I'd just like to come on." His agent didn't like that. He was a wonderful guest, so cooperative. We had 'em all — Ronald Reagan, Jane Wyman, Marlene Dietrich — all the big stars.

Did you have a favorite among the stock company?

Bea Benaderet, Elvia Allman, Hans Conried — they were all so completely dependable. You *knew* — I mean, they could come in without a rehearsal, and you'd just hand them the script. I was a great admirer of Bea's. She was a wonderful person, a fine actress. Very bright. I used to just sit in the control room — that's why I made up my mind, if I could ever do a show for Bea Benaderet, I would do it. She was so good, so dependable, she would come in and give the show a lift.

Didn't you audition her for Granny in The Beverly Hillbillies, *before you cast her in* Petticoat Junction?

She insisted on it. I thought it was ridiculous. I always trusted Bea's judgment on scripts 'cause she was just great — I showed her the script of *The Beverly Hillbillies* pilot. Before I showed it to *anybody*, I showed it to Bea. And she said, "I'd love to do the part of Granny." And I said, "Well, Bea, I see Granny as a kind of little, dried up..." She said, "I'd love to try it." To me, Bea was — too attractive. In fact, my exact words — I said, "With those tits you'd never be able." When Irene Ryan did her test, Bea said, "That's Granny. Forget me, that's Granny." But Bea was so good, so perceptive, so sharp; I really respected her judgment of other performers. She just had a fabulous perception.

CREDITS

Radio: *The Nighthawk Frolic* (singer only), *Happy Hollow* (actor only), *The Musical Grocers* (also singer), *Fibber McGee and Molly; Dan Dunn, Secret Operative Number 13; Melody and Madness, The Joe E. Brown Show, The Rudy Vallee Show, The Burns and Allen Show.*

TV: *The George Burns and Gracie Allen Show, The Dennis Day Show* (also producer), *The Ray Bolger Show, The Bob Cummings Show* (also creator-producer), *The Real McCoys, The Beverly Hillbillies* (also creator-producer), *Petticoat Junction* (also creator-producer), *Green Acres* (executive producer), *The Return of the Beverly Hillbillies* (TV movie).

Film: *Lover Come Back, Bedtime Story, Dirty Rotten Scoundrels*, The Beverly Hillbillies***.

* Henning received screen credit but had no involvement in the remake of *Bedtime Story*.

** Henning was not involved in the feature film based on his TV series.

CHARLES ISAACS

Jimmy Durante was one star among many who hesitated to appear on television in the early days of the medium. Years later, Charles Isaacs recalled the comedian's lack of enthusiasm at a meeting for the proposed show. " 'Gotta memorize all that stuff,' he growled, 'and worse than that, I gotta read it before I memorize it.' " Somebody had to write all that stuff before Durante could read it, and that somebody, more often than not, was Isaacs.

Born in Canada, Isaacs grew up in Minneapolis, where he attended the University of Minnesota's School of Journalism. The Twin Cities was also where he got his start, writing commercials for a film company, and items for newspaper columnists like Cedric Adams, "the first reporter to be arrested for not revealing his sources." The transition from unpaid jokester to professional comedy writer took many years — at one point he served as a correspondent for *Radio Guide* — but he eventually found his niche.

Isaacs, who seemingly was destined to write for television, thought in terms of visual humor from the outset of his career. One of his very first jobs was creating material for Merrie Melodies and Looney Tunes. "I'm not a cartoonist, so I sat with them — the guys had a big storyboard, and I would make suggestions for a gag. I would describe the visual, and what the gag would be — and if they liked it, they'd draw it."

Beginning with *The Log Cabin Jamboree* (aka *The Jack Haley Show*) circa 1937, Isaacs wrote for nearly every comedian on radio. Among their ranks were Edgar Bergen, Rudy Vallee, Milton Berle, Spike Jones, Oscar Levant, Al Jolson, Dean Martin and Jerry Lewis — to name just a few. "God almighty," said Isaacs, "I worked so damn many shows — it's the old joke, 'He couldn't hold a job.' "

While he was certainly capable of sustained employment — notably as Jimmy Durante's head writer for four years on *All Star Revue* and *The Colgate Comedy Hour* — the story was much the same in television. In addition to writing TV shows for Eddie Cantor, Alan Young, Dinah Shore, Red Skelton, Dean Martin and Johnny Carson — among many others — Isaacs scripted specials for Victor Borge, Jonathan Winters and Bob Hope. He produced several shows and created three series of his own, not to mention a "wild" half-hour pilot starring Dan Rowan and Dick Martin that preceded *Rowan & Martin's Laugh-In* by a decade.

Isaacs was busy working on a screenplay when I first called for an interview. On a subsequent evening when I phoned, he again expressed regrets that he was too busy — then proceeded to talk to me about his work for three hours. What took place was practically a monologue, which kept me glued to the phone with a fine-tuned ear until nearly midnight. As we decided to call it a night, Isaacs remarked, "Someday maybe you'll read this all back to me and I'll tell you I don't believe a word of it." Sorry, Charlie — as Orson Welles might have said, "It's all true."

How did you break into writing for radio?

I used to write little things — vignettes and one-liners — and send them into the *Minneapolis Journal* and the *Minneapolis Star*, to the columnists, and they would use them. And I began hearing them on radio, like on *The Phil Baker Show*. So I wrote letters East, trying to get them to buy from me. Obviously, they had a clipping service that clipped jokes for them out of newspapers and magazines. That was a common thing in those days. So I felt that maybe they would pay me. I had no luck until I wrote a sketch — the first sketch I'd ever written — and mailed it to Fred Allen. And I got a letter from him saying that he thought it was a funny sketch and would play well, but they were going off the air in about two weeks. But if I had any odd thoughts, get in touch with him in the fall. So in the fall, instead of getting in touch with him, I decided I had to go to New York.

This would have been in the mid-1930s?

I think it was the fall of '35. Since it was the Depression, I didn't have any money. I was doing odd jobs, everything from mowing lawns to helping truckers haul stuff — anything. I finally had about fifty or sixty bucks, but I wasn't quite sure how I was going to get to New York. I just wasn't getting enough money together...

But you eventually got there.

A friend of my brother's got me a pass on a cattle train. I went by caboose; I changed cabooses about 14 times. I got to New York and I went over to NBC. I knew that Fred Allen was up on the eighth floor, and I found out when they were rehearsing. I finally joined a tour group; when we got up on the eighth floor I sneaked away from 'em. When you're young, you do those things — I walked into the rehearsal — today I can't believe I was that kind of aggressive kid. I pushed through the doors and I bumped a music stand, and the whole goddamn line went down like dominos. And Allen was rehearsing with Minerva Pious, and he looks over and says, "What is this?" So all eyes in the place turned to me, and I said, "I corresponded with you, Mr. Allen, from Minneapolis, about material..." And he says, "Well, wait outside."

You certainly had chutzpah.

I must've sat there for an hour and a half, in that lobby-like area up there, and finally I see everybody leave — except Allen. I figured he'd gone out a back door. But pretty soon he and Portland Hoffa came out. I just sat there, because I was so embarrassed. And Portland looks over, and she says, "There's that boy." Allen says, "You wanted to see me?" At that point I didn't. But I showed him the letter he had written me. I think he was scared — shitless is the word — that he had become responsible for this young jerk from Minneapolis. He said, "Go over to Young & Rubicam Advertising and see Pat Weaver." So I went over to the agency and told the receptionist that Fred Allen had sent me. Pat Weaver came in; we talked, and he asked me what I had done. I said I'd written this and written that — and of course I said I had contributed to *The Phil Baker Show.* I was hoping he wouldn't follow up on that. I said I had worked for this comedian — in those days, in Minneapolis we had an announcer on CBS named Clelland Card...

Yes, he was on WCCO.

Yeah. I had written a few little things for him. When I got through with this litany of stuff, Weaver says, "You know, if you're going to claim all those credits, you better grow a moustache and wear glasses." I looked about 16 at the time.

How old were you?

I was about 19 or 20. "Well," he said, "we're pretty well set now, but keep in touch." By this time I was also wondering just how long I could last. I was paying only about four bucks a week at the YMCA — but even though this was Depression times and things were cheap, I knew that sooner or later I either had to get to my goal or that was it. David Green, a high-powered publicity man who handled people like the Yacht Club Boys and Goodman Ace, said he'd get me to meet a few people, if in return I would write some one-liners for him to put in columns as quotes from his clients: "So-and-so said this... heard at the Stork Club..."

The same way Woody Allen got started.

This was kind of what I did — it touched on what I had done in Minneapolis, in a sense, except there they used my name half the time. Which was great. Anyway, Green finally called me and sent me to see Teddy Bergman (who later became Alan Reed), who was on *The Harvester Cigar Program*, I think. Bergman was very nice; he read a couple of my sketches and he sent me to the producer, a man named Walter Craig. He was the meanest sonuvabitch. He said, "I don't need a writer. I'm the writer." Anyway, I kept knocking on doors, and I finally ran out of money. I was literally starving.

I assume you eventually got some work as a writer.

No, as a matter of fact I got a job as a busboy — graveyard shift, $2 a night. I saved up $19.50, which in those days was bus fare back to Minneapolis. I went to the university for a year, but we just didn't have enough money and it was too tough; I was working at night in a chemical plant. I quit, and just went into odd jobs until I had enough to pay my fare out to California.

So it wasn't until you came out here that you actually got started in radio?

Yeah. I submitted material to a guy at William Morris Agency, who turned out to be a nice enough guy. But first I got a job through a friend, working on gag and story at Leon Schlesinger Productions. I was getting $14.75 a week; that was in '37 or '38, before the cartoonists' strike.

Was there anyone who took you under their wing, and taught you the craft of comedy writing?

No, it was trial and error, I guess. A man named Al Boasberg — he wrote the "Buck Benny" sketches for Jack Benny — he died about the time I arrived out in California. I had a couple of sketches I'd written, and I took 'em to the Lyons Agency, which handled Benny. And I wrote a letter to Benny saying perhaps there would be a chance for me to write, since he lost a very fine writer and so on — whatever I said was probably more stupid than that. About a week later I got a call from the Lyons office, to go to a Mr. Haley's home in Beverly Hills. I had to hitchhike out there; I didn't have a nickel. I didn't who the hell Mr. Haley was, or what I was doing. The door was opened by a butler, and I walk in and suddenly I realize it's Jack Haley. I had no idea — that's how stupid I was. He had a show for Log Cabin Syrup with Wendy Barrie and Frank Morgan. I was put on at $35 a week.

You finally struck it rich.

I was elated, but it was tempered by the fact that I was broke. I hitchhiked back to the rooming house, and there on my bureau was an envelope from a film company in St. Paul. I'd forgotten I'd written some two-minute scenarios for commercials. They sent me a check for $17.50. The landlady got so excited when she saw that check, she invited me to dinner — that was quite a dramatic moment for me.

I would think so.

I struggled through several years, more or less. I lasted about two weeks and got fired from *The Jack Haley Show*. Then I got a job with a guy called Tizzie Lish [Bill Comstock] on *Al Pearce and His Gang*. He was a grey-haired middle-aged man who dressed in drag. Tizzie Lish walked out   this is radio — wearing a funny, ragged kind of skirt, and he would have a ratty fur thing around his neck. He would do crazy recipes and things about housekeeping. And he got screams.

People listening on the radio couldn't have known...

When Eddie Cantor was doing radio and working with Harry Von Zell as the announcer, or maybe earlier with Jimmy Wallington — he would do a joke sometimes and run over and leap on the announcer, and the announcer would have to catch him. Cantor would leap up and throw his arms around him, and bring his legs up around the guy, and that would get a scream. People wouldn't know what the hell was going on. Cantor was strange. I worked on his TV debut, and that whole experience was funny — but he epitomized the tough little guys who came up...

The hard way.

... through vaudeville, burlesque or the New York East Side, and some of that hardness was — they also had starved probably, so they were very tough and very nervous — and again, we were live then, everything was live, both in radio and then TV.

Did you work with Cantor in radio?

No. Well, maybe on the Al Jolson-Oscar Levant *Kraft Music Hall*. But no, I didn't work steady with him. Anyway, I worked for Tizzie Lish for a few months, then a fight developed between Al Pearce and Tizzie, and I was off. I ran into a guy who had a little advertising business near NBC. I said I'd like to write for him. He said, "I don't really need anyone. But," he said, "do you think you could write for Edgar Bergen?" I said, "Sure. Do you know him?" He said, "No, but I have a girlfriend who's on a switchboard at the Cocoanut Grove, and she'd have his phone number." So she got me his home number and I began calling. A woman named Hanrahan kept telling me that he didn't need another writer. Finally she told me to come out — I guess they got sick of me calling — and he put me on *The Chase and Sanborn Hour*, briefly, for about 25 bucks a week. Which was like a million dollars to me.

Was Zeno Klinker writing for Edgar Bergen then?

Yeah. But I don't ever remember meeting Zeno. I understood Zeno worked in his bedroom; he sat on his bed, with the shades drawn and the lights on. I heard he was a kook. There was another writer named Royal Foster. But I didn't work with them; I guess you would've called me an apprentice. I went over and talked to Foster about the premise he was going to do, then over to the library in Hollywood. I'd get a book; if he was going to have Bergen talking about antiques, I'd get a book on antiques and get nomenclature I could use for a joke. I think damn near my first joke — I forget how we got into it — Edgar Bergen says, "I was thinking, on the hall table I would put an old tankard." Charlie says, "Skinny Dugan's dad is an old tankard." And Bergen says, "No, Charlie, a tankard is a beer mug with a lid." And Charlie McCarthy says, "That's old man Dugan."

Did Bergen function as an editor of your material?

Oh, God, Bergen was in on everything — certainly. He wrote, too. Don't forget, he already had been doing his act for a long time.

Radio was probably eating up the material faster than he could come up with it.

Oh, sure. That's what happened to all these guys. He had Royal, he had Zeno, and he had another guy, at least for a short time. None of us were called into any script meetings or anything — at least I wasn't, let me put it that way. Just turn the stuff in and...

You would each do your material individually and turn it in to Bergen?

I think so. It's possible that Royal Foster sat with him. Royal was a little more normal, I think, than everybody else. I'll tell you when this was — this was just about the week that he had the show with Mae West.

You mean the show that was so risqué it got Bergen knocked off the air? Did you work on that?

I worked on the show, but not on the "Adam and Eve" sketch. I had to write truckloads of material for Bergen. As a matter of fact, I wrote some stuff with W.C. Fields. I remember, because he used it in a movie.

That would have been You Can't Cheat an Honest Man.

The joke I had was in the middle of a thing with Fields. W.C. Fields says, "As I look back on my life, I get a lump in my throat." And Charlie says, "Probably a cork." Then years later I got a call that he wanted me to contribute something — I was not crazy about him, because I thought he was a cheap sonuvabitch.

Who, Edgar Bergen?

Yeah. In the earlier period, when I came up with a continuing idea for him, he gave me $50 and then I never got rehired on his show. I was kind of annoyed at that, because they continued to use the idea. I worked like a dog on the show, and it wasn't until I gave him a premise where Charlie was blackmailing the guests who came on — he started a little newspaper and was blackmailing them — that I got a raise. Bergen began using that as a runner, because it made an easy thing to involve Charlie. And he raised me fifty bucks. Then he dropped me, 'cause he said he wouldn't need any more material. However, some years later he asked me to come back and do some material for him, which I did.

What did you do after you left Bergen in 1938?

I was pretty good at squirreling away a dollar or two. I got a little bachelor apartment for 35 bucks a month. It was unbelievable what small money it took to get a semi-decent place; they weren't ratholes. Anyway, a guy knocked on the door of my apartment and said, "The manager tells me you're a writer." I said, "Well, I'm supposed to be. I'm not working right now." It was Paul Henning. We got to be very friendly. Paul had been working on *Fibber McGee and Molly* in Chicago, with Don Quinn. He came out, then he sent for Ruth, his girlfriend; they got married, and we were all very close.

Did you collaborate with Paul Henning?

Yeah, Paul was my partner at that time. Paul got me on *The Rudy Vallee Show*. I was starving; he rescued me. We had some strange experiences — I had written a script and sent it to *The Joe Penner Show*. A small envelope comes to me about three weeks later; it says, "Congratulations. You are now a member of the Joe Penner Fan Club."

Edgar Bergen and Charlie McCarthy participate in a World War II recycling campaign.

Great. What about the script?

Never heard about the script. Then Paul and I got together and wrote a script on spec for Robert Benchley, who was doing a show [*Melody and Madness*]. They had writers, of course; Martin Gosch was the producer. An agent got us up there, George Gruskin of the William Morris office. Gosch said, "Oh, I love young writers," all that stuff. We gave him a script, and a week later we got a call from the Morris agency; they were sorry but the script they were going to do was kind of similar to what we had. And obviously Marty Gosch was going to use pieces of our script. Instead of paying us a lousy couple of bucks, he wanted to steal it. Well, we raised hell. We said we would sue William Morris, we were going to sue everybody. We finally settled for $75, for the two of us.

This script was for Robert Benchley?

Yeah. Of course, Benchley wasn't involved in that. I later met Benchley at Armed Forces Radio; he was a lot of fun. Anyway, I forget various things Paul and I did. I did some work for Jerry Lester on the Rudy Vallee *Fleischmann Yeast Hour*, monologues — my writing on that thing was sporadic. There wasn't much money; now Paul was married, and we were kind of in trouble. Don Quinn had decided to move to Santa Barbara, and he had three months to go on his lease on this lovely unit off Sunset Boulevard, near Schwab's drugstore. He told Paul he could have it, live there for three months. So they moved in and invited me in. And the day we moved in, we found the kitchen cabinets were stacked high with canned goods, everything you can imagine. Quinn apparently knew we were broke, and had filled the cabinets with food. He was some guy. So we lived on that, and on cheap vegetables. You'd get a head of lettuce for a nickel, tomatoes for two cents — things were so cheap, because it was still coming out of the Depression, prior to the war.

I thought Paul Henning had told me everything.

We used to walk to the Egyptian Theater, to Bank Night. They used to have those things where they gave away stuff, where you might win some money. We would gamble our few cents we had on winning Bank Night. Finally, the three months ran out, and I moved to an old boardinghouse near the Pantages Theater on Hollywood Boulevard. They rented me half of the front porch for two dollars. They had an old metal bed out there, and there was a chair; I could put whatever I owned on it. Then one morning Paul came hammering on the porch screen — he had sold an idea for *The Rudy Vallee Show* [for Sealtest]. He not only sold the idea, he got me on the show. But he had to push to get me on there.

Henning had to push to get you on the show?

Yeah. They had Norman Panama and Melvin Frank; they hadn't planned on another writer. What happened too is that Vick Knight, the producer, had a crony named Sid Fields, who was Mr. Guffy on *The Eddie Cantor Show* — who was not a writer. But Knight thought Fields would somehow come up with real solid old jokes or something.

I think old is the key word. The Abbott and Costello TV shows have the credit, "Written by Sid Fields."

Sid was not of any help, really. One time he told Panama and Frank he was giving Paul and I a lot of jokes, and he told us he was giving them jokes. He was full of crap; he wasn't giving anyone any jokes. It was kind of ridiculous, the whole damn thing. But I really owed Paul a lot for that — he got me that break. We went to New York with the show. At some point we found out Knight was leaving to produce a new Eddie Cantor radio show — he didn't tell us — and he was just walking away from us. And Ed Gardner was coming in, with Abe Burrows, Keith Fowler and Frank Galen. So there was quite a squabble. But in those days there was no Writers Guild. We all eventually left. But Ed Gardner decided he needed the help; he asked Paul to come back on.

But you left the show.

I went immediately back to California. Out of my measly money I'd saved a few bucks, so I spent my time laying on the beach. Then the Vallee show came back out here and Gardner asked me to come back on, so I came back. Then Bob Hope's manager, Jimmy Saphier — who also managed Jerry Lester — asked me to come over to the Bing Crosby *Kraft Music Hall* and write for Jerry, who was going to be on every week. He knew I'd written some stuff for Jerry before. So I was now working on the Vallee show with Paul, and at night I'd work on monologues for Jerry. Then they began asking me to write for *Kraft*, so I was writing sketches that included Jerry and Bing and the guest star, and the monologue.

Did you work with Carroll Carroll on Kraft Music Hall *?*

Not really. Carroll was the head writer; he didn't have anything to do with my material. He kind of left me to my own devices — except in the sketch, if he thought that Bing should say something differently. Carroll liked to do that language that Bing used. Bing would get flowery, in kind of a humorous way.

All that flowery language emanated from Carroll Carroll, then?

Yeah. That was Carroll's. It gave Bing a certain character. But I was responsible to try and make a funny sketch, and a decent monologue for Jerry Lester.

Was Ed Gardner the head writer on the Vallee show?

You might say he was, except Ed didn't really do any writing. Actually, Ed was kind of a martinet. In some ways, he was very funny. Other ways, he'd be a little rough. He was a character, let's face it. Poggenburg was his real name. He used to say, "I'm doin' pretty well for Ed Poggenburg, born upstairs of a bakery."

I've heard stories...

Wild stories. Anyway, I was doing the *Kraft Music Hall* with Bing Crosby and the Rudy Vallee Sealtest show, and then Jimmy Saphier said he'd give me a raise if I would drop the Vallee show. I had asked for raises on the Vallee show, 'cause I was getting paid a lot less than the other guys. I was still a kid as far as they were concerned, I guess. So I asked for a raise, and they wouldn't give it to me. I said, "To hell with them." There was a tug of war, though, because Paul Henning was not only a writing partner, he was like a brother, really; he and his wife had really been wonderful to me. So anyway, I left the Sealtest show, and stayed with *Kraft* until they ended that. When the show finished, I went to write for Ransom Sherman.

The zany comedian who gave Garry Moore his start.

Jimmy Saphier was managing Sherman then — this was the winter coming into 1942. I started to work with Artie Stander, and we were doing a good job; we not only wrote our share but we rewrote the script the night before the program. Everyone was saying how improved the show was, and Jimmy suddenly decided he wasn't getting enough material to look at. In other words, the Bob Hope technique of "Everybody writes the same thing, then most of it goes into the waste basket." I said "I don't want to do that, so I'm leaving." Jimmy says, "Well, if you want to come back at any time, just call me." I left and I got a call immediately from Corny Jackson at J. Walter Thompson — they were having trouble with the Ballantine Ale show [*Three Ring Time*], with Milton Berle and Charles Laughton.

Berle and Laughton? There's a bizarre combination.

Laughton I guess was quitting, or quit. I came on working for J. Walter Thompson as head writer, and Berle immediately bristled, because he felt he was head writer. But the show had been doing so bad. It was a funny thing — he had his own staff — Ray Singer and Elon Packard and I forget who else. I was independent; I was working for the agency, and they were working for Berle. But we worked on the same show. I was nevertheless head writer, I had to put the script together.

Was Berle difficult to work with?

He would race through material. I could understand everyone being a little nervous, being live on air — and you've gotta get those laughs — but some guys didn't take it out on the writer. Berle would say, "Don't tell me that that's funny," and he'd pull out the proverbial roll of bills to show you how much money he had. I'm not saying he couldn't — I saw him work and get big laughs — but nevertheless, with new material, I felt that I had the right to give him a little guidance as to what we saw in it.

To protect the material.

To make sure he understood — because it wasn't the formula that he used so often. I'd say, "Milton, you see here, we put a line and then a couple of dots where you should pause, then another line, a couple of dots" — for a little, almost a soliloquy. But I said to him, in this case, "We think you can get three laughs here." He says, "You telling me how to read?" And I said, "Well, Milton, you're kind of racing through it. You ought to give it a little chance." So he turns to the control booth and he yells at the producer, "Morrie, send this guy home." And so naturally, I had some words to say to him — and that happened a few times. But I was with it 'til the show went off.

It sounds like you certainly earned your paycheck.

Berle got very upset one time. I was head writer on Dinah Shore's one-hour TV shows, and Berle came in. He had this writer, Hal

Collins, following him around with a gag file; he started inserting old jokes. I'm not against someone putting an old joke in, if it's a good old joke and it hasn't been used lately. But you can put a joke into a routine and it can ruin the next three jokes that were there. And Berle didn't use his judgment on that — well, maybe he didn't have any judgment, didn't understand he was ruining the next couple of jokes.

You worked on many other radio programs after you left the Berle show.

After Berle went off the air, George Gruskin of the William Morris office got me a job to write for Herb Shriner on *The Camel Caravan*, in New York. While I was writing for Herb Shriner, I was told I was going to be drafted, so I got on the train and came back out here. Paul Henning met us at the station. We were still good friends. He said, "You're not going in the Army." I said, "What do you mean?" He said, "I called Rudy Vallee, who's the Coast Guard bandmaster..." I began being pushed in a direction that I really hadn't planned on going. So, I rushed down to Long Beach and got sworn in, and I'm in the Coast Guard. I get finished with boot camp, and I'm transferred over to Hollywood and Vine — with Jess Oppenheimer in public relations — where I'm writing programs for the Coast Guard band.

Was that part of Armed Forces Radio?

No, it was a separate thing entirely. Then they had me doing other writing — recruiting announcements and so on. Then they sent me down to Long Beach Naval Hospital to interview some Coast Guardsmen who had returned from Guadalcanal, all shot up. And I felt terribly ashamed, because every morning I'd have breakfast at the Brown Derby on Vine Street, with all the Special Service guys; it was like not going to war at all. So I went over to headquarters and said, "I want sea duty." I ended up going to Pacific Gunnery School, then on to a fleet of patrol frigates — Navy ships that were manned by the Coast Guard. Next thing I knew I was off to the South Pacific, as a gunner.

You eventually ended up at Armed Forces Radio.

Elliott Lewis had asked my wife [actress Doris Singleton] to let him know when I was in. I was transferred from my ship when I got back from the Philippines; they transferred me to Hollywood, and I finished out the war at AFRS.

Did you work under Elliott Lewis there?

No, I worked *with* Bill Morrow, Al Lewis, Sherwood Schwartz. We didn't really work under anybody; you worked with somebody, or you worked alone on a script.

And you worked primarily on Command Performance *or other shows?*

I worked on all of them — you traded around. You worked on *G.I. Journal, Command Performance, Jubilee*; you were kind of circulated from one to the other. Depending, of course — if Jack Benny was there, Bill Morrow usually wrote for him. I worked on a Benny guest spot with Morrow. I worked with Al Lewis on a Robert Benchley spot. I remember Benchley coming in — we did the shows at the Hollywood Canteen — and I said, "Gee, it's terrific to meet you" — I thought he was a wonderful character. I said, "Thank you for doing the show." He says, "Oh, I don't mind. The only thing is, I don't like to come to this neighborhood." I said, "Oh?" He said, "There are no bars."

I believe you wrote for Fanny Brice when you got out of the service.

That was right after I got out. At that point, I had now had some rough edges knocked off me, and it looked like I was going to go on and up. While I was still at AFRS in the summer of '45, I got a call from Freeman Gosden and Charles Correll to contribute to *Amos 'n' Andy.* Like everybody else, I wanted to get hold of some money. I'd been making $66 a month in the South Pacific, so I contributed to the show. They'd give me a storyline and I'd write a scene a week, and then write another storyline to contribute — which they'd do or not do, depending on which one they liked. There were about four or five other writers.

You were really in demand when you left AFRS.

I got out of the service in the fall of '45. I immediately got called by Jess Oppenheimer, who was on the Fanny Brice show. Ray Stark, her son-in-law, was my agent on the show; I guess that's the only way I was able to get on that show, let Stark be the agent. So I went over and joined Oppenheimer and Everett Freeman on *The Baby Snooks Show,* and I got a pretty good salary there considering what I'd been making. But I was very anxious to get something going, so I was taking everything I could get — which in one way was good, in another was it was tough on my health, working night and day. I did one helluva lot of stuff until I fell on my face, and was told by a doctor if I wanted to live another year I'd better lay off. So I slowed down then, and just did one show at a time, for the most part.

You must've been very well established before you went into the service.

I'll tell you something, I probably had just gotten established.

What was Fanny Brice like off the air?

Fanny was another performer who came up the hard way. I remember when they felt the show needed — there was a meeting — Abe Lastfogel, Jess Oppenheimer, Ray Stark, Fanny and myself. I think Lastfogel said, "Sponsors always get nervous if there's a drop of a half a point in the ratings." He says, "Fellas, you just have to work a little harder. And Fanny, you'll have to watch it," and so on. And Fanny says, "I'll do anything. I just want to keep this great big house." Like suddenly she was going to lose everything. By this time, she was quite rich. I just did the one season with *Baby Snooks.* I probably killed the show.

You also wrote a pilot for Spike Jones in 1945.

I was going from one show to another then; I was doing about four different shows. Spike was very pleasant. He was very — not frenetic, but it was almost like, "Let's get going, let me get out there with the cowbells." Even though he was on solid ground with his music, Spike wanted to have a semi-storyline. But it was a very short script; he had a number of things he wanted to do musically.

The script you sent me was funny, but it was rather strange for Spike Jones. It had nothing of the zany musical humor one associates with him...

That's true. But Spike wanted a college premise. It was a jokey-joke kind of show. There was a lot more material and joke routines in the first draft, which was really what Spike was interested in. It's like anyone else — when I worked with Oscar Levant later on *Kraft Music Hall*, he would keep yelling, "Give me more lines." And I told him, "You're doing a five-minute concerto." Levant said, "To hell with the concerto, I'll have more jokes." Spike wanted to be funny. Of course, if you were doing strictly a variety show, in those days you would hammer in every joke in the world — you cut exposition to the bone and got right into quick little stand-ups that were hung on a thread of a story.

Don't worry about the exposition, just get the jokes in there.

Yeah, but you had to let the listening audience know where the hell you were. Remember, Bob Hope used to say, "Well, here we are at the door of this beautiful girl..."

Yes, you had to set the stage.

On *The Rudy Vallee Show*, I was writing a spot for John Barrymore and Billie Burke. There was sort of a college theme, so we had a thing where John knocks on her door and he says, "Oh, I wonder if she'll remember me when she sees me in my freshman beanie and my turtleneck sweater. What will she say?" So you hear a door open, and you hear Billie Burke say, "Ooohh, a turtle!" These were the set-ups you did to let people know what the scene was, where you were and so on. We cut that to the bone on Spike's show. You had to take what would be a well-developed scene — not Shakespeare but definitely a cohesive funny little scene — suddenly you're chopping like hell, because you've got limited time, and you're also trying to make room for music...

Right, Spike had to get two or three numbers in there.

I did a show called *Johnny Mercer's Music Shop*. There again was, in a sense, a similar kind of thing to what Spike was doing; it was trying to squeeze in a lot of music, but have something going in comedy. I probably didn't suggest the college campus idea for Spike because I preferred that we would do more stand-up type thing — even if it was little vignettes — rather than try and put a storyline through. There was so little time to do that, and you had to squash it down so; instead of being able to get something rolling, you had to trim it back.

In any case, it didn't work. The show never got beyond the pilot stage.

It seems to me that whole thing went very smoothly. I remember getting laughs. Spike was very happy afterwards. Everybody seemed to like it. I guess we were elated because Spike was happy.

Do you have any idea why the pilot wasn't picked up?

I think maybe you said it. They maybe didn't think it was the right format for them. In those days, there were a lot of shows — musical shows — where they practically went to the mike and said, "And now, a wonderful number I heard when I was in Keokuk [Iowa] and I thought I ought to try it tonight" — and boom, into the music.

Just as you barely establish the scene, they cut to a piece of music...

Yeah. So from that standpoint, I preferred the stand-up kind of thing. A good example is the Walgreens show. I did a big special for Walgreens with a tremendous cast, with Groucho Marx and Bob Hope and a bunch of people, and they even wanted a story in that. Hope had a radio station in the desert — that was the idea — and anyone who showed up out there came on as a guest. It was a framework, in a sense. So I wrote a lot of narrative pieces that were literally little bits of monologue to kind of set up what came. But then I'd go immediately into the stand-up, with the personalities. As broad as possible. But by the time we got to recording the show, that narration had come down to one or two hasty lines. And thank God. Because at least then, we got right into solid laughs. We didn't have laugh tracks in those days.

This is an almost a legendary show — how did it come about?

Manny Mannheim and I were called in to write the special — we did it two years in a row — they had already booked Bob Hope, and they decided they needed another comedian. We were in this meeting with the ad agency handling Walgreens; someone had already started negotiating, I guess, for Jimmy Durante. The agency man said, "This is not possible. Durante's been on for Rexall, and he's too identified with them." Everyone was pitching, and I said, "How about Groucho Marx?"

Art Linkletter was also on this show.

They put Art Linkletter in a little segment on the show. It was a piece of *People Are Funny*. That was just a section, it had nothing to do with Groucho — but when we did the show, Art's producer, John Guedel was in the wings. And the big spot I had written for Hope and Groucho became in my estimation almost a shambles, except the audience was screaming their heads off. Because Groucho began ad-libbing. It's a thing he did a lot in those days.

One of the fastest mouths in show business.

Later I had Groucho on the Al Jolson-Oscar Levant *Kraft Music Hall*, and he did the same thing to Jolson. He'd talk over 'em, and the audience loved it. And of course we were live on the air, but this Walgreens special was being recorded on wire. Anyway, Hope lay down on the floor with a standing mike, to get away from Groucho — and of course it was all visuals. He was doing a radio show, but there were all sorts of visual things going on with the two of them. Meanwhile Groucho was getting screams with his interruptions of the script and so on. And John Guedel had been looking for someone to do an idea he called *You Bet Your Life*. And that's how that happened; he saw Groucho out there ad-libbing.

Apparently Marx and Hope were both ad-libbing.

Well, there was a lot of ad-libbing. There were a couple of off-color ad-libs — off-color for those days, not for today. With Groucho, part of that routine of talking over other people was to do what he felt was the Groucho character — that was more important than reading the lines perfectly. The Jolson-Levant piece I wrote was a little more cohesive, but included that interrupting style. I thought it was a lit-

Peggy Lee conspires with Al Jolson to entertain *Kraft Music Hall* listeners.

tle cleaner than the Walgreens piece — but still Groucho ad-libbed. There'd be a joke that he would do right — and it would get a scream — and he would say, "Gee, I was wrong about that one." Meaning, "I didn't think it was very good." But I didn't like that. I don't like to see scripts put down.

Too much hard work goes into them.

There are people — Victor Borge was one — who ruined some good material, just to try to prove to us that he was right, that the material wasn't right for him.

This was on television?

Yeah, it was a TV special. Again, I had the greatest respect for him when he did his own act. My God, he was hilarious. Even Milton

Berle. When I went to New York to do *Camel Caravan*, and I'd fin-ished with Berle — we weren't on the best of terms — I was walking down Broadway and ran into his brother, Phil Berle. He said, "Come over to the theater tonight and say hello." He was at the Strand Theater. You heard the biggest laughs imaginable — packed house, screaming. I got in the wings. There was Berle, sweat run-ning off him as he worked. They screamed every time he opened his mouth. He came off stage and saw me, and he stopped. He said, "Now don't tell me how to read a line." I must say, when I saw him out there and heard those laughs, I realized, there is something these guys developed, or had — being in front of people over and over again — they had something.

You have to respect talent.

Without mentioning names, I've worked with people in rather recent years, who read in the columns that they're stars — *bullshit*, they're stars. They're manufactured; they're synthetic. They've been given sometimes some funny lines to say, and they've learned enough to get the line out so you can hear the line. If it doesn't get a laugh, one will be inserted — and nobody at home knows the differ-ence. And maybe where they missed it's been edited out. There's a lot of artificiality today, in my estimation. I'm biased, certainly. But they're not stars in my mind, they just aren't.

At what point did you write for Jolson and Levant?

I worked for Bob "Bazooka" Burns, then I went to the Jolson-Levant *Kraft Music Hall* for two years with Manny Mannheim, which would have been maybe fall of 1947. Somewhere in there — because Manny worked with me on the Walgreens special. We did two years there, and after that I did the Dean Martin and Jerry Lewis radio show...

Did you write for Oscar Levant, or did he write his own material?

Oh, no. Manny and I wrote the pieces, wrote everything. There were times when Levant would say, "Why can't I say this here?" And maybe you'd have a line that was kind of humorous — but he was often more cerebral than what our audience probably would accept.

Sometimes we'd say okay; to humor him, in a sense, we'd put the line in. I remember a case where we didn't think it was going to get a laugh, and it didn't — it was kind of vague. We knew what the joke was, but we had a feeling that it was a little hip for the audience, and it didn't play. Oscar was just mortified afterwards; broken-hearted, practically. He says, "Why didn't that work?" I said, "Well, Oscar, it was very clever. And maybe that audience wasn't clever enough to understand it." And he says, "Why did you let me do it?! Why did you let me?" I said, "Because you were threatening us, if we didn't put it in."

Probably a lot of the things Levant came up with were too hip.

When we were putting the show together — in the original meetings — Jolson would say, "Oscar, we don't want any trouble on the show. We gotta like each other." Oscar says, "Why don't we start out by hating each other and slowly grow fonder?"

I think he was one of the great minds of our time.

He was terrific. Unfortunately, the poor man was pretty sick. I liked him, but sometimes he kind of bugged the hell out of you. He was quite crazy at times. Again, I respected him because — you weren't talking to some piano player from a bar on the pier. He was a helluva musician.

Would Levant participate in the writing sessions in any way?

No. Manny Mannheim and I wrote the script alone. It was sent back to New York for an okay, and — outside of Levant saying, "Couldn't I say this here?" — that's all. You see, you didn't have a helluva lot of time in those days; it wasn't like you were taping a show three weeks in advance. You came out of the show, after it had been on the air, and the next day you were talking, "What can we do next week?" Don't misunderstand — there were shows in existence where people were fighting all week, and were up all night.

But there wasn't much room for that sort of thing in radio.

I must say, maybe I had a little too much ego at times — "I'm right and they're wrong," that kind of thing. Maybe I was being defensive, too, about what I'd written. I sometimes came on pretty strong. Whether it was Jolson or Berle or Durante, any of 'em. As much as I got mad as hell at them, and it really bothered the hell out of me because I didn't like to see a script suddenly falling apart because they wanted to do this and that — there was also the pressure of time. You'd be coming up to a show and suddenly there's very little time left. There's hardly time enough to make any repairs; they're asking for the world. I'd get pretty sore sometimes, because I knew it was going to be impossible — and also I felt it didn't need that much of a change. Yet, as mad as I got, I had tremendous respect for how these people came to where they were.

They certainly earned it.

Christ, even Al Jolson. Jolson could be pretty rough. But when I saw that man standing in the wings in his turtleneck cashmere sweater, a little grizzled looking — and kind of slumped, sort of tired — I would look at how he summoned up that strength. Ken Carpenter would give him his cue to come out; this would be a minute before the show, just to give him a little warm-up time. Carpenter would say, "And here's Al Jolson." The audience would start applauding — and Al would stand up, head up, chin up, chest out, and stride out to that stage like a 20-year-old, and the people would go wild with him. And he would go down the aisle, into the audience and shake hands, all that stuff. To see him out there with that audience...

This was only a few years before Jolson died.

Most of their earlier shows, most of these guys did some pretty formula jokes; I won't say that we didn't do some. But now and then we thought a little bit wittier, a little bit smarter. Jolson would be a little worried, 'cause it wasn't something he recognized as a formula. But I'll say this — even if he was not sure of things in the script — by God, he'd give it his best.

Dean Martin and Jerry Lewis were so visual, it's difficult to picture them on radio.

I took over the show; I don't know who the guys were, but they had to turn in a resignation. I remember the one writer I kept — Jack Douglas. I loved Jack; he was one of the most wildly creative guys that was ever in this business.

What set him apart from other writers?

I didn't care if Jack wrote three pages of bizarre nothing, there was always something that would come out of it. The fourth page would have something brilliant on it, something that nobody else would even think of — he had such wild imagination. You remember Jeff Chandler, the actor?

Yes. He started his career in radio as Ira Grossel.

Well, Jeff did a lot of Indian pictures. Jack figured everyone knew Jeff Chandler was always in a forest or something. So in Jack's mind, that meant that he could do a line like "Put out your camp fires. Let's keep Jeff Chandler green." It's a pretty wild thought — kind of like a Smokey the Bear joke, but it's Jeff Chandler. I guess some people didn't understand that; they had to remember Jeff was in the woods all the time, in his movies. Jack Douglas wrote outlandish things.

Did Martin and Lewis tend to do a lot of ad-libbing?

Not really on radio. They stuck pretty well to the script.

What were they like away from the microphone?

Well, Dean was pleasant, he was always nice, he was friendly. Jerry could be friendly, but he was not always sincere. Jerry was kind of an odd combination of ego and — I remember a little kid [Donny Richards] who was on the show, about 10 years old, and Jerry got jealous 'cause the kid got big studio laughs. When there was a scene where several people were near the mike, he would try to crowd the kid away from the mike. It was pretty goddamn stupid to try — and literally hurt the show — the poor kid was yelling his lines from off-mike. Bob Redd was producing; he gave Jerry hell, but it didn't particularly matter. Jerry would show moments of being friendly, but he was a very odd man.

This was early in their career, of course.

This was when they first really burst on the scene, practically. A man at NBC, Norman Blackburn [director of programming], called me and asked if I would take another writer [Hal Goldman] with me and go to Chicago where Martin and Lewis were appearing, and talk to them about a television show. This was right at the end of '49, probably right after the radio show was off — I'm guessing it was about then. When we got there, their agent, Abby Greshler, says, "Never mind the damn TV show. These guys need an act." Because they were doing an act that was not at all cohesive. Actually, the act was funny 'cause it wasn't cohesive. But what he really wanted was material.

I believe you ended up writing a lot of material for Martin and Lewis and not getting paid for it, then suing them.

Right. As a matter of fact, Earl Wilson printed in his column a good part of their hit act in New York. Abby and Jerry kept saying, "We're not using the material." It didn't matter whether they used it or not — they had to pay for it. But in this case, it turned out they were using it and lying about it. I guess I didn't blame Dean as much, 'cause Dean didn't seem to enter into these discussions. He had a very easy, nonchalant way about him. Years later, when I did Dean's TV show, he was just the same; nobody I knew who worked with him disliked him. Where on the other hand, some of them had questions about Jerry. I guess Jerry was a little more temperamental. Jerry could do things — he walked off a show I was doing once. I was head writer. And it infuriated me, 'cause I'd spent a lot of time going over to Paramount and giving him ideas, page after page of different suggestions on what he could do on this show.

This was a television show?

A variety show. He finally okayed one idea, and then when we were rehearsing, he suddenly said, "I don't want to do the show" — and he walked out. Hardly professional. This was years after I'd sued him. He once apologized, I will say that — he came up to me and he said, "You know, we were kids then, kind of wild and..." He said, "You were in the right." Which I thought was at least something.

The comedians were very demanding in those days...

Looking back, the writing was pretty damn good at times. Remember, there were no laugh tracks. There were no retakes. It was on the air live, and goddamn it, you had to get your laughs, or — in those days without a strong guild — you could get fired. The comics would throw fits if they weren't getting laughs. Bob Burns raised hell about a script one day. He said, "The script stinks." I said, "Jeezus, we think it's fine, Bob." Burns says, "It's not funny. I'll do it — I have to do it — but it's not funny." So he goes out, and he gets screams. I'm standing in the wings. And as he came off the stage, reverberating with laughs, I said, "Well, Bob, you got laughs." He said, "Of course. I had my fly open, the whole time I was out there." They wouldn't give an inch. His fly wasn't open, but he couldn't say, "I was wrong." None of them did. Not with their egos. Groucho Marx — even though we were pretty good friends — could be murder. He drove you crazy. He'd say, "I don't know if this stuff's funny." Once, he said, "Well, what do you think?" — about the script — and I said, "I don't know, Groucho. I wouldn't go out in front of millions of people and do the kind of stuff I write."

How did you make the transition to TV?

I went into television in 1950 with Jimmy Durante. I had just come off Martin and Lewis' radio show; I must have reached some kind of stature. Abe Lastfogel called me, from William Morris. I went over to meet with him and Durante. They were talking about doing a one-hour show, and I said sure. Jackie Elinson and I did an awful lot of work on that show. We threw out a lot of stuff, put stuff in, took it out, put it back, threw it out.

This was in New York?

Yeah, we went into New York. I lived in various hotels: the Windsor, the Algonquin, the Warwick. Jackie and I would sit in the room writing, and one day we got a call to come over to rehearsal, something was wrong. I went over and Durante was saying, "I don't like what's happening." I said, "What's the matter?" He says, "I don't feel comfortable with this." Joe Santley was the producer — in fact, the director too, even though there was a camera director — and Joe was one of the sweetest men in the world. I had great respect for him, 'cause he had one hell of a background. But Joe was a great

Charles Isaacs, Jimmy Durante and Carmen Miranda during a rehearsal for Durante's first TV program.

guy for beauty; he liked to stage things in a pretty way, and what Durante wanted was a little slam-bang feeling to make sure the jokes worked.

How did you resolve the problem?

I said, "I know what's wrong." There were three cameras, and none of them were in the right place at the right time. Joe says, "Do what you want." So I restaged it. The crew laughed like hell, and of course that told Durante it was fine. Before they set up the next scene, he leans over and he says, "Stick around." And from then on I was staging most of the sketches. I'm not going to claim I was a natural-born director, but I knew where the joke was. After all, Jackie and I had written them, written the visual. I had a lot of visual feeling; when I used to fool around with the guys when we were writing, I used to do visual things. I'd do gags, just for fun.

You must have done a lot of visual gags in radio.

There were things — in radio, I gotta admit, it was pretty much stand-up. Bang, bang, bang. You would do what we call picture jokes. But your audience had to imagine that. Nevertheless they presented a picture in the mind, that's true.

Was it hard for you to adapt to writing for a visual medium after all this time in radio?

No. It was just a case of learning fast. With Durante, I just *knew* that the camera had to see *that*. I just knew it should be that way. So TV sort of triggered and expanded what I used to kid around doing — I did some crazy athletic things — I used to hang by my toes from beams. I must say, that I think we did more inventive things than *Your Show of Shows*. Remember, Durante wasn't a Sid Caesar. He wasn't an actor; he was a personality. We tried to bend his personality into situations, but he was Jimmy Durante at all times. We got some tremendous raves for some of our shows. I don't know whether the appeal of our show was as universal as Sid's; they got one helluva lot more publicity.

Did you have any difficulties with Durante?

I remember getting mad at Durante, because people would be interviewing him and they'd say, "What are you going to do when you run out of material?" And he'd say, "I don't know." I really got mad; I was ready to quit. I said, "What do you mean, run out of material? Jackie and I are writing our tails off. We're writing the show — you're not doing your act." Except when he was at the piano, or doing the music. The sketches were new. In fact, we were putting new joke lines in the music routines he did.

I think this is a common thing with comedians. Jack Benny is the only one who ever really acknowledged his writers.

Yeah, moreso than others. I said to Durante, "Goddammit, we don't get credit for anything." He got a Peabody Award, he got an Emmy — Jackie Elinson and I didn't even get a certificate. It really was crap. I thought it was terribly unfair. Everybody, beside the money, wants a little pat on the back. We were up in the hotel room in a meeting with Jimmy, in his room at the Astor Hotel. Jimmy remembered I had yelled at him that "nobody seems to know Jackie and I write the show." While we were sitting with him, a hotel maid came through with a vacuum. And Jimmy says, "Hilda, this is Charlie and that's Jackie. These are the boys that write my material." And as she went out, he says, "You see, I give you credit."

Would you say TV was more your medium than radio?

I think they both were. I've always been strong on dialogue — I still am. Even on my screenplays, when they're turned down, someone always mentions the dialogue. I think I was quite well rounded.

What was it like working with Red Skelton on his TV show?

Skelton was mean-spirited. Insulting, autocratic.

Moreso than Milton Berle?

Well, in a strange way, you could fight with Berle. But Berle was the kind of old-fashioned guy — what they used to call a *haimishe* kind of guy — who would say, "Aw, c'mon, let's go have a sandwich." You could make up with Berle. Because underneath, he wanted to be friendly. Skelton just thought you were nothing. He hated to have to talk to you, even. Skelton was really the one who felt that he should get all the writing credit.

What was the most difficult part of writing for radio?

I suppose like everything else, getting the premise. Once you knew what you were going to write, whether it was a sitcom or stand-up, or sketches. In those days, we tried to have a little story in our sketches, so that we could have a situation — to find a good situation for laughs. So it was getting, in a sense, a premise. Once you got that — most of us who seem to be reasonably able to write dialogue — then you could go. And also, then getting a blackout to the sketch. Making sure you had a funny get-off. It's the same today in anything — what's the idea?

What was the most satisfactory of all the radio shows you did, the most satisfactory working experience?

I can say that working with Paul Henning back in those days was wonderful. It was a great feeling I had for him and his wife, Ruth. That was from a friendship standpoint. As far as the show itself — it's kind of hard to say. I enjoyed doing the *Kraft Music Hall* with Crosby, because Bing was quite the big star in those days, and having guest stars — I suppose, in a way, having important people doing my lines. But then, despite problems, maybe the later *Kraft* show. There again, we had a lot of guest stars. It was quite an interesting set-up — you had Jolson, you had Levant, you had Groucho. I suppose you could say it was big-time. The funny part of it — this whole conversation has been rather immodest — but it's kind of interesting to look back, when we're supposed to look forward.

This has been quite an education for me...

Well, I should have gone back to when the writers used to carve their jokes in stone — and put so many grunts to a line.

CREDITS

Radio: *The Phil Baker Show, Al Pearce and His Gang, The Log Cabin Jamboree, The Texaco Star Theater, The Chase and Sanborn Hour, Melody and Madness, The Royal Gelatin Hour, The Rudy Vallee Show, Kraft Music Hall* (Bing Crosby), *The Ransom Sherman Show, Three Ring Time, The Camel Caravan, Johnny Mercer's Music Shop, Command Performance, G.I. Journal, Jubilee, The Baby Snooks Show, The Spike Jones Show* (pilot), *Amos 'n' Andy, The Screen Director's Playhouse, The Sad Sack, The Bob Burns Show,* Bob Hope-Groucho Marx special, *Kraft Music Hall* (Al Jolson & Oscar Levant), *The Martin and Lewis Show.*

TV: *All Star Revue, The Colgate Comedy Hour,* Ed Wynn special, Ben Blue special, *The Alan Young Show; Wide, Wide World* (specials: also producer, director), Jonathan Winters special, *The Duke* (creator-producer), *The Emmy Awards, Hey Jeannie* (creator-producer), *The Thin Man* (script consultant), *The Johnny Carson Show, The Gisele MacKenzie Show* (also producer), Bob Hope-Roy Rogers special, Rowan and Martin pilot, *Give My Regards to Broadway* (Jimmy Durante special: also producer), *An Evening with Durante* (special: also producer), *Victor Borge Special, The Dinah Shore Chevy Show, The Shirley Temple Show, The Real McCoys* (also producer), *The Tycoon* (creator-producer), *A Salute to Stan Laurel* (special), *The Red Skelton Show, The Hollywood Palace, The Dean Martin Show, The Bobby Darin Show, Harold Lloyd's World of Comedy* (special), *Newcomers, It Pays to Be Ignorant* (also producer), *Wait Till Your Father Gets Home* (animated series), *Imperial Grand Band, The Tonight Show, Alice* (executive story supervisor), Bob Hope specials.

Films: Looney Tunes and Merrie Melodies cartoons (gags), *You Can't Cheat an Honest Man* (additional dialogue), *Love Happy* (additional dialogue), *Digby — The Biggest Dog in the World* (story only), *Squeeze a Flower.*

Theater: *Somebody Up There Is Down Here.*

IRVING BRECHER

Irving S. Brecher was born in New York City, January 17, 1914. As an enterprising high school student he earned $6 a week as a reporter for the *Yonkers Herald,* in addition to writing for the school paper.

In 1933 he was working as an usher at a Manhattan movie theater when a young comic named Milton Berle admired the teenager's chutzpah and gave him a chance. Brecher broke into radio scripting a program for dialect comic Willie Howard. A show for Berle followed, and unexpectedly led to an opportunity to write for motion pictures when the program moved to Hollywood; he made his less-than-assured screenwriting debut with *New Faces of 1937,* which co-starred Berle with Harriet Hilliard (pre-Ozzie and Harriet).

His fortunes rose when Mervyn LeRoy put Brecher under personal contract for $650 a week. "I worked without credit and wrote comedy scenes for his production, *The Wizard of Oz.* There was no other assignment around and so I did that. LeRoy told me there'd be no credit because there was a script," Brecher recalled. "But I polished the scenes for the three comedians, Bert Lahr, Jack Haley and Ray Bolger." His "small contribution" to the film included additional gags for Frank Morgan, who had the title role in the film.

Brecher also wrote Morgan's material for *Good News of 1938* — Metro-Goldwyn-Mayer's Maxwell House-sponsored radio show of the moment — which featured MGM stars like Judy Garland as regular guests. (While he surreptitiously scripted Al Jolson's *Old Gold Show,* he ultimately focused most of his energies on the movies.)

LeRoy then assigned Brecher to write a pair of films for the Marx Brothers, *At the Circus* and *Go West.* He was particularly reluctant to accept the latter job: "I don't know how I survived it," he told writer Lee Server. "LeRoy asked me, I tried to refuse, but goddamn it, I did it again." As a result, Brecher became the only writer to receive sole credit on a Marx Brothers film — twice.

He won equal renown for *Shadow of the Thin Man* and *Meet Me in St. Louis,* an unhappy endeavor that nevertheless garnered him an Oscar nomination. The film's producer, Arthur Freed, employed

Brecher on several projects; *Yolanda and the Thief* and *Summer Holiday* were even less pleasant — and less successful — efforts on which they worked together.

Brecher was the only MGM writer allowed to work on outside projects at the time, notably *The Life of Riley,* a 1944-51 NBC radio series about a lovable *schlemiel* which he created, wrote (sans credit, to pacify the studio) and produced. It eventually became a feature film and an Emmy-winning television series. After licensing the show to others for a further lease on life, he returned to TV with *The People's Choice,* a sitcom about a city councilman and a talking basset hound. He followed it with the films *Cry for Happy* and *Bye Bye Birdie.*

Irving Brecher graciously received me in his West Los Angeles apartment. His physical and vocal resemblance to his friend and associate, Groucho Marx, could have been intimidating, but he was friendly and receptive — especially allowing as I wanted to talk about something other than the Marx Brothers, the subject of most interviews. He was in a somewhat somber mood, though he couldn't resist the occasional wisecrack.

Was there anyone who taught you the craft of comedy writing?

No. I never went to college, you see. I started putting down what I felt was amusing, in either a letter I would write to a friend, or saying things to make friends laugh. And also I wrote a column in the high school newspaper, *Crimson Echo* — Roosevelt High School was the name of the school, in Yonkers — and I tried to be amusing in some of what I wrote. But I never had any formal instruction. I don't think too many writers ever did learn anything, except by their own experiences — I suppose it's a gift, like other people never have to take a golf lesson, but can hit the ball a mile. Anyway, I never had any opportunity to get instruction.

Were you an avid reader of, say, Robert Benchley or James Thurber?

I had serious vision problems in those days. I did some reading; I read humorous magazines, like *College Humor,* which was a great magazine of its day. And I read things like Ring Lardner. I was enchanted with humor. I can't say anyone was a model. I liked Benchley, I liked Lardner. And I did like S.J. Perelman, who I thought was just great, and whom I met later when I was at MGM. He also briefly was at MGM — he hated writing movies. He and Groucho Marx were interviewed in London by Kenneth Tynan, who asked them, who were the fastest wits they knew. The reply: "George S. Kaufman, Oscar Levant and Irving Brecher." They inflated me to the point where I walked on air. Coming from S.J. Perelman — I lived on that for days.

Were you a particular fan of radio shows?

As a kid, I recall listening to Ed Wynn. I thought he was funny at the time. I also liked the humor of Goodman Ace. And the Marx Brothers — I particularly liked *Flywheel, Shyster and Flywheel*. The Marx Brothers knocked me out, their movies. The first movie I ever saw with them was *Animal Crackers* — it killed me.

Did you intend to write for radio in the beginning?

Oh, no. I got a job working for a second cousin who owned a motion picture theater on 57th Street in Manhattan called the Little Carnegie Playhouse, next to Carnegie Hall, which ran foreign pictures. It was the depth of the Depression. And I wound up as an usher and errand boy, working for 18 bucks a week in the theater. And I would occasionally send out a one-liner — we didn't call 'em one-liners then, we thought of them as gags — but if something occurred to me I thought was amusing or printable, I'd send it on a penny postcard to Walter Winchell or Ed Sullivan, who were columnists of the day. And once in a while, one would appear in the column, which would thrill me no end and make me very important in my circle of friends.

Would they generally put your name on it?

I'd see my name in the paper. One day while I was taking tickets at the theater, the reviewer from *Variety* — Wolfe Kaufman — came in to review the new film that was showing. Apparently he had seen some of the lines that had landed in the paper with my name attached. And he said, "A couple of those lines were pretty funny." I said, "Thank you," very flattered of course. I was at the time 17. He said, "Bob Hope used them at Loew's State Theater the other day; I went there and saw his show." And I was thrilled. I thought that was just great. I said, "Did the people laugh?" He said, "Yeah, they laughed." He said, "You know, there are people who get paid for doing that sort of thing." I said, "Really?" I was pretty naïve at the time.

Did you make contact with Bob Hope, about his using your jokes?

No. I was flattered when I heard about it, and as I say naïve enough that I didn't realize this stuff could be sold. But at that time I'm sure other comedians were picking up material, as well as buying from their own writers. There were some writers, I learned later, who were making in those days, big money. In those days if a fella got $500 for a script, that was like maybe $5,000 now.

How did you start selling your wares?

Wolfe Kaufman told me that there was a market for that sort of thing if you could get somebody to buy it. So a friend and I — Al Schwartz — we decided to take a crack at that, see if we could get into that business and get some bucks. And we took a small ad in *Variety.* At that time there was a new, very brash comedian coming up fast called Milton Berle. And he had a reputation which he imposed upon himself and referred to constantly in his act with braggadocio — that of stealing other people's material. So I wrote a one-inch ad, which cost $15, and gave it to my friend from *Variety,* Mr. Kaufman, with the promise that I'd pay it off over a period of weeks. That's how tough it was — $15 was a lot of money. And he printed it. The ad said: "Positively Berle-proof gags, so bad not even Milton will steal them." With the telephone number of the theater.

What was the result?

We went about our business. The following week, on a Wednesday, I was working the addressograph machine in the theater, and the telephone rang. I answered, "Little Carnegie Playhouse." And a man's voice at the other end said, "I'd like to talk to Irv *Bretcher.*" I thought it was a friend of mine, who I told about taking an ad — I said, "Lee, I'm busy working, and the boss will come in any minute, I can't fool around on the phone." And I hung up. The phone rang

again, and now the voice was very firm, and said, "Nobody hangs
up on Milton Berle." Then suddenly I began to shake, when I realized it could possibly be — and it was — and briefly he said, "If
you're so goddamn clever with your ads, be at the Capitol Theater
tonight, I'm being held over — and bring me some of your material." I hung up the phone kind of in shock.

Did you have any material prepared?

I called up Al Schwartz and said, "We better write some stuff." I
told him what happened, of course. He was also thrilled, excited
and frightened. We got together while I was working in the theater;
we had the daily newspapers, and we got some topical one-liners
that we put down on paper, and I typed them out. We went over at
midnight, after the show was over that Berle was doing, and submitted a page of these gags to this young, brash comedian. First
time I'd ever been backstage in a theater. And he read them and he
said, "Go over to the Park Central Hotel and see Charlie Morrison;
he's my agent, he'll give you a check." And we ran all the way. And
this man, Charlie Morrison, gave us a check. We didn't even *look* at
it. We ran outta there, then we looked at it — it was $50. We just
couldn't believe there was that much money in show business.

You were rich...

Now, what happened was, Schwartz's parents insisted that he was
not going to stay in show business; he was going back to college,
and so on. And I was left to work for Berle, sporadically, at very little money at that time. I started writing for him in vaudeville, in
1933. Whenever he played a different theater, he'd call on me, and
I'd write some one-liners, and it was real starvation. But one day he
got an offer to do radio, on the Yankee Network for Gillette. And the
writer he wanted — a famous writer named David Freedman, a
very brilliant fella who wrote for Eddie Cantor and a lot of other
comedians — he was not available. Berle called on me, and I went to
Boston. I wrote a program for him partly on the airplane and in the
hotel. We got to Boston a day before the show, and that's when the
whole thing started, my dip into radio — on a long-term basis.

This was not the first show you worked on, though.

It was not my first venture into radio, but my first real job. Then Milton Berle and I parted, and I picked up crumbs writing with another guy — I joined up with a fellow named Alan Lipscott in 1934 or early '35, and we wrote some little things for vaudeville acts. But we wrote a radio series called *Folies de Paris* with Willie and Eugene Howard. We wrote something called "The French Lesson," which Willie Howard did. Very funny man. And Fifi D'Orsay was the woman on the program; she was an ex-movie star who'd been in *The Big Parade.*

I believe Willie and Eugene Howard were among the first comedians on the air. Did they go over well on radio?

I didn't think so. My impression is that there was very limited popularity. I may be wrong, but I don't recall them as being a strong radio force, and they had limited exposure. The program had no audience — it had a brief run, 13 or 26 weeks, and they were off. Willie Howard was too parochial. He had a New Yorkese Jewish accent. Hilarious comedian on stage, absolutely wonderful. He did great impersonations.

Did Willie Howard edit your material? Did you work with him?

Willie was a breeze. A wonderful little guy. He had a brother who was — a pest. No talent. Show business knew that Eugene Howard was a lightweight and made jokes about him. And they also knew that Willie Howard was a genius, but loyal to his brother. So he kept him — Willie was a good-hearted guy. It was a brother act. The way that Eugene would justify his existence was to be a pest, and make believe that he knew all about it — so he would stick his nose into scripts that we had done, and when he was all through carping and criticizing, Willie would say, "I like it." And that was the end of it.

After that, you went to work for Milton Berle again?

Then I went back to Berle when he needed me, and I was no longer working on the Willie Howard program. Berle wanted me individually to do this thing in Boston, on the Yankee Network in the summer of 1936, two or three shows. Which I did. And the result of that was, he was signed by Gillette for a series on CBS, a 45-minute program. It began in the fall of '36 and lasted through May '37.

Milton Berle exchanges quips with aviatrix Beryl Markham on
The Gillette Original Community Sing.

This was The Gillette Original Community Sing?

Yes, and I was the only writer. I must tell you — I look back at it
now, I don't know how I did it. 45 minutes. Of course, it wasn't all
writing, there were songs involved. But there was at least 25 minutes of text every week. Milton and I have remained good friends —
and Milton still, when we're together, introduces me saying, "This is
the only guy I ever knew who wrote a radio program every week all
by himself."

*Did Berle function as an editor? Did he say, "This is going to work for me,
this isn't..." ?*

Not too much, as a matter of fact. If he had trouble saying a line, or
he thought, "This might be not be that funny," I would certainly go
along with that in most cases. If I couldn't sell him that it was, I
would replace it. But that didn't happen too much. Once Milton
trusted me that I was doing a job, we would have brief discussions

about what I was going to try to do for the following week's program — occasionally, he would suggest something that he may have used sometime before, to include — but essentially I think he left me pretty much on my own. And he was very supportive, and would defend what I did, against opinions of the sponsors or the agency. Milton was very good to work for.

Could you assess Milton Berle as a radio comedian?

He didn't make it really in radio, and the reason was not that he's not a very funny man — obviously he is. But I think one of the reasons was he worked very fast, with a kind of a nervousness that's part of his characterization. And what came over — what you heard were the jokes — but you couldn't for some reason grab his personality, which, when you see him, is totally different. Certainly television was his métier. Milton Berle's visage, his grimaces, his body language, is all something that was captured brilliantly in TV. But in radio, it didn't go. We used to get tremendous laughs in the studio — but that's not good enough. Except in my case, what happened was, producer-director Mervyn LeRoy liked the Berle program so much that he signed me to write movies. But he was the exception, apparently. Because after that one season, the series came to an end. So that was radio, as far as I was concerned.

Bert Gordon played a character on that show similar to the Mad Russian he played on Eddie Cantor's show.

Right. I called him Misha Moody. Pretty much the same character. Gordon had done a lot of Jewish-accent comedy around New York, in vaudeville. Funny guy.

You wrote a movie with Berle and Gordon about the same time as the show.

During that period Milton made a movie called *New Faces of 1937*. And while I was writing his radio show, I was forced to write the final script of that movie. That was the first time I went near a motion picture studio. We came out to Los Angeles — the show was moved to the Coast because he had to work in the movie, and I was put on salary — I was writing the radio show and the movie at the same time. I nearly collapsed at the end. I managed it. It was exciting, but the movie was not very well received. Someone said recently they were going to run the film at a Milton Berle festival; they asked me to come down. I said I'd come, but I'd bring a bodyguard.

I believe you wrote for one of Al Jolson's radio shows.

Secretly. What happened was, I'm out on the Coast, I'm under contract to MGM, and I'm not supposed to do anything except work for MGM. A very dear friend of mine — G. Bennett Larsen, who produced the Berle program that I did — comes to me, pleads with me, he's got Al Jolson signed to a program for Old Gold Cigarettes, I believe. They are in trouble with the ratings because they can't get the material. Would I write the show? And I told him my problem. Well, I finally caved in because I felt I owed Ben Larsen a great deal; he'd been wonderful to me in my experience with the Berle program. And so I said, "I'll get another fellow in, and I'll work with him at night. But nobody must know." And I did that. I brought in a fellow named Alex Gottleib. And I wrote the program, and Gottleib contributed, and Jolson's ratings started to take off. At a certain point I finally said to Ben, "I just can't do it any more." And he accepted that and went on from there.

How did you find Jolson to work with?

I found — when he was down, and the rating was low, Al Jolson was the nicest fellow in the world. When the rating got up, he was not a very nice fella. Arrogant, difficult — most talented man I've ever known. He knew I was involved, so I had some personal association with him, out at his ranch. Never went near the studio. The meetings were not unpleasant, but when Al was winning, he was rough. When he was losing, he was a delight.

Jolson had a reputation as an egomaniac.

Jack Warner had a wonderful line about actors and their egos. I have to quote him. He said a lot of things he thought were funny that were not funny — but this line fit. Warner said, "One actor on his ass is worth two on his feet."

While you were at MGM you also did a show called Good News of 1938.

That's right. Louis K. Sidney, a producer who at one time ran the Capitol Theater in New York, asked for me to write part of the *Good News* radio show that MGM was starting, using their people. I started Frank Morgan on the air, and wrote that show for a good number of weeks. I used to have to take him from a bar where he was busy slurping martinis, into the studio. I don't know how he did it; he got loaded before each broadcast. Frank Morgan drank three, four, five martinis, and I would steer him to the studio, and he would go on, and he would giggle in his delivery, and get the jokes over and all that, and then when he was finished, he'd go to sleep. The presence of the audience somehow took care of the martini effect. He was a very good performer.

Fanny Brice was on the show as Baby Snooks. Did you write for her?

No. Phil Rapp wrote for her. I did Frank Morgan, and the guests — that's where I first worked for Jack Benny. I did a show for him. He had a big piece of that particular program, and we ended up being very close friends. I was crazy about him, as a person. I always thought his — his and Fred Allen's — were the best comedy shows, ever, on radio.

Did you ever write for Benny's show?

Jack liked the *Good News* program so much, he said, "One day, we're going to have to work together." I said, "I would love that." It didn't seem a possibility at the time. When his gag man, Al Boasberg — the guy who started him off — died suddenly, Jack called me in. His program was being written by Ed Beloin and Bill Morrow but Boasberg was still part of the team; he would come in and polish all the scripts. He was a very funny man. When he died, Jack asked me to come in and sit through their rehearsals, and punch up the script if I thought of things that could be inserted. I did that for a couple of weeks, but I was uncomfortable because things were already established. The writers' noses got out of joint; they resented me, and I felt it. I didn't need it, I was doing motion pictures, so I did a couple weeks of that and told Jack it wasn't going to work.

Radio success was a long time coming for Groucho Marx.

You took a long hiatus from radio to write screenplays.

It was after the *Good News* show that Mervyn LeRoy asked me to write a Marx Brothers film, which I did, called *At the Circus.* And then I wrote a second one, *Go West,* and that was enough for me. 'Cause I'd written both of them by myself, and that was unusual; nobody'd ever done that. And I paid the price — I wound up with a tic. And the depression of writing a film for the Marx Brothers, who were wonderful people and friends of mine, but left all the decision-making about "Is the script okay or not?" to Groucho...

Among the three of them, I can imagine...

Groucho, who was my best friend, nevertheless hated the business of acting, and used every excuse not to work. Whereas Chico, who was always broke, wanted to shoot everything *today* — let's go. And Harpo was a fey, beautiful person; whatever Groucho decided was okay with him. So Groucho would read the script that I would give

him, and he would say, "It's very funny," and so on and so forth,
"but..." And I would have to debate, and not insult, and be diplo-
matic and change a few things. Eventually we'd go to the sound
stage. And that happened with two films.

The Marx Brothers had a hard time translating their humor to radio.

I didn't think they worked in radio. The program [*Flywheel, Shyster
and Flywheel*] was not successful. Again, they're visual. Now, Ed
Wynn worked, even though he was a visual comedian and wore
funny hats and one thing or another — but his program worked.
And Eddie Cantor. His show worked because he sounded like a guy
you knew. He would appeal to the heart. He had a certain warmth,
and spirit. And it worked. But the Marx Brothers didn't work.

I think Groucho's later show...

You Bet Your Life? That was different, because by then he was so well
known from films, when you listened to radio, you saw him, in
your mind. With all due respect to Groucho, who was very clever
and very witty — and said a lot of very funny things, particularly at
parties or when you were alone with him — most of what he did on
the show was already written.

You went back into radio in 1943.

I had just written the two Marx Brothers films. Groucho had been
canceled on the radio and couldn't stomach that degradation, that
blow to his ego, and he wanted to go back into radio. And he said to
me that he wanted me to come up with some program. I demurred,
because I was under contract to MGM, and I just had no real interest
in doing radio. Movies were far more exciting. But he leaned on our
friendship. So I said, "I've got something in the trunk that I wrote
years ago, long before I came to Hollywood — just a treatment, an
idea called *The Flotsam Family*. About a guy and his family who floats
along, getting into trouble, and so on." He said, "So maybe you
could do it for me." He prevailed, really pushed. I wrote a script, and
it was auditioned — they made what they call an audition record.

Did anything come of it?

An advertising agency, BBD&O, financed the record — couldn't have been more than a couple thousand dollars. They did it in a Hollywood studio with a live audience, and while it got a lot of laughs — because the audience loved Groucho — it did not ring true, because he was playing a man of flesh and blood. And Groucho's character is not — when you paint a mustache on with burnt cork, it's not really flesh and blood. So it didn't sell. About a year later, I saw a short Hal Roach film called *The McGuerins of Brooklyn.* And there was a man in there I'd never seen before, who struck me as an interesting character; his name was William Bendix. And I thought maybe this old script that Groucho did could be made with him, if anybody — a radio sponsor — wanted it. So I contacted Bendix's agent, who said, yes, he'd be interested in a radio show, and I rewrote the script — not drastically, but I changed the title from *The Flotsam Family* to *The Life of Riley.*

"The Life of Riley" was already a well known phrase.

Oh, sure. It's part of the English language. And it had been used on other vehicles before. It came from Ireland; it meant total ease, nothing to worry about. But it seemed to me that it was a contrast toward what the life of this character really was — nothing but trouble. Anyway, we made an audition record with William Bendix. And they laughed. But nothing happened. Nobody bought it. Six months later, I received a phone call from Chicago, from a man who was with the Leo Burnett Advertising Agency, representing the American Meat Institute. They were looking for a radio show, and he had come across a platter which had my name on it.

The audition record no one bought...

The man had been trying for days to locate me. He didn't know who the agent was or anything, but he finally got me through the Writers Guild. And he bought *The Life of Riley.* I had to break the news to my agent, William Morris, which eventually got 10% for not having found a buyer. And they made over a million dollars, because the program started in 1944 and ran for years, then became a television series starring Jackie Gleason first — and after that I

William Bendix and Irving Brecher rehearse *The Life of Riley* with actors
Tommy Cook and Paula Winslow.

licensed the property to NBC, and it became a big show for William
Bendix. I had nothing to do with the making of that.

The radio program wasn't that popular in the beginning.

The show became a hit after Digger O'Dell, the undertaker, became
part of it. That turned it around. The whole thing moved up.

*I believe the undertakers' union caused some sort of a ruckus. They didn't
care for the jokes...*

The undertakers were aroused and threatened. My secret friend in
the advertising agency was for keeping O'Dell on, which was not
what his client wanted. He told me that one of threats was that the
undertakers would stop patronizing the Meat Institute — the various people under that umbrella — from which they bought the ren-
derings to make soap, to wash bodies. Isn't that cute?

The soap they used was made from the fat...

That's right. I persisted in keeping O'Dell on. Then the tide turned, because we began to get positive letters — and they react so quickly to letters. Such idiots. That's what made the difference. After the negative reaction from the undertakers, at their next annual convention they invited Digger O'Dell [actor John Brown] to speak — which he did.

The show was eventually sponsored by Proctor & Gamble.

After 78 weeks — one and a half seasons as it were — we were dropped by the Meat Institute, which had no longer any interest in the program. They wanted to go classical. It was just an institutional thing; they had nothing to sell. And the powers that be there — the Protestants whose wives wanted some shit on Sunday afternoon — they happily dropped us. Proctor & Gamble picked us up and put us on at night, and that was the beginning of the great success of *The Life of Riley.*

Did you encounter any problems in trying to adapt the radio series to tele-vision?

I did all radio scripts. I rewrote all the radio scripts for TV, and there was no Guild provision for paying writers. I'm pleased that I was able to do what writers didn't thank me for — I gratuitously sent a check for each program that I used, to the Writers Guild. Sort of the beginning of the residual. Not a great deal of money, 'cause there was no real money. But I was using radio scripts, and the writer's names were on them.

It wasn't your idea to do the TV series...

Pabst Beer [the show's then-sponsor] wanted me to go into televi-sion. I didn't want to for reasons of my family life being on the West Coast, and I was in motion pictures out here, and doing a radio show. They said, "We're going to cancel. We want to get a foothold in television." This was 1949. This was after I had made a feature picture called *The Life of Riley,* which had turned out to be quite suc-cessful at the box office. Finally they cajoled me — or threatened me, whatever — with cancellation, and since the radio show was very lucrative, I fell into the trap and said "Okay." Then I went to New York and auditioned a number of actors —because Bendix was not available — and found nobody.

William Bendix was unavailable? Wasn't he tied to the show?

Bendix was under contract to Hal Roach, and Roach thought he would not let Bendix go into TV, which would probably soon blow over. I was forced to find some replacement, and Pabst said, "Anybody." Apparently they really didn't care about anything, except getting a time slot. I finally took a man that my agent said I shouldn't touch, named Jackie Gleason. The reason they were wary of him was because he was very irresponsible. He was also a heavy drinker, he was always in debt, and generally they felt it couldn't work. But I was desperate so I took Gleason, who was happy to have a job.

Wasn't there a TV pilot with Lon Chaney Jr. before the Jackie Gleason series?

I made a pilot before I took Gleason, in New York, with Lon Chaney Jr. In desperation. It wasn't any good. Chaney was too big, too powerful. I looked at it, I showed it to the Pabst people, I said, "I don't want to do this." After that I got Gleason. His salary was an immense $500 a week. The entire package — in the light of today's prices, nobody will believe this — but the entire package that I was to deliver would be paid for by Pabst, for $8,200. The biggest salary was Gleason — the rest of the money was for actors, for a script that I would write, for my producing, for a director, et cetera, and the cost of the film.

Was the Gleason series done in New York?

Well, when it got time to really think about shooting, I was very concerned about the need to have to fly back and forth from coast to coast every week, to try and put on — I knew this had to lead to a heart attack. So I went to the head of NBC, Niles Trammel, and appealed to him to let me do the show from the West Coast, which was impossible then because there was no coaxial cable — but I would put it on film. His associate, Pat Weaver, who was a wonderful man and a friend of mine —but nevertheless loyal first to NBC — said, "If we let Brecher put this on film, he doesn't need a network. With film, all you have to do is mail it to each local station — and put us out of business. Whereas with live television you need us." Weaver was opposed to it. But I implored Niles Trammel, and he bent. He said, "Okay, you can put it on film, but you'll have to pay the excess over the $8,200 that Pabst is supplying." So I agreed, not knowing what that cost would be. And the upshot was that I put it on film out here in California. For 26 programs, the excess over what Pabst paid me was $2,000 a program average — $52,000. That's what it cost me to make the series.

Cheaper than a heart attack.

The day that we won the Emmy for the best comedy on television was the day we were canceled by Pabst — who hadn't told us that what they really wanted was a time slot to put on prize fights, which is what they eventually did. So Gleason and I parted, and the next thing you knew, Gleason was on his way. He went to Dumont, and from there he went to CBS and became the giant that he deserved to be, because he was very talented.

Did it occur to you that Ralph Kramden had more than a little similarity to Chester Riley?

Well, it was obvious that he was doing *The Life of Riley* in a different sense, without children. And *The Honeymooners* was pretty close to *Riley*. It didn't really hurt me. It kind of made me feel smugly pleased, that he would flatter us by topping what he did. But, that's part of the business...

He also borrowed from The Bickersons...

Yes, he did. My friend Phil Rapp sued Gleason. I don't think he won anything.

Then of course Riley was reborn as Archie Bunker.

Carroll O'Connor paid me a lovely compliment. One day I went to a party at Groucho's house — this was the second season of *All in the Family*. And in the distance I saw Carroll talking to Groucho. A few minutes later, I got a tap on my shoulder. It was O'Connor. He said, "I came over to thank you." I said, "For what?" He said, "We're doing your program with freedom. We're doing *The Life of Riley* with the freedom you couldn't have." I said, "I think that's very generous of you. I think you're doing better than we ever did." He knew that he was doing Riley. But you can't copyright a characterization. And I didn't invent dumbbells. I just used one in terms of Riley, and it did pay off.

George Burns [was] a good friend of yours — why do you think Burns and Allen were more successful than most vaudeville comedians in making the transition to radio?

They were beloved on the radio. Gracie was a most adorable character, appealed to everybody — such a flake, and so sweet — I don't know how they could have missed, just letting her be what she was. George [was] very sharp; he knew how to present her, and be there. He allowed himself to be put down — he often [talked] about how unimportant he was, in terms of her, and how the success could not have happened without Gracie.

You never worked on their show.

No, I didn't. I took George in as a partner, an investor, in a series I did for television called *The People's Choice*. That was the only time we've done anything together. Occasionally after that I'd supply him with some little things, but not on a regular basis. A guy I really loved, and never worked for — would have loved to — was Fred Allen. I thought he was great.

You devoted a substantial part of your career to writing for motion pictures. When you look back on it...

You forget the pain — like having a baby, I guess. I wrote some good ones, like *Meet Me in St. Louis*. I worked on *Ziegfeld Follies*. I wrote *Shadow of the Thin Man* with William Powell and Myrna Loy. Powell was very bright — in terms of actors, he was more literate than a lot of others. In retrospect, I had a good time at MGM. When you were doing it, it wasn't always fun. An awful lot of terrible pressure.

Would you say there was more pressure writing for radio, or movies?

There's more pressure writing for movies. Radio, there wasn't enough time between programs to fool around. Whereas in movies, the producer is insecure in his own judgment — and many of them were — they were too timid to go to bat, so they would say, "I like it but..." And then they'd start again, with somebody else. I was fortunate, or unique, in the sense that every script I wrote, during the time I was doing films, was the final script that was shot. I wasn't followed by anybody. Many writers didn't have that happy experience. It was kind of an unusual experience. Maybe that's because I didn't write that many pictures.

CREDITS

Radio: *Folies de Paris, The Gillette Original Community Sing, The Jack Benny Show, The Old Gold Show, Good News of 1938, The Flotsam Family* (pilot), *The Life of Riley* (creator-producer).

TV: *The Life of Riley, The People's Choice, The Many Loves of Dobie Gillis.*

Film: Easy Aces short subjects (narration), *New Faces of 1937, Fools for Scandal* (additional dialog), *The Wizard of Oz* (additional dialog), *At the Circus, Go West, Broadway Melody of 1940, Shadow of the Thin Man, DuBarry Was a Lady, Ship Ahoy, Best Foot Forward, Meet Me in St. Louis, Ziegfeld Follies, Yolanda and the Thief, Summer Holiday, The Life of Riley* (also producer-director), *Somebody Loves Me* (also producer-director), *Cry for Happy, Sail a Crooked Ship* (also director), *Bye Bye Birdie.*

Theater: *Sweet Charity.*

NORMAN PANAMA

"Filmmakers are beginning to go for any kind of gimmickry or packaging that seems likely to arouse interest," veteran writer-producer-director Norman Panama lamented late in his career. "Part of the trouble today is that comedies are in the hands of directors with no writing experience. They have the visual pyrotechnics but no real empathy with characters."

Panama was born in Chicago, April 21, 1914. In his early years he worked as an usher at the Chicago Opera House and dabbled in songwriting, reportedly selling a couple of tunes. "One was called 'It's Lousy But It's Commercial.' I don't remember the title of the other one, but it was just as lousy as 'Lousy,' " he once told a publicist.

He studied law and political science at the University of Chicago, where he met Melvin Frank — with whom he would embark on a long and profitable collaboration — in a class on the history of American drama. "The first thing Norman and I ever wrote together (that was accepted), was a check for a month's rent on an apartment we shared when we were both going to the university," Frank remembered years later. "Although we were studying law, we knew we wanted to be writers." Recalled Panama: "We took an apartment over the summer, and wrote a play. Nothing ever happened with the play, but on the basis of that, we decided to come out to California and see what would happen."

Upon their arrival in Hollywood, a friend arranged a meeting with Milton Berle, "who said he would be happy to look at any comedy material we would care to submit. He loved our stuff and said so — the day before his radio show was canceled." The fledgling writers ended up "freeloading" off the hospitable comedian for several months, supplying him with jokes to entertain his pals in exchange for food. Berle also aided them in finding an agent, who gave them a chance to write for an up-and-coming comic named Bob Hope at $80 a week — for the pair of them.

Panama and Frank helped launch Hope to stardom, on the maiden season of *The Pepsodent Show* in 1938. They went on to write for Phil Baker, Jimmy Durante (on a piecemeal basis, in between jobs) and Rudy Vallee, toiling profitably — if unhappily — in radio for a few short years before the movies beckoned. A story treatment for Hope called *Snowball in Hell* (retitled *My Favorite Blonde*) netted the team $7,500 and a contract with Paramount Pictures. Although "we had no basic choice in what we did" as contract writers, they were finally pursuing their dream.

Following nearly a decade of "strange detours," during which they wrote and produced *Mr. Blandings Builds His Dream House* at RKO, Panama and Frank became "a double triple-threat team" at Metro-Goldwyn-Mayer. MGM's chief of production, Dore Schary — their former boss at RKO, and an Oscar-winning screenwriter himself — gave the team the opportunity to produce and direct their own scripts.

"We had to become producers so we could see what we wrote," Panama recounted, noting that he and his partner were tired of being blamed for "whatever was bad," while also seeing much of their script cut. When Schary asked them how two men could co-direct, they devised a unique system; according to Frank, one of them would act as spokesman for the team and call the shots, communicating non-verbally with the other. They started by tossing a coin, then alternated in the role.

Panama and Frank eventually formed their own production company, Parkwood Enterprises. The collaborators went their separate ways in 1966, parting amicably after three decades and nearly 30 films together, not to mention three Oscar nominations. The split was "purely for economic reasons when we found we couldn't put together enough properties as a team." Panama announced a number of stage and film projects in the ensuing years, most of which failed to get off the ground; those that materialized did little to enhance his reputation. The last effort to reach fruition was *The Glass Bed*, a 1980 novel about a young comedy writer in 1930s Hollywood.

Despite illness, Panama graciously consented to a telephone interview for this book — to the surprise of his agent. It was with considerable effort that he spoke; he occasionally had trouble talking, but continued at some length. He appeared to realize he had a unique perspective on Bob Hope that no one else could offer. When contacted a few years later, however, Panama could not recall having granted the interview. "I never cooperate with anyone," he insisted.

You began your collaboration with Melvin Frank at the University of Chicago. Did you have a playwriting class together?

No, we were just two geniuses on the loose. It seemed to come instinctively to us; we had both done some writing, Mel had written a novel. And I used to write in high school and college, plays mostly. It was just two guys who thought quite a bit alike, enjoyed writing — and had a 25-year collaboration.

Was writing for radio something you aspired to?

No. It was uninspired. But we were big radio fans.

Did you come to California hoping to write for the movies?

Yeah, we were hoping to get in the movies. Mel and I didn't work in radio when we first came out, in '37 or '38. We had no credits at all, just some letters of introduction to various people in the business that didn't amount to anything when we got out here — just a lot of spirit of adventure and a lot of chutzpah. We futzed around for almost a year until we finally made a connection with the Bob Hope show.

This was his first season on NBC...

He had just gotten his first radio show, *The Pepsodent Show;* he'd been doing a monologue for Lucky Strike before that, I think a five-minute spot. We'd never seen him work, actually. When we got a chance to write some material for him, we went to a movie theater in West Los Angeles where they were playing *Big Broadcast of 1938.*

How did you come to write the material for Hope?

We sat on our asses in a little apartment on Fernwood Avenue in Hollywood, and submitted material to every top comedy show. Usually the same jokes reworked. If it was *Fibber McGee and Molly* one week, it would be the Al Jolson show another...

Were you under contract to Hope's agency, Lord & Thomas?

No. We didn't have any formal contract at that point; we were just on Bob's payroll. He paid the writers himself. He had seven or eight writers on the show. He'd gone to New York, when he got the show, and picked up some writers, some more out here. Mel Frank and I were totally fresh and untouched. We didn't even know all the jokes we came up with were file jokes.

Unlike Hope, most of the shows had a sitcom-type format.

Bob was more or less unique in terms of his style of comedy. The monologue was kind of his — he came out of vaudeville, where he did a lot of one-liners. His monologue was always his pride and joy, and still is to this day unfortunately.

Did he say at the outset, "I don't think a sitcom is going to work for me; let's go with something else"?

Not really. The word "sitcom" was unheard of, anyway. I suppose Jack Benny's *Jell-O Program* was a sitcom in a way — at least it had a story, or it had characters. On our show, Bob would open up with a monologue, then there'd be a cast spot — he'd work with the members of the cast, and Skinnay Ennis, who had the band. Then there'd be the guest spot, which would be the big spot. There was a guest every week — Judy Garland, picture people mostly. Our first show was for Groucho Marx — that's what established us. Mel and I were sort of the specialists on the guest spot; we did about 20 or 30 of 'em.

Groucho was the guest on your first show?

It wasn't Bob's first show, but it was the first show Mel and I did. Hope came back from the East and did two or three shows before we had the famous meeting at Paramount when he gave us a two-week job with a two-week option. And our first one was Groucho.

Hope initially signed you for just two weeks?

That's the way it worked. They were so jammed with writers, and struggling for a formula — and Mel and I were very fresh, only because of inexperience. These two kids came in off the street virtually — we were a smash right away. We wrote Groucho, and the next week I think was Chico, and so on — by the end of the fourth week, he signed us to another contract. In those days, they used to be signed at 13-week intervals. I think there were 9 weeks left. So there was a 9-week deal, then a 13-week deal, then another 13 — that was it for the first year.

Bob Hope was so new at the beginning, he really didn't have an established character when you started...

That's true. Bob's style of comedy was kind of revolutionary and new to radio in those days; there wasn't anybody exactly like him. Jack Benny did character comedy. Eddie Cantor and those people did the schtick that they did. But not the Peck's Bad Boy with the impish grin who would tell a joke and then say, "Or..." and tell another joke. This was the style — it was basically unique to Bob. And it caught on. The show was very successful.

Would you say he was most responsible for that style, or did the writers help him develop that character?

No, Bob's delivery and style was his own. We just conformed to it. We used to have to read our material to Bob every Saturday. There was a fraternity of writers against Bob...

Against Bob?

In a nice sort of way. He was the ogre, he was the enemy. He was also the professional who got the most out of the joke. But there was a great amount of sympathy among all of us writers, because of the horrendous hours and the number of jokes that Bob wanted, and everything else.

What sort of hours were you working?

About 70 or 80 hours a week. But it was marvelous training, and we were just a couple of kids. Matter of fact, it was a lucky break for Mel and myself. We hadn't wanted to write radio comedy; we thought we were serious playwrights. Took a few years to prove that.

Jerry Colonna horns in on *The Pepsodent Show,* to the discomfort of Frances Langford and Bob Hope.

After about three years of radio, we wrote an original story called *My Favorite Blonde* and sold it to Paramount, and we were in pictures from then on.

Most of the writing for Hope would have been done at home?

We had a little bungalow in Hollywood, and we used to work there. The shows used to be planned — the way it worked was, the show broadcast on Tuesday night. Then we used to meet at the advertising agency, after having dinner somewhere around midnight, and plan the next week's show, and divide up who would write what. Mel Frank and I were a team, Milt Josefsberg and Mel Shavelson were a team — those were the two teams — then there was Al Schwartz and a couple of other guys. We'd work out an outline for the next week — it might be that Santa Anita [Racetrack] was opening. And everybody would write horse jokes. Or maybe it was the opening of the football season. Whatever the topical thing of the week was would be the basis for a show.

It must have taken a while to figure out what worked for Hope and what didn't, what fit his personality...

Well, we were learning about his personality at the same time we were writing it. It wasn't as formalized as that. It was all seat-of-the-pants flying on this particular show.

Hope was also learning about it himself I guess, finding out what would work.

And getting the confidence. Bob knew he could tell jokes; that's where he came from.

Do you recall any of the early shows where Hope might have done something, and then said, "That doesn't really work for me — let's not use that type of thing again"?

The joke formula "Or..." came out of that. 'Cause before the show, Hope used to warm up the audience. He'd do five or ten minutes of monologue. And one night he told a joke, and nothing much happened — and he said, "Or..." — and told another joke, or switched the same joke a different way, and got a big laugh. So "Or..." became for a while part of his arsenal. It's just a formula for a joke — in other words, if you tell a joke and it lays there, you go on to your next joke, if you're doing a monologue. Instead of going on, Bob would tell the joke, lay the egg, and say "Or..." — and tell another joke. Or a joke like it. Or repeat the joke and see why didn't it get a laugh.

I understand Hope was lightning quick, if anybody flubbed a line or dropped a script.

He could make the most of it. But it was very bad practice because of the fact that radio after all was not a visual medium. And the audience at home said, "What the fuck are they laughing at?" It happened once in a while, but what was more likely was the laughter you would get from the sound effects — the sound effects man running down the stairs, breaking the glass, the car zooming away...

On The Spike Jones Show, *Jones and the band did a lot of visual gags for the studio audience.*

There was a difference between *The Spike Jones Show* and *The Pepsodent Show.* Not that one was any better than the other, they were both about the same. Bob's personality came across — as far as he was concerned, it was duality. His stature as an actor and a comedian was developing in pictures, and at the same time radio was an absolute cinch for him.

I believe there was a weekly pitch session at Hope's house.

That's right. We'd lay out the show at the ad agency, we'd all have our assignments; we'd go away, and then come back with the material. We would get together on Saturday night at Bob's house out in Toluca Lake [near North Hollywood]. He'd usually be at a party somewhere, he'd come in at midnight or one o'clock. He'd order a half pint of ice cream [and eat it] —11 writers around the room looking at him — we used to make jokes about that.

You'd spend all night at his house on Saturday?

Not all night. He'd come in late, and we'd spend an hour or so. We used to read our material. I was a pretty good reader; I used to read like Groucho Marx. The other writers complained that we had an edge because I was doing Groucho and sounded so good. And it was partially true — but it wasn't intentional, it was just the way we used to present our material. What Bob would do is check off the jokes that he liked — he was getting like five or six shows, because we were two teams of two, and so on — and don't forget, we were all writing on the same subject. So now there'd be like 15 or 20 monologue jokes on Santa Anita. Bob would check off what he liked, or he'd give numbers to the jokes that he liked — a "3" would be a big one.

Then you would put the show together?

We would then go home, around one o'clock or whenever we finished, and put together the spots. Bob always did his own monologue; that was his baby. He always wanted more monologue jokes;

he was insatiable about that. Mel and I would put together the guest spot — Bob and Groucho, or whoever the guest of the week was. We'd put that together, and someone else would do something else, then we would deliver the material to him in Toluca Lake the following morning — Sunday morning — we'd gather out there, he'd read the material and check it off again. And we would take it into NBC and get it mimeographed for the preview that night. After the show that night, it was back to the advertising agency to play the record of the show — and the final editing — and we were off from then until the show Tuesday night. Although he always said, "I need a few more things for the monologue."

You would make a transcription record of the preview?

Right. And then listen to it, and you could tell which were the strong jokes — we'd rewrite some of them, or cut some of them. The record was made on Sunday night, the revisions and the rewriting and all that crap went on Monday, and the show was broadcast at 7 o'clock on Tuesday. We used to have to sit out in the audience and mop up the jokes, too, by the way.

You had to sit out front and laugh at the jokes?

Yeah. There were about eight writers, so it was a fairly decent body of people. They spread us out under various microphones — this was the origination of the short and sincere laugh.

Of the whole group on the Hope show, I think Milt Josefsberg might have been the only seasoned writer.

Milt wrote for Walter Winchell in New York; he met Mel Shavelson and they came out here. Some agent picked them up and brought them out because they were damn good. All the writers had experience except Melvin and I myself; we were just a couple of hopeful amateurs.

How was Bob Hope as an editor?

Well, he was the czar. It was his material. We didn't say, "Hey, Bob..." We might suggest a reading to him, if a joke didn't come across or something, in one of our private sessions putting material together. But by and large, he knew what he wanted.

Would you say he was pretty sharp as far as what worked and what didn't?

Oh, yeah. Thoroughly professional. Bob was and is a great comedian. I'm not talking about pace now, I'm just talking about delivery. About conception. Of course he was quick. He recognized the fact that he owed a tremendous amount to his writers, and he always had a very big writing staff, so big that there was very little money to go around.

Hope reportedly made paper planes out of the paychecks, and sailed them down the stairs.

That's true. Not always, but the Toluca Lake house had a kind of winding staircase; his bedroom was on the second floor. He used to make paper airplanes out of them once in a while, if he was in the mood for that. And you'd stand below and grab for your check. It was humiliating. We didn't all know what each of us was making — so there was a certain amount of desperation about grabbing your paper airplane. We had to protect our own sense of privacy; he used to say whose it was and then flip it down the stairs. But there wasn't any rancor to it. It was sort of a tasteless whimsicality.

Was that whimsicality typical of Hope?

To be frank with you, we were working our asses off so much — and happy to be working on a top show — I don't know. We came along as a fresh new thing, Mel Frank and I. It was our first show.

You quit to work for another comedian named Phil Baker.

Mel and I left the Hope show at the end of the first season, and went to New York to write *The Phil Baker Show,* for about four times the money. Phil was a vaudevillian and a star on Broadway in shows like *Night in Spain,* various Shubert revues. He had a classic act with an accordion, and a stooge who used to heckle him from the box. While Baker was playing the accordion, he would accompany the jokes with a little arpeggio. A very funny act, by the way. But his radio show was dying when we got there. I think whatever quality points the show had came from the Andrews Sisters.

How could they afford to pay you four times as much?

We weren't making much with Hope. I think we were making something like $250 or $300 for the team. The opening salary with Baker was something like $1,000 a week. And there were tickets on the Superchief, which was a big inducement — to travel first class.

Your stock was on the rise...

Mel and I signed with the William Morris office. I hate to keep mentioning the money, but the money *was* much different; the show was in trouble and we were the two bright boys, these new kids on the Coast. There were three or four other writers on the show who of course resented our coming in — I don't blame them. They sat on their asses mostly while we sweated our way through the summer. It wasn't the happiest time for Panama and Frank.

Would you say Baker was ineffectual as a radio comic?

Ineffectual is probably too harsh a word. Phil knew where the jokes were. His style was a gentler style than Hope's, not as staccato, not as abrasive. When we left the Hope show, we were exhausted from having written that thing all year, and we were in steamy New York with a show that was dying. We were walking down to Radio City with Phil one afternoon, and Oscar Levant came along — Oscar was at the height of his popularity with *Information Please*, the big quiz show. Phil introduces us to Oscar. He says, "Have you heard my new show?" Oscar rather politely said, "Yes." Then Baker said a stupid thing like, "Well, what did you think of it?" And instantly Oscar said, "I'm thinking of bringing over a string quartet and livening it up."

I believe you then went to work for Rudy Vallee.

The Baker show went off the air, so there we were in New York without a show. We came back to the West Coast, and did *The Rudy Vallee Show*, in which Rudy played a different character from history

James Cagney and Rudy Vallee apparently have something to sing about on Vallee's popular variety show, 1935.

every week, and a musical comedy. This was a new show, for Sealtest. Abe Burrows was on the show — Abe and Frank Galen were sort of a team, Mel and I were a team. And Paul Henning was on the show — in fact it was Paul's idea, *The Rudy Vallee Show* that we all did. Paul brought it in as an original idea, the format, the characters...

Ed Gardner also worked on that show.

Ed Gardner was the so-called — I guess he was producer of the show. And a very tasteful and dynamic — a breath of fresh air, as far as we were concerned. Ed came on the show, and we began having some fun again, writing it. But we were determined to get the hell out of radio.

Did you learn anything from working with Gardner on the show?

Just never to compromise; that things could always be a little sharper, a little better. A little more tasteful. He was a sophisticated man. We appreciated him, and liked working with him.

Could you assess Rudy Vallee's contributions as writer or editor?

He never wrote a line, never edited a line, and never really could tell a joke. He had absolutely no talent, and the show deservedly went off the air. But he was a legend in a way, because of his background and his early meteoric success; he lifted radio too, at a point. Vallee wasn't one of our all-time favorites. He barely deigned to recognize anybody on the show.

John Barrymore was a regular on the show. Were there any problems with his drinking?

As writers looking for premises, we wrote about his drinking naturally. And we were on for Sealtest, which was a dairy. It was a clean family-type show. So they said, "No more drinking jokes. And no more dope" — I think we wrote some marijuana references or something. And John heard about it, and he said, "I understand the boys are having a problem getting material for me. If it'll do you any good, you can tell them that I rarely bathe." Maxie Rosenbloom used to be on the show too. They gave whatever life there was to the show. Before it went off, Mel and I wrote *My Favorite Blonde* for Bob Hope, and we got back on the track that we came out for originally, which was to write movies — I'm not depreciating joke writing, which is not easy.

You had evidently left Hope's radio show on good terms.

We remained friends. Bob wasn't too happy we left him because of the Phil Baker thing, but they offered us three or four times the money, and he said, "I can't stand in your way." Through the years Mel and I wrote quite a lot of Bob's movies.

What medium do you think captured Hope better, radio or film?

John Barrymore gleefully mocks himself on screen in *The Great Profile*, with Gregory Ratoff looking on.

It's hard to say, because he was so good in both. He never really believed in himself as an actor. The many pictures that we did with him, we used to say, "Bob, for Chrissake, you don't need a pocketful of jokes. The medium is different." He'd say, "I know, I know..." But he'd always rather have a pocketful of jokes. And he used to try to force them into situations. In *My Favorite Blonde*, we did a pantomime sequence for him in the club car of a train in which there are half a dozen spies in the room, and each one takes a look at him in turn. And his reactions were marvelous, but he didn't know that.

He didn't know his own strengths?

Mel and I pointed it out to him later. We said, "Bob, you're getting laughs because it's a reactive medium. The audience doesn't laugh at you, they laugh at the reaction to what's happening — that's why you don't have to tell jokes."

He was so used to getting the laugh with the joke on radio...

On radio and on the stage. He got two or three very good reviews in New York before he got into radio. His sense of timing came naturally. He had to be convinced that he didn't have to have jokes, and he became a better actor because of it. Later on during the pictures, he used to bring in jokes from his writers for scenes.

Just in case there weren't enough in the script.

A lot of them were good of course, but most of them didn't fit the situation — the medium was so different — we'd rewrite the jokes that were now being submitted by his staff, to try to protect the material in the movie. We didn't want a joke on every line, if we were playing a situation or trying to develop a character. When Mel and I did the *Road* pictures, the characters kind of developed themselves. Hope was Hope, Crosby was Crosby, Lamour was Lamour — although each story was different. The characters were the same.

Was it difficult to segue from writing for Bob Hope as a radio comic, to writing for him as a movie comedian?

Well, the style of writing was entirely different. In a movie, he had to play a character. Even though the character in a *Road* picture might be a [stereotype] of some kind. The last picture I did with him was *How to Commit Marriage,* he and Jackie Gleason. That was probably the closest thing to his radio persona, that he did in his movies. It was wonderful working with them — they were two great comedians who came out of different mediums. This was away from the formula stuff that they did on their radio and television shows. Here they were playing two characters.

As opposed to simply throwing jokes at each other.

The principal example of this is the picture that Mel and I did with Bob and Lucille Ball called *The Facts of Life,* in which they played characters. We originally had written the thing for Olivia de Havilland and some stray leading man [William Holden] — we couldn't sell it to Metro at the time. Later Mel came up with the idea, "What would you think about *The Facts of Life* with Hope and Ball?" I said, "I think that's a great idea." We went out to see both of them at their homes and in one day we put the picture together.

Lucille said, "No jokes, now; we're going to play characters." And Bob agreed. It gave the picture what distinction it had, which I personally thought was quite a lot — away from the pocketful of jokes.

Was it more difficult writing movies than radio shows?

It was quite a radical transition. Radio is a form of your imagination; you have to bring something to it to appreciate what it was. Now we were dealing with a visual medium — one picture, they say, is worth a thousand words. The writer who came out of radio and into pictures had to go into a decompression chamber and discover the camera tells the story, and it is a reactive medium. Not so in radio. Film is strictly reactive.

I take it writing for movies was more satisfactory.

We were satisfied. That's because our horizons were always broader than what we were doing. The plays we wrote back in college were serious plays. They had comedy in them, of course — we couldn't stop that, or didn't want to.

You and Mel Frank wrote the screenplay for the film version of Duffy's Tavern. *How did you translate it from radio to film?*

We had a helluva lot of trouble on that picture. It was a very hard assignment. Mel and I wrote three or four different versions of it for Buddy DeSylva, who was head of Paramount. DeSylva and the executives out here had never heard the radio show. They almost fainted when they saw some film tests that were shot in the East, back at the studio. DeSylva said, "Oh, my God, what are we going to do now?" I remember his absolute panic at how terrible it was going to look on the screen.

How did you resolve the problem?

We said, "Well, the charm of the thing is its unwashed, sort of strange eccentric look. And that's what you bought. And if it doesn't work..." DeSylva said, "What the hell, we'll take a crack at it. If it doesn't work, we'll junk it." The picture turned out to be an all-star revue with everybody in town and that saved it — it didn't save it, but it was releasable.

You once said when you got into movies you "escaped from radio."

It was a mildly humorous way of saying it was a salt mine. It was death for anybody who... if you had sensitivity and you could write beyond it, and write character, you could never be satisfied writing for radio. You could, depending on what you were writing for radio, but if you were going to write situation comedy, that's pretty grim and one-dimensional. It was a little bit mechanical.

Could you assess your strengths as compared to Mel Frank?

It was a collaboration in which we never knew or took credit for each other's work. It was kind of a magic machine of give and take.

Did you each write different types of jokes, different types of material?

No. Mel and I had different strengths, but we sublimated our egos to what was coming out on the written page. We were a composite of almost the same personality, strangely enough — a composite talent. My strength might have been the fact that I could type better than Mel, and change a typewriter ribbon. We were together for over 25 years. We were one person. Producer Arthur Freed at MGM used to pass one of us in the hall and say, "Hello, boys."

CREDITS

Radio (in collaboration with Melvin Frank): *The Bob Hope Show, The Phil Baker Show, The Durante-Moore Show, The Rudy Vallee Show, Command Performance.*

Film (with Frank): *My Favorite Blonde* (story only), *The Princess and the Pirate* (uncredited*), *Star Spangled Rhythm, Happy Go Lucky, Thank Your Lucky Stars, And the Angels Sing, Duffy's Tavern, Our Hearts Were Growing Up, Monsieur Beaucaire, Road to Utopia, It Had to Be You, Mr. Blandings Builds His Dream House* (also co-producer), *A Southern Yankee* (story only), *The Return of October, The Reformer and the Redhead* (also co-producer/co-director), *Strictly Dishonorable* (also co-producer/co-director), *Calloway Went Thataway* (also co-producer/co-director), *Above and Beyond* (also co-producer/co-director), *Knock on Wood* (also co-producer/co-director),*White Christmas, The Court Jester* (also co-producer/co-director),*That Certain Feeling* (also co-producer/co-director), *Li'l Abner* (also co-producer/co-director), *The Jayhawkers* (also co-producer), *The Facts of Life* (also co-producer),*The Road to Hong Kong* (also director), *Strange Bedfellows* (story only), *Not With My Wife You Don't!* (also producer-director).

Film (without Frank as co-writer): *The Trap* (also co-producer and director), *How to Commit Marriage* (director only), *The Maltese Bippy* (director only), *I Will, I Will... For Now* (also director).

TV (without Frank): *Coffee, Tea or Me?* (TV movie: director only), *Barnaby and Me* (TV movie: director only).

Theater (with Frank except as noted): *Utopia, Inc.*, sketches for Shubert revues, *Keep Off the Grass, Li'l Abner* (also co-producer); *The Thirty-First of June* (without Frank).

* Panama and Frank wrote an incomplete screenplay and several story outlines for this project in 1941; their material apparently was not used.

SHERWOOD SCHWARTZ

"Sherwood Schwartz. He sounds like Robin Hood's rabbi." With those eight words, Hal Kanter once introduced his fellow comedy writer at a testimonial dinner, to an audience of their peers. Recalls the honorary rabbi: "I was supposed to speak — it was hopeless — they laughed for 20 minutes. I just said, 'It looks like I'm not going to able to follow my own name.' Then I sat down. There's was nothing else I could do. Kanter introduced me with that, and it's followed me everywhere I've gone."

Schwartz was born in Passaic, New Jersey, on November 14, 1916. He was pursuing his studies at the University of Southern California with the intent of becoming a doctor when fate — in the person of his older brother, Al Schwartz — intervened. A golden opportunity to follow in the footsteps of his sibling, as a writer for an up-and-coming comedian named Bob Hope, threw the younger Schwartz into a quandary.

Remembered writer Norman Panama: "Sherwood came down to the theater where we were broadcasting one night, and said he had a dilemma — should he go to medical school, or should he become a comedy writer like his brother Al? We thought, 'For God's sake, you must be kidding, you gotta become a doctor.' Naturally, he didn't take our advice, and became a wonderful comedy writer.' "

Schwartz followed up his apprenticeship on *The Bob Hope Show* with a stint in the Army. By a stroke of luck, he fulfilled his duty by working for Armed Forces Radio Service, where he wrote for virtually every star in Hollywood. After the war, he returned to Radio Row, where he toiled in the service of *The Adventures of Ozzie and Harriet*, *The Alan Young Show* and *The Beulah Show*.

I Married Joan introduced Schwartz to television, where he eventually found his fortune, creating not one but two critically lambasted — yet phenomenally popular — shows. The first of his "cult classics" was conceived as an escape from the confines of writing for *The Red Skelton Show*, to which he devoted seven years.

Schwartz sold the idea for *Gilligan's Island* to CBS on the spot in 1963, but the show barely managed to make it on the air. When network president Jim Aubrey pushed for "a charter boat that would take people to different places," the creator told him it was an idea for a show, but not his show. The castaways spent three years in prime time and have been syndicated non-stop ever since.

The writer's 1969-74 ABC series, *The Brady Bunch*, likewise found an audience that strongly identified with the show. Like *Gilligan*, the program has been reborn in a spate of TV movies; it has also returned as a live stage production — which recreated original episodes word for word — and even a feature film, which spawned a sequel of its own. (The movies' co-producer is Sherwood's son, Lloyd Schwartz, with whom he wrote *Gilligan's Island: The Musical*; his daughter Hope Sherwood co-wrote music and lyrics for the latter).

"I honestly think I could sit down and write a show tonight that the critics would love, and I know it would be canceled within four weeks. I *know* what the critics love," Schwartz once said, in response to the pounding *Gilligan* and *Brady* have taken over the years. "[I] write and produce for people, not for critics."

Like many successful television writers, you got your start during the Golden Age of Radio.

The Golden Age of Radio didn't last all that long. But the funny thing is this — anytime I'm in the car, I listen to news — I get more out of that than news on TV. It's always fresher — 'cause it's immediate. That's the great thing about radio, anyway. Its immediacy. It always was.

As Norman Corwin says, "It was the shortest Golden Age in history."

He knows whereof he speaks. I guess it was from '35 or so... by '50 it was gone. I came into it in 1939. You know what Satchel Paige said. "Don't look back, somethin' may be gainin' on you!" I don't do that; I don't look back.

Did you have much interest in radio prior to that? Were you an avid fan?

No. I liked it. I am not obsessive about almost anything. That's why I'm sometimes amazed — I frequently bump into people who are so obsessed with *Gilligan's Island*, or *The Brady Bunch*, which I cannot understand. There are people who want to know everything there is to know about those shows. I'm very happy about it. But I don't quite understand it. Makes me a little nervous sometimes.

What's your earliest memory of listening to radio?

My earliest memories are a crystal set, when I was a little kid back in New Jersey. I guess my early memory is Roosevelt and his Fireside Chats. He was such an enormous figure in history, even to a little kid. But a President is impressive — at least he was in those years. I remember *The Jack Benny Show*, I remember *Lux Radio Theatre*. I remember the scary ones; I think kids remember the scary ones more than anything else. The creaking door — Arch Oboler — I remember him, and his shows. They had an enormous impact. They still do.

Your introduction to radio was by way of your brother, Al.

Yes. My brother was on *The Bob Hope Show* the 1938-39 season, the first year of the Hope-Pepsodent show. Bob had been on radio previously, but this was his big opportunity. That's when Bob really took off and became famous. It took off like a skyrocket, that show. And my brother was on it the first year. I was at USC, getting a Master's Degree in guess what?

You were going into medicine.

Yes, that's right. A Master's in Biological Sciences. I had about a month left over. And it didn't seem to me to be very difficult to write comedy, and I had no money — so I said to my brother, "If I write some jokes, would you show them to Bob?" And he said, "Sure." So I wrote some jokes, and he showed them to Bob, who liked them — and the last month of *The Bob Hope Show* that first year, they used some of my material. And then he said to me, "Why don't you come on the show?" So the following year, in 1939, I became a writer all of a sudden. I've been writing ever since.

Had you toyed with the idea before that, since your brother was writing for radio?

No. Although I had little adventures in writing. When I was in high school, a friend of mine was a very good mimic; he could imitate

Bob Hope and his gaggle of gagsters, 1939. Seated left to right: Milt Josefsberg, Hope, Mel Shavelson, Jack Rose, Dick McKnight and Norman Sullivan. Standing: Al Schwartz (left) and Sherwood Schwartz.

anybody. They had amateur hour in theaters; they had a movie and then they had amateur hour. So we went to several different places, sometimes once a month. I would write the material and he would do it. He would do impressions and use my material, and we would divide the money. I was 16 at the time. But I never had any ambitions to be a writer; it was just something I felt I could do, but that was not my interest. Then I started to do it, and it did become my interest, and my life. I've been writing for over 50 years. My fingers are getting tired.

How did your brother get started?

Al had a strange career. My mother always wanted him to be an attorney, and he thought he wanted to be an attorney — but he didn't really, once he got into law school. He always wanted to write jokes. And he wound up going to law school, and writing jokes, which he used to send into the columns. Walter Winchell used to have jokes. It was a two-way street — they'd [print] my brother's name and his joke, so he would get a little publicity, and Winchell would fill up his column.

A lot of writers started that way.

Yes. Many writers. Then Al sold some jokes to Milton Berle. A lot of people in those years who wrote comedy started by selling jokes, piecemeal — five dollars a joke, maybe $10 — to comics. Finally, at my parents' insistence, Al finished law school, passed the bar, gave his diploma to my mother and said, "Here, I'm a lawyer, now let me go do what I want to do." He went to work for Berle on a steady basis, then heard about *The Bob Hope Show* and joined the show. I was going to USC and living with my brother; I saw what he did, and I became involved just because I was there.

Did you more or less learn the craft of comedy writing from him?

I don't really know. It just never seemed hard to me. At the end of the term, I finished my thesis — "The Effect of Vitamin E on the Damage and the Germinal Epithelium in the Testes of the Rat, Caused by Irradiation" — I went right from there to Bob Hope. An unlikely step.

A quantum leap.

I'm glad that I didn't become a doctor, for a very strange reason — because I don't think I'd be alive today if I were a doctor. Because I know how — I have a certain personality, and if I have a sick script to worry about, I'll be up all night. If I had a sick patient to worry about, I think it would just destroy me — if one of them died, or something like that. I mean, I've had a script occasionally that died, but that didn't kill me. But I think if a patient died it might. So — it's just as well that I became a writer.

Of course, you have it all within your power to correct a sick script — whereas you can only do so much as a doctor, and it's out of your control.

You're absolutely right. So you have to face a different kind of rigor mortis with a dead script, than you do with a patient. You can always revive a dead script, but people, when they go, they go.

Speaking of which, when you did the Sunday night rehearsals of the Hope show, a lot of the jokes didn't fly.

That's what the previews were for. Bob Hope really invented a new way of writing comedy. Jack Benny had two writers originally — then all of a sudden, Bob had seven guys, I think. Or eight guys. At that time, nobody was doing that. Sometimes there were teams of writers — he would get I guess four or five scripts. So what that gave Bob was an opportunity at any point — since we always wrote the same show, we always had the same outline — we gave him the choice of moving from this script to that script to get the best parts of each.

He would throw out the premise, or the writer would come up with an outline?

He would start — the writers would come up with various ideas, and then he would approve one basic line for the show. Hope was very involved with the writers. In those years. I don't know how it was after that, because I was there for four years, and then I went into the service.

You couldn't have asked for a better training ground.

The Bob Hope Show was one of the great training grounds for writers, because the nature of the show demanded lack of words. Even within the confines of a monologue joke, it had to be in and out, as soon as possible. Superfluous words were killed off, immediately — Hope had no use for them. He had a rhythm in his speech, and you learned that rhythm. An extra "the" was cut out. You learn to write bare bones kind of dialogue. No fat. So you kill phrases that have no meaning — and that hurts sometimes. You learn spare writing. That's why I don't think I could ever be a novelist. To write about the color of the changing mountains due to the sunlight that's fading, and all this kind of stuff — first of all, you don't need it in films, because you see it — you don't have to write about all that stuff. But I would be too impatient.

Who was on Hope's staff when you arrived in 1939? Norman Panama and Melvin Frank had left the show by that time...

Panama and Frank were only there the first year, then they moved on; I was there just at the end of that year, the last month of it. So I didn't get to meet them very often. Mel Shavelson and Milt Josefsberg were a team, and my brother and Norman Sullivan were a team. This gave Bob an opportunity to look at five scripts that were basically the same story, that had different jokes. Everybody wrote different jokes. He would pick one from here and one from there, then various groups of writers would put it together, using the material Bob liked. Then we'd do this preview that would run an hour and a half, and unless a joke got an enormous laugh, it was cut. Because we had an hour and a half to trim down to a half hour.

How was the preview structured? Hope took parts of scripts...

Parts of different scripts. But it was just one long script. So that every scene, which should have been three pages, was nine pages. And it ran very long. Then you cut that down. So you really had the cream of the crop that was left. We used to grade the jokes — unless it got a "3" with a check next to it [the joke was dropped].

How much depended on the audience, as opposed to what you guys thought was funny?

What we thought was funny was on the page. If the audience laughed, it was good. If they didn't laugh, it was not.

It was what got the biggest reaction, rather than what Hope or anyone else thought.

Absolutely.

If Hope thought it was a great joke and it didn't get the reaction...

Then it was gone. And that's why Bob played no favorites when it came to jokes, regardless of his politics — he would do a joke about Democrats just as willingly as a joke about — anything. If a Republican joke got a bigger laugh than a Democratic joke, that went in. They were only a very few things — he would not do jokes about mother-in-laws. He wouldn't do that. He loved to do jokes that he felt were a little esoteric. If it included some term that he was not familiar with, he would always do that joke — 'cause he wanted to show the writers that he was up on everything. So that was a way to get jokes into a script.

As far as what went into the 90-minute preview...

But then it was dead, after that. If he didn't like a joke, it was not done.

Would you try and use it again later on? Rewrite it with a different twist on it?

You might. But not if the audience didn't like it. 'Cause that was his test. He would put himself second to the audience. We'd spend all day building up to this preview on Sunday night. And after the preview — it would be 10:30, 11:00 o'clock — we would always gather at what was then Lord & Thomas, the advertising agency. All of us, including Bob. It was really grinding. He was meticulous — it had to be just right. We would be there frequently until five in the morning, looking for just one joke sometimes. So that those scripts were honed and polished — and *big*, in terms of audience reaction.

I've been told Hope was a pretty good ad-libber.

Yes. Very few people give him credit for that. Because he had so many writers. But the truth is, he was so smart — he knew that nobody could ad-lib perfectly all the time. So he felt much more secure with writers. But that does not mean he can't ad-lib. 'Cause he can; he's a remarkable man. Bob is just as much at home on a stage as he is in his own living room. There is no trepidation, no nervousness, no nothing. He walks out as though he owns the audience, and the audience reacts as though they know he owns them. It's a two-way street — they both agree.

Any particular recollections of Hope's talent for ad-libbing?

Something does come to mind with Elvia Allman, who was Cobina on the Hope show. One time, she was not in that character; she played a different character on the show. And on the preview night — Bob was a desk clerk , and she was a guest in the hotel — and she was supposed to say, "Send somebody up right away, there's a man peering over my transom." She said, instead, "Send somebody up right away, there's a man peeing over my transom." And Bob said, "Tall son of a gun, isn't he?" There was a huge laugh. For those who don't think Bob can ad-lib — you can't do better than that.

Many people — especially movie personalities — were uncomfortable on radio.

It's funny, but a lot of performers, on sound stages — where they don't see the microphone, and don't have to talk directly into it — are fine. But put a microphone in front of them, they get very rattled. One day I wrote a script for Armed Forces Radio — I think it was for *Mail Call*, with Clark Gable. And Gable was terrified of microphones. So he would never do radio. But they prevailed upon him because it was for the Armed Forces, to do this show. He and Bob Hope had exchanged little black books, so each one was going to have a choice of the other one's dates — that was the idea of this show. Bob wound up with Margaret O'Brien, who was 9 years old, and Clark Gable wound up with Dame May Whitty, who was 82. It was just a funny idea, each one tricking the other with a phone number.

How did Gable manage this "command performance"?

Bob came out and did an opening monologue, and Gable came out — this was an all-servicemen audience, some 300 servicemen. Gable was so nervous, the script he was holding — his hand was shaking so hard that you could pick up the rattling. Which he didn't know, but Bob knew. And then he couldn't talk. His tongue got stuck in his mouth. So Bob put his arm around him, and said, "Clark, these guys are friends. We're going to have fun together." He said, "I think we should start over, and I think we should have fun." Bob is so at home with the microphone, and with audiences, and of course Gable wasn't.

They weren't on the air live — they recorded these Armed Forces shows on transcription discs and then sent them out for broadcast.

That's right. So they started over, and Bob did the first part of that scene with his hand holding Gable's arm so it wouldn't shake. It took him about two or three minutes, then everything was okay. It was a remarkable scene of a man helping somebody overcome this stage fright. It sounds strange to talk about Clark Gable and stage fright in the same breath, but he was terrified of microphones.

Could you describe a typical writing session for Bob Hope?

Well, a writing session, with all these eight people, was not for jokes. That was to outline the show itself. It was a pitch session about what is a good topic, what's topical right now. It would be in a room at the advertising agency. Somebody would say, "You know what's important this week? Why don't we do a thing about this?" And the funny thing about comedy writers is that they appreciate what's funny but don't necessarily laugh. Somebody will say something that's very funny, and it will be greeted by the other writers saying, "Hey, that's great." No laughter — 'cause they know it's funny.

And where did you write? At your individual homes?

That's right. We'd do a take-off on some song that was popular. But it could be a movie, it could be something else — very often we would do satirical sketches of some movie, and that would be the idea. And then we'd all go away, and write our version of that story, breaking it into segments that composed the show. Then we'd gather — the material would be sent over to Bob, to look at — then we'd have a meeting, and he would discuss what he liked and didn't like. Then different writers would then put together different parts of the show.

Your brother was the head writer on the show, wasn't he?

Yeah, the first year I was there. But Bob truly was the head writer because he made all final decisions by himself. He seldom came up with jokes, because he didn't have to. He had the jokes handed to him. So he would just pick and choose, and this was more valuable. As valuable as a writer is — and believe me, I know — nevertheless, the guy who knows what material is proper for him, is in a sense the head writer. He has to be. Bob was an excellent editor. He didn't have to write jokes — 'cause he knew which jokes were best.

How long would it generally take to do a script, once you had the pitch session?

It would take you the week, because in those years you didn't have to be ahead, like in television. No sets to build. That was the wonderful thing about radio. All you have to do is say, "Here we are in front of the Taj Mahal." And you go from there — in everybody's head was a better Taj Mahal than anybody could build for you anyway on the stage. So you didn't have to spend eight days filming it. It used to take maybe four days, five days; we'd take off a day and then we'd gather and discuss the next script, then go off and write.

What other recollections do you have of writing for Hope?

Because I was the youngest kid on the show, when I first came on there — among my duties, when we used to work until 3, 4, 5 o'clock in the morning — he would sometime during that night send me down to get a pineapple sundae for him, at the Pig & Whistle on the corner of Hollywood and Vine. It was open all night. He used to give me 35 cents to get him his sundae — and he liked it a certain way, he just liked vanilla ice cream and pineapple syrup on it; no whipped cream, no cherry. So I used to get it. He'd eat his ice cream; the writers would sit around and watch him. Then I didn't see him for a couple of years...

During the war.

...I was in uniform. I was in New York on a mission, for some show or other, and *The Bob Hope Show* was emanating from New York, just by coincidence. I said, "I ought to go and say hello to the guys, and to Bob." So I went to the NBC building — there's a drugstore on the corner — so I stopped in there and I got a pineapple sundae for him, the way I always used to get it. Now, I'm in uniform, he hasn't seen me in some two years; he's sitting in the room with the cast, all rehearsing, and I come into the room. I was behind him. I tapped him on the shoulder and I said, "Bob, here's your pineapple sundae." He said, "What took you so long?" Two years. Further evidence of this man's...

How much were you paid by Hope?

I started at $50 a week. Which I guess was all right; I'd never written anything for anybody before then. Then it was in 13 week cycles; it was $75 and then $100. You couldn't put that staff together later on for I don't know how much money. But the whole writing budget was like $1500.

He apparently paid everybody at different rates...

Well, in a way it was depending on what your experience was. And I was completely inexperienced. I not only didn't know how to type when I got out here, I didn't have enough money for a typewriter. I found a secondhand typewriter, which cost I think $55 or something. But I didn't have $55. So Milt Josefsberg was the co-signer on my typewriter. Milt was a very nice guy. Bob's writers were a bunch of nice guys.

Did you work with a partner on the show?

I never did. I probably would have written with my brother, except he already had a partner [Norman Sullivan] and they wrote together. So I wrote my own scripts. I really don't know how that happened, but I know that I always worked alone.

Who was the biggest joker on Hope's writing staff?

Jack Douglas was funny. He was kind of a character; he worked alone. He never was satisfied with the audience's reaction. If he had a pet joke, and it didn't get a laugh, he would scream and carry on and curse the audience. Everybody else accepted the fact that the audience laughed at what they believed. But not Jack Douglas. He believed he knew better what was funny than the audience. He would try to insist on certain jokes remaining in, even though the audience didn't laugh too hard.

Would the various writers write different types of jokes for Bob?

I guess you have your own style, but I don't think you know what it is. I think other people know your style better than you do, because it's something you do, and you do it unconsciously. You write a certain way. There are certain jokes that I think I could pick out as Jack Douglas jokes — 'cause they were off the wall. I mean, he wrote material that is just different. I will never forget a joke of his which amazed me, 'cause the audience *did* laugh at it. He said — this was a satirical commercial — he said, "This is the only toothpaste in the world that contains John Charles Thomas." What does that mean?

It is an off-the-wall joke, but it's funny.

That's what I mean. That's the kind of jokes he wrote. Usually either the audience laughed a *lot* at one of his jokes, or they didn't laugh at all, 'cause they couldn't comprehend it. John Charles Thomas was a famous opera singer at that time. But what he was doing inside a tube of toothpaste is something else again.

Would a lot of Jack Douglas' material find its way into the final script?

Yeah, very often. Jack once wrote a joke about Jerry Colonna calling in — he's an engineer building bridges — and he said, "Good news, Mr. Hope. We just finished the Mississippi River bridge. It took us 55 years." Hope said, "My goodness, 55 years to build a bridge across the Mississippi River?" Colonna said, "Ohhhh, *across* the river." What a great joke that is. Not duplicable on television.

No. You could only tell that joke on radio.

There's where radio will continue to shine — in the mind. There are a lot of jokes, particularly Jerry Colonna-kind of jokes — I love Colonna jokes, which, by their very nature, are off-the-wall kind of humor. And I wrote quite a lot of Colonna jokes — but not like Douglas — mine are more grounded in reality. That same show contained a joke that I wrote, when Jerry said, "We just finished building a bridge from Nashville, Tennessee, to Lincoln, Nebraska." Hope said, "Colonna, it's absolutely impossible to build a bridge from Nashville, Tennessee, to Lincoln, Nebraska." Colonna said, "It is?" Hope said, "Yes." Colonna said, "Boys, take her down." Now, again, there's no way to do that — except in radio.

The best radio jokes were visual.

Visual. That's right. I once wrote a joke about an escaped lunatic. Again, it was Jerry Colonna who was searching for this escaped lunatic. Hope said to him, "Can you give me his description?" Jerry said, "Oh, yes. He's very short, very thin, and he weighs 350 pounds." Bob says, "350 pounds?" Colonna says, "Why are you so surprised? I told you he was crazy." How are you going to have such a person? There's no way to legitimize something that's only in the mind. And that was radio's great contribution, the stimulation of the imagination — which you don't get, you have to show things on television.

Did you have any trouble with the censors then?

I never personally had trouble with censors, even in television. I guess I have — and I don't think it's necessarily good — I have a built-in sense of my own. You become accustomed to knowing what's going to be accepted or not accepted, and there's taste at stake too. I can only tell you, at the start of each TV season, somebody from the censorship department would gather all the producers together, and the associate producers, and give a lecture on what he's going to allow, and what he isn't, and so forth. This ABC censor gathered all the producers together. And then he said, "Is there anybody here from *The Brady Bunch*?" Three of us raised our hands. He said, "You're excused." So I have never had trouble with censors. Maybe that's wrong — maybe I don't stretch in those directions — but that's how *I* am. I'm not saying everybody should be that way.

How did you come to work for Armed Forces Radio, other than being drafted?

Well — your life is sometimes touch and go — particularly in those war years. I left *The Bob Hope Show* in 1942 or '43, after four seasons. I was up in San Luis Obispo, California, in basic training — the next day my unit was shipping out. I didn't even know where — they don't tell you that. My group, Special Services — we were slated to go to the Aleutians, which is the worst place to be sent. That evening, orders arrived for me to come down to Hollywood to Armed Forces Radio Service. On my application — all the papers you filled out — I said that I was a writer, and they were just staffing the AFRS division, and they sent for me. Had that order come a day later, I would've been gone — I'd have been in the Aleutians. Timing.

I believe the AFRS headquarters were at Sunset Boulevard and Western Avenue in Los Angeles?

Originally. Then we moved over to Santa Monica Boulevard, near Gower. Every day you had to be there at 6:30 a.m. for roll call, and 10 minutes later you were supposed to be writing jokes, or writing scripts anyway. We had about the same size staff as Bob Hope, now that I think about it. They had about seven or eight comedy writers, turning out I don't know how many shows a week. I'll tell you who was there — there were a couple of guys named Jerome Lawrence and Robert E. Lee. They would write one part of *Command Performance,* the dramatic part, and then the comedy writers would write the other part.

Was there a head writer at AFRS?

No. We were all privates. Col. Tom Lewis was head of the whole operation. And the majors and captains and all those people came from ad agencies. The writers were privates, or corporals. As were the performers — although some of them were lieutenants also.

Was the operation run like an army base?

It was an army base. We used to line up at 6:30, and it was very difficult to go your office and start writing scripts immediately. So what we started doing — we would line up, and then we would go off and have breakfast. We'd get back an hour later, and then start work on the scripts. Well, the army doesn't take kindly to rules and regulations being broken by privates and corporals, so they brought in a regular army captain. People think that unless you're physically writing, you're not writing. You can stare out a window for 20 minutes, and you're writing; it's all going on in your head. Well, he didn't understand that at all. So he said, "You're supposed to be at your desk, writing, at 6:32" — or whatever, right after roll call. So, we really didn't pay any attention.

It was business as usual, as far as you were concerned.

The next day we went out and had breakfast, and then came back — and when we got back, sure enough there was a notice that all of us were put on KP. The captain said we had to get into fatigues and pull all the weeds out of the officer's parking lot. So we were pulling weeds in the parking lot; the officers started to arrive and they said, "What are you guys doing?" We said, "Well, we were naughty, and we're being punished." So they said, "Who's writing *Mail Call*? Who's writing *Jubilee*? Who's writing all the shows?" We said, "We were put on KP; we were told we had to do this." So the major — "Pete" Peterson, who was a very nice guy — went to see the captain, who was this hard-line army guy, and he said to him, "I have news for you, Captain. If men pull weeds for a living, you can punish them by making them write jokes. It doesn't work the other way around." That's my favorite memory of AFRS.

Did you write for Jubilee?

Yeah, that was the black AFRS show. It was a variety show. They had wonderful black entertainers. In today's market, you couldn't do a segregated show like that. It would be crazy. But in those years, what the hell, they had separate latrines for black and white. A different time in American life. So we had Lena Horne and other great black performers.

Was it different writing for that show than Command Performance *or* Mail Call?

No. The writing, so far as the AFRS shows were concerned, didn't make any difference — whether it was *Jubilee* or *Mail Call*, you just wrote as funny as you could write.

How was it decided who wrote what?

I would write with one guy one week, and another guy the next. I don't remember any organization — I remember just writing this and writing that. Somebody would say, "Hey, you got a minute?" In a given week, you could be working on three different shows. We had a show called *G.I. Journal*. It was a newspaper format. There would be a cooking column, and an advice to the lovelorn column. There would be a different editor, like Bing Crosby would be the editor one week...

All the stars were involved in Armed Forces Radio.

That was the great thing about writing in that milieu — you could get anybody. There were three agents who had been drafted, who would contact all these people and find out their availability. They knew the stars personally; they knew who represented these people.

So you would find out who was available, and then write to fit the star?

I'd mostly just write. And then we'd get the stars to fit as well as we could. Because we could almost get anybody. Don't forget, this was radio — they didn't have to learn anything. They just had to come in on an evening and read the script.

Did you work with Jack Benny or Fred Allen at AFRS?

Oh, sure. We did quite a few things with both of them; they were guests on different shows. They were both terrific people. I must've written for 100 stars. Every star you can imagine. And it was all going on in one week, sometimes. And all different things. Bob Hope was so generous, so was Bing Crosby, so was Kay Kyser.

Would Fred Allen write his own material when he was on Command Performance?

No. Fred Allen was a great writer. Nobody could turn a phrase better than Allen; he was brilliant. But he understood the time constraints that we were under, going from show to show and doing things as fast as we were, and trying to keep everybody's character in proper perspective. He may have changed some lines here and there, but never made a fuss about it. He did the material. Most of the stars did. I remember an unpleasant situation with Eddie Bracken, who thought that army writers could *never* be as good as civilian writers — forgetting the fact that we were all civilians to begin with. And he just wouldn't do the skit, so we got somebody else.

Did any of the guest stars surprise you, in what they did?

I remember one specific time when Bing Crosby and Bob Hope did a spot with Frank Sinatra, and this is just when he was taking off in his career. And everybody felt sorry for poor Frank, being thrown in with these two huge stars. Well, they started ad-libbing, and it was Frank who put both of them away. It was really — nobody expected it.

Are there any other guest stars who stand out in your mind?

For the most part, they were just super cooperative. I remember an incident with Jerome Kern. We did a show — I guess it was *Mail Call* — to satisfy certain requests from servicemen. Somebody wanted the biggest, most important songwriters to each sing or perform his own favorite song. And Jerome Kern was high on the list. He was the dean. The most important older songwriter we could get was Jimmy McHugh, who — at the drop of a hat — loved to sing. But Jerome Kern was a very shy person. I called him and he said no, he doesn't do that. I said, "What do you mean, you don't do that? This is for the army — and you certainly rank among the most important songwriters of all time." "Thank you, but no." He said even the thought of appearing in public, he gets a fever blister. He said, "I just don't appear." Well, we wanted him...

So you didn't take no for an answer?

Jerome Kern's real fear, it turned out, was that nobody would know him. He said, "Sure, they know Hoagy Carmichael, they know Johnny Mercer" — who were [appearing] in the same show — "They know those people, but nobody's going to remember me." I assured him they would, and it went back and forth. Finally he agreed, just to come on and say, "Thank you very much. My favorite song is 'Smoke Gets in Your Eyes' " — which it was. I said, "That's all you have to say."

And did Kern show up?

It came the day of the show, and the announcer introduced him. We saved Jerome Kern for last, 'cause he was the most important one, whether he thought so or not. Everybody else got a terrific hand — Hoagy Carmichael did "Star Dust," Johnny Mercer I think did "Blues in the Night," Jimmy McHugh did "Sunny Side of the Street" — they all did their favorite song. And then they announced Jerome Kern. And he came out, and the audience went *crazy*. They applauded, and screamed, and gave him a standing ovation — he was the only one. They stood and just cheered and yelled, and Kern stood in front of the microphone, and cried. Tears were streaming down his face; he couldn't talk. So he never said anything. He just walked over to the piano and he played the song. He was so humble that he couldn't believe what was happening. Most people overestimate themselves. Kern so clearly underestimated his importance, and the love of America for him. Young or old, everybody knew his songs. *Show Boat* is forever.

You left AFRS in 1946. How had the industry changed during the war?

Prices had gone up. I was in the army for three years. I did *Ozzie and Harriet* when I got out of there. It was completely different — when I went in, if you got $150 you were making a lot of money. When I got out, people were being paid $350, $500 for writing. There was a dramatic increase, somehow, during the time I was in. All of a sudden I was making twice as much.

You didn't feel so bad about not having made any money during the war.

Well, I gained more than money. 'Cause I learned to write for anybody and everybody. We all did. And it had to be funny, no matter who it was — if you were writing comedy. Very often you had dramatic performers who wanted to do comedy. You could do that for them, and they could do a lot for you. So, it was a good arrangement. It was invaluable experience for me as a fairly young writer at that time.

And you couldn't be fired from AFRS.

No. Well, if you wrote a bad script they could take you out and shoot you.

Do you recall any writers...

Who got shot? No, I don't. I mean, that's "desertion" if you write a bad script. And you can't demote a private. So where were they going to put us?

Your next show was The Adventures of Ozzie and Harriet — *quite a departure from* The Bob Hope Show. *How would it compare in terms of the way it was put together?*

In the case of *Ozzie and Harriet*, there I think we had three writers, and we each wrote a script. Ozzie was a damn good editor. He fancied himself a writer. And I don't say he couldn't write. But he was better as an editor. Again, he knew what he wanted, and he knew what was good for him, and for Harriet. I would write a script, and Ben Gershman and Sol Saks — we each turned in a whole script. It was a shared full script. In other words, a script could be 35 pages — so we'd each turn in a 22-page script. But then Ozzie would take the 66 pages and distill them down and make bridge lines of his own, to put it all together.

So no one writer was doing a complete script on that show?

You'd do the entire story, but if a scene were going to be four pages, you would write two and a half — you'd get it over with a little quicker, 'cause you know someone else is also writing the same story. Ozzie would pick and choose and put them together.

Would you come up with a premise, or would you have a pitch session?

A pitch session. Which Ozzie was involved in — moreso than Bob Hope. Ozzie was directly involved in the initial pitch session.

Was Harriet Nelson involved at all?

Not at all. Ben Gershman and I talked about that, how little she had to do with anything. And Ben once said, "That's what we know. But in the wee horizontal hours of the night..." Who knows what happens, what kind of input?

The Adventures of Ozzie and Harriet moved to ABC in 1949.

Paul Henning tells a story about Burns and Allen, about George changing his mind — or having it changed. Gracie would never say a word in front of the writers, but...

That's exactly how it was with Harriet. She was seldom in the room even.

Did events in their lives have any influence on the storylines at all?

No. My concern at that time was strictly as a writer. Later on, when I became a producer, my relationship with a show changed in that I just didn't worry about a script, I now had more contact and more important relationships with the actors. I didn't become a producer until television. I don't even know that I attended rehearsals. I wrote the script and gave it to Ozzie and he'd change it around — meanwhile the writers got together and started getting ideas for the next episode, so it was strictly writing.

You worked on Ozzie and Harriet *for about...*

About a year and a half. Then I went off and wrote with my brother Al for a year on *The Alan Young Show*. That was not successful — it only lasted a year.

Alan Young doesn't have as distinctive a personality as, say, Bob Hope.

Well, he has a softer — most of the comics that succeed are brash. And back-away kind of comics like Alan Young — or Wally Cox, who was very successful — are softer personalities. They take a step back when they walk into a room. They're never as immediately successful as more powerful kind of personalities. It's the old business of the squeaky wheel — getting the attention. That's how it is with the comic. Them that makes the loudest noise generally get noticed.

Alan Young seemed to excel at reacting to people.

That's right. It's the same with Jack Benny. He wasn't an actor, he was a reactor. He reacted to everything that was going on around. Alan wasn't indistinct. He was just — it's the difference between extrovert and introvert. A guy who comes on strong and a guy who's laid-back. You have to tailor your writing to fit that character. We didn't originate it — we were told what the show needed, and tried to fulfill the demands of the show...

Jim Backus played a character called Hubert Updike III on The Alan Young Show— *sort of a prototype of Thurston Howell III on* Gilligan's Island.

Yes. He was doing Hubert Updike's father, really. As soon as I thought of Thurston Howell, I could not get Jim Backus out of my mind. I had also worked with him on *I Married Joan*. He had a great voice — I knew he could be that character. I called Jim and said, "How would you like to be in this show?" He said, "Great. Send over the script." I said, "No. If I send the script over, you won't want to do it." His availability had happened so suddenly, I didn't have time to flesh out his part as well as I wanted to. Finally when he got the [pilot] script, he said, "My part is shorter than the wine list on an airplane."

The Alan Young Show *was the first time you actually worked with your brother Al. How did you work together?*

Fine. Thanks again to that army experience — I worked with seven people sometimes in the course of a week. You get used to different styles — writers have different ways of working in a room. If you're a head writer, you have to be very careful in the knowledge of different people's sensitivities. But I'm very flexible. Always have been. I don't say that it's a virtue, it's just how I am. I can adjust myself to someone's style or working habit. I don't know whether that's due to bumping around from one thing to another in terms of writing with so many people in the army, or that's just how I am. But it's never been a problem with me to work with anybody.

How would you describe your brother, as a writer?

My brother was only really happy when he was writing. He loved it. He adored it. In that way, he's similar to Larry Gelbart — whose happiest time is when he's writing. And that was my brother Al — he was a very mild-mannered person — shy, and *loved* writing. When he wrote a great joke, that was his greatest joy. He never, of his own volition, quit any job. Because if it meant writing — he was not that interested in the amount of money, or the glory, or fame — he loved writing, that was it.

Did you and your brother have similar writing styles?

My brother loved big jokes. Great big jokes. That's from his very early days with Milton Berle. Picturesque jokes Al loved, too. I think he once wrote one of the great jokes of all time — this guy was so poor that he couldn't afford to put cheese in a mousetrap. So, he put a picture of cheese in a mousetrap. And caught a picture of a mouse. Great joke.

You would write more subtle material?
I think I was a little bit more flexible in terms of non-jokes. I'd write straight lines too. I'm very interested in straight lines. Which puts

me out of keeping with the current vogue in television. Joke, joke, joke, joke. Everybody that comes into the room has got to top whatever remark was last made.

No set up, either. Just the punchline.

No set up. That destroys character. It destroys the shape of scenes, it destroys plot. What you wind up is like a fighter who does nothing but left jabs. There's no haymaker, there's no big punch. You're so busy with joke, joke, joke, joke, there's no build up to a big joke. And I think that's to the detriment of comedy on television right now.

You went from The Alan Young Show *to* The Beulah Show.

I was there for three years. Hattie McDaniel was terrific. She was marvelous.

The part of Beulah was originally played by a white man, Marlin Hurt.

That *was* strange. I remember how surprised I was that it was a white man. Well, go figure. It was radio. Edgar Bergen was a ventriloquist; on radio he was a big hit. On radio you couldn't see it anyway, whether his mouth moved or didn't move. It doesn't make any sense at all. But he was a major hit. And Charlie McCarthy wasn't a laid-back guy. He was a fresh little bastard.

Was there any pressure from the NAACP on The Beulah Show, *or any problems with the censorship board?*

No. The one thing that we always made very sure, is that everyone in that show who was black was employed. Beulah was employed, she was a housekeeper; her best friend, Oreo, was a housekeeper; her boyfriend was working someplace. There were no shiftless... no bad-image blacks.

That was one thing you couldn't do.

I wouldn't. I just wouldn't; it never occurred to me to do it.

You alternated with Hal Kanter on the scripts — how did that work, exactly?

Hal had his team and I had my team. And he would write one week's episode — there was a continuing story, so we would know what each other was doing, but we would not be working together. We decided — I decided on my storyline, Hal decided on his. We somehow meshed, so it made sense from one week to the next. It was a daily show.

So you basically had two weeks to do a week's worth of scripts.

Yeah. That was a lot of pages — only 15 minutes, but that's an hour and 15 minutes a week. He was the head writer one week, and I was the head writer of the next week's show. Hal would just want to know how it ended. And I wanted to know how he ended his, so I wouldn't violate anything...

What do you think Hal Kanter's strengths are as a comedy writer, if you can particularize?

It's hard to particularize. But he's more witty than necessarily funny. Which is not to say he isn't funny. 'Cause he's a very sharp-witted person. Rapier sharp. Very quick-witted. Just about as quick as anyone else I've met — much more so than I.

You also wrote for Danny Thomas on radio.

Briefly — that was an unhappy experience. Again, a writer's trapped by what he's told to do. Danny's format was pre-ordained. It was there when we got there — that's something I did with my brother. It was a guy who talked to himself. Again, it was a laid-back comic. We were told that was his great characteristic. He was a mailman, or whatever — he would say to himself, "Why didn't I speak up? Why didn't I tell 'em what I really thought?" And he never would. He would get jokes off that fact, that he didn't speak up — and next time he's going to — which of course he didn't. That kind of comic doesn't work. Or if it works it's a rarity, let me put it that way.

That was the character Thomas played on Fanny Brice's show, wasn't it?
Exactly. And we were told to extend that into his own show. And we did that. He had that character — which we were told, that's what we had to

write. So you really can't blame the writer if he's fulfilling the requirements of the show. He's not free to say, "I don't think that character's going to work, let me tell you what to do." They say, "Let's get a writer who'll do what we tell him." Doesn't work that way.

How would you assess Danny Thomas as a radio comic?

I think he was a great storyteller. I think that's where his great talent lie. Not in one-liners. He used to tell these long stories in his night-club act that were marvelous. And I think that's where he shone, actually. But the television show that he did allowed him to take advantage of that. 'Cause he played an entertainer. So he was brash in his own family life, and that was better suited.

He just didn't click on radio.

No. That was an unhappy experience. Because I think he blamed my brother Al, and blamed me, for writing that show. But that's what we were told to do. Funny, I never thought of it, we were trapped by that same problem in *The Alan Young Show*, a laid-back, shy, introverted comic. The same thing happened in *The Danny Thomas Show*.

You didn't have that problem when you and you and your brother later wrote for Red Skelton's TV show.

Oh, no. He's not a shy, wilting comic like the other characters were.

At what point did you go into television? Did you say, "Well, radio is dying..."

I knew radio was dying because my brother and I had just about sold a new radio show, with Sheldon Leonard and Alan Mowbray in it. And suddenly Proctor & Gamble said, "We've changed our minds. We're putting our money into television." And that's when the big sponsors starting pulling their money out of radio. That was in 1950.

You could see the writing on the wall, then.

Oh, yeah. Graffiti. Right after *Beulah* I went into television. I did *I Married Joan* with Joan Davis for two years. They needed a writer and I came on the show. I left there to finish a play — I'd started a play during the off season in television. I didn't want to go back for the third year, 'cause I got all excited about the play.

How did the atmosphere of working in TV differ from radio, especially in the beginning?

Well, I still worked at home. I was not on the set. It became different — you became closer to the performers, because you saw them for a whole week. You'd go on the set — it's not like radio where you rehearse for an hour, then you go on the air. It's very different. The timetable changes; you become closer to the actors and the show. You become closer to the show itself, as a writer, 'cause you visit the set; you work with the people.

Which was more stressful, radio or TV?

I guess television. Also mixed into that is the fact that I became a producer in television, which I had not been in radio. You just have more to do. I wasn't the producer on *I Married Joan*. But Joan Davis *demanded* a writer on the set with her at all times. Joan was a great believer in writers. A lot of performers aren't — they think they can change everything around. But she felt if there was a line she needed, or a better ending for a scene, she wanted a writer right there to discuss that with her. So that was very stressful. Being on a set when she says, "Wait a minute" — to the whole company — and turns to you and says, 'Give me a better finish."

What do you think makes for a great radio program?

The same thing that makes for a great television program. To be different enough from everything else that's on the air, and — whether it's comedy or drama — to impact you in a way that no other show does. I think you need that to be great. There are certain shows that are great because no show like it was ever done before. *Gunsmoke* was one of a kind — in both mediums. Sometimes first is best. A perfect example of that is *I Love Lucy*. That was the first domestic comedy, really, in television, so I think it was the best. But you have to have everything. You can't just have a great performer. You have to have a great writing; you also have to have a good director. But I think above all is concept.

CREDITS

Radio: *The Bob Hope Show, Command Performance, Mail Call, Jubilee, Melody Round Up, The Adventures of Ozzie and Harriet, The Danny Thomas Show, The Alan Young Show, The Beulah Show.*

TV: *I Married Joan, The Red Skelton Show, My Favorite Martian, Mr. and Mrs.* (special), *Gilligan's Island* (creator-producer), *It's About Time* (producer),*The Brady Bunch* (creator-executive producer); *Big John, Little John* (producer only); *Dusty's Trail* (producer only), *The Brady Bunch Hour* (producer only), *Harper Valley P.T.A.* (producer only), *The Brady Brides* (also creator-producer), *The Bradys* (co-executive producer).

TV (animated: executive producer): *The Brady Kids on Mysterious Island* (special), *The Brady Kids*, *The New Adventures of Gilligan, Gilligan's Planet.*

TV movies: *Rescue From Gilligan's Island* (also co-producer), *The Castaways on Gilligan's Island, The Harlem Globetrotters on Gilligan's Island, The Brady Girls Get Married* (also co-producer), *The Invisible Woman, A Very Brady Christmas* (also co-producer).

Film: *The Wackiest Wagon Train in the West, The Brady Bunch Movie* (co-producer only), *A Very Brady Sequel* (co-producer only), *Gilligan's Island: The Movie.*

Theater: *Mr. and Mrs., The Real Live Brady Bunch*, Gilligan's Island: The Musical, Rockers.*

* Based on original scripts for the TV series.

BOB WEISKOPF

"Television comedy is no good today. The funny people aren't around. Jackie Gleason is dead, Jack Benny is dead... by and large, most of the comedy shows are done with people who aren't very funny. They don't amuse me. If I were starting out today," asserted Bob Weiskopf, whose son is a TV comedy writer, "I'd be in a different line."

Weiskopf, who was born in Chicago in an era long before television, fell into comedy partly as an accident of geography. The Windy City — or at least the University of Chicago — was a breeding ground for funsters, as he remembered it. "We'd sit in the class laughing and telling jokes. 'Did you hear Ed Wynn last night?' It was delightful if the other guy had missed it, 'cause then you could quote all the jokes."

Along with Wynn and Benny, Weiskopf and his college pals listened faithfully to Fred Allen — whom John Steinbeck called "unquestionably the best humorist of our time" — never dreaming that he would end up in the comedian's employ for nine long and happy years. It was the most satisfying of his experiences in radio, at the opposite end of the spectrum from his stint with one of Allen's rivals, Eddie Cantor.

Writing for television in the 1950s was a wholly different experience for Weiskopf, not only because the medium was in its infancy, but because he chanced to meet — and team with — fellow comedy writer Bob Schiller. It was a fortuitous partnership that would change both their lives and careers. Prior to the teaming, Weiskopf generally soloed at the typewriter, except for one year on *The Fred Allen Show* when he was paired with Nat Hiken, the future creator of *The Phil Silvers Show*. "It wasn't bad, but it wasn't great, so we didn't do it after that," he observed.

Weiskopf and Schiller reached the pinnacle of their partnership writing for *I Love Lucy*, which they followed up with *The Lucy-Desi Comedy Hour* and *The Lucy Show*. Their relationship with TV's other favorite redhead was far less pleasant. "Red Skelton had a pattern. He would fire his head writers every two or three years — his attitude was, 'Gotta keep 'em fresh.' He viewed his writers as adversaries," stated Weiskopf. "That's the way some of those guys were."

More palatable was their job scripting *The Carol Burnett Show*, and their long tenure writing for Norman Lear on *All in the Family* and *Maude*. On the latter show they often found themselves borrowing from real-life experiences. "Norman would say, 'Use that, it's wonderful.' Norman used to love that — if you said, 'We had an argument the other day, and I said such-and-such,' he'd say, 'Jesus, let's use that. That's terrific stuff.' And we would use it."

My interview with Bob Weiskopf took place in his beautiful home in Malibu, Calif., amidst a prodigious library of his bound radio and television scripts, an array of writing awards and the souvenirs of a lifetime. His home survived the mudslides that occurred within a week of the interview; sadly, everything was destroyed in the Malibu fire the following year.

Did you originally intend to write for radio?

No. There were a bunch of fellas in Chicago, four or five, who reportedly were kind of funny. Said funny things. Two of them wanted to become writers — Norman Panama and Melvin Frank. I introduced them to each other. I lived next door to Norman, and I knew Melvin through a friend; Mel and I went to the same high school. They took a flyer, came out here to the [West] Coast...

Where they joined Bob Hope's staff.

Meantime, I was working in advertising. I was doing reasonably well, making about $50 a week, which was a lot of money. Norman and Melvin really nudged the hell out of me to give this a shot, this kind of thing [comedy writing]; they claimed I could do it better than they could. I finally got courageous and quit my job — I thought my old man was going to kill me, for quitting a $50-a-week job. I just came out to the Coast on a flyer, there was nothing left in Chicago. There were a couple of shows there, but nothing happening...

A lot of shows originated from Chicago before the war...

I wrote some questions for a quiz show, but that was about all. My contacts were in California. Norman and Melvin helped me get various appointments; I wrote some jokes and things. One of the appointments was with Eddie Cantor's producer, and I got a job with Cantor; I was only out here two or three weeks, I think, when I got the job. That got my feet wet, and that was it.

Did you write for anyone before Cantor?

I wrote two jokes for Bob Hope. First time I ever sold anything — I've never been paid, to this day. That was my first professional thing on the air. I remember them quite well, 'cause I'm a sports fan. That was the year the Rose Bowl was Nebraska and Stanford — and one of the jokes I wrote for Hope was, "I have seats on the Nebraska side — it's about three miles this side of Omaha." That was the joke. Then I got this job with Cantor.

Did you ever write anything else for Bob Hope?

No, I didn't work for Hope. I did guest shots for him. Mel Frank had a cousin in Chicago, Myron Frank — he and I wrote a script at the request of Mel and Norm, when Hope was at the Chicago Theater playing on the stage. Hope loved the script and asked us to write another one. He didn't like the second one too much, and accused Panama and Frank of having written the first one. That turned us both off.

You got the job with Eddie Cantor by showing him a few pages of jokes?

I wrote a couple of pages of jokes, and they were interchangeable, pretty much. I think some of the same jokes I showed to Hope, I showed to Cantor. Cantor's producer said, "You'll hear from me." I subconsciously gave him the wrong phone number. He couldn't find me, so he sent a telegram. He wanted to see me right away; he sent a driver with a limousine out to get me. Next thing I know I'm in a big Beverly Hills mansion, with about 20 guys in a room, and Cantor. He was a bastard, which I didn't know at the time, 'cause I was naïve as hell, and new. It got around to "How much money do you want?" I said, "How much do you want to pay me?" And he said, "No, how much do you want?" We were like two school boys. I was making $50 a week in Chicago; I figured, I'll tell him I was making $65 and he'll give me $75. So I said I was making $65 a week. He said, "I'll give you $50." And I took it.

As you say, you were quite naïve...

When I spoke to Panama and Frank, they hit the ceiling. They said, "Why didn't you call us?" — 'cause I didn't have an agent or anything. I said, "You guys were busy. This thing happened; I didn't know what to do."

I've heard a lot of stories about Eddie Cantor...

One time Cantor locked his writers in the train, he wouldn't let 'em out. 'Cause he claimed they were goofing off. That's before I went with him. These guys went on a train, and they got to Chicago, and they got up in the morning to have breakfast. They got to the other end of the car, and it's locked. And they got furious. So they wouldn't work. They didn't work the rest of the trip, 'cause he locked 'em in — wouldn't let 'em get out to get breakfast. That's the kind of guy Cantor was.

They were going back East to do the show?

In those days, the comics were all from the East, originally. They loved the climate out here. But as soon as the weather got warm in spring, they'd go to New York for the final 13 weeks. The season used to be 39 weeks. So I went to work out here for Cantor in January 1941. But in March, just two months later, the show moved to New York for the final 13 weeks.

To what extent did Cantor actually work with his writers?

Very little. He would read the script and complain here and there, or maybe laugh — "That's a good joke," and so on. When we had readings and stuff in his apartment in the Warwick Hotel [New York], I used to have to go to the john — I'd go in there and laugh like hell, 'cause I couldn't laugh in his face. Once, he hated the script, and he jumped and almost hit his head on the ceiling, because it was very low. And he yelled at these guys: "With you boys, this is just a stepping stone to movies. But this is my whole career. Where am I going to go?" He was practically in tears, complaining about the script.

He didn't really function as an editor, as Jack Benny did?

Not really. He had a producer who did that, Vick Knight. But someone finally must've told Cantor that radio producers didn't do very much — which they really didn't, outside of clocking the show. One year Cantor was in Lindy's. Vick Knight had been fired; it was in the papers. Somebody he knew said, "Eddie, what's happening? I read Vick was fired." Cantor says, "You know who's going to be my producer next year?" The guy says, "No." He said, "Nobody." Someone told Cantor he didn't need a producer. So he saved money, didn't have one.

Did Cantor give you pointers on the type of thing that would work for him?

He really didn't know — he couldn't. When I came on the show, it was shortly after he did a flop movie called *Forty Little Mothers*. And every week there was a joke in the show about how bad this thing was. And one day Cantor said, "No more jokes about *Forty Little Mothers*." What happened? He got one letter from a lady in Nebraska: "It wasn't a bad picture." That was the end of that. All he needed was one letter.

Did you work on the show alone, or with a partner?

I came on the Cantor show by myself. John Rapp worked with Lester White and Buddy Pierson — the three of them worked together. So Cantor put me with Joe Quillan and Irving Elinson. We got to like each other. We were all veterans; they were wonderful to me. The only trouble was — and it was big trouble — Joe Quillan was nocturnal. He slept most of the day, and he worked most of the night. And I almost said, "If this is the way it goes, I'm not going to do this for a career." I once said to Izzy Elinson, "Why don't we work — you and I — during the day?" Izzy said, "I've never learned to type." And he wasn't trying to be funny.

Did you know Cantor to ever do any of the actual writing?

Not really. He would throw in a joke — a terrible joke. These guys didn't know humor, that kind of humor. Once Cantor brought in a joke: There's a phone call. He says, "I'm tied up." "You can't come over?" "I'm really tied up." And he had ropes around him — that kind of thing. We didn't put that in the script. We used to have previews on the show. He didn't forget — nobody put in the joke about being tied up. So he came back to his apartment at the Warwick after the preview, and everyone was in fine spirits 'cause there were — they used to count 'em — there were 212 laughs. Somebody said, "Great show, tonight, Eddie. 212 laughs." Cantor's response was, "There would've been 213 if you boys had put in that rope joke."

He had somebody clocking the laughs?

Yeah. Most of the writers would mark the script — if you got two checks, it was a big laugh. Three checks, it was an uproarious laugh. The writers came to preview and checked the jokes; that was the purpose.

Was the script reworked after the preview?

Yeah. It was all done in those days really from joke to joke to joke, pretty much. Basically, if you were lucky, you'd have three or four good jokes, and if you were overtime, you had to eliminate a joke or two. Maybe you could use it in the future, maybe not.

You would meet at Cantor's apartment and put the script together?

Actually, I think we gave it to him at a certain time, then he and Vick Knight, the producer, would put it together, and then we'd meet on Sunday at five o'clock. One time I was at Cantor's, the usual Sunday afternoon at 4:30 or 5:00, and the other writers weren't around, weren't there yet. He asked me to call them. So I called them — one was out to dinner, and so forth — he said, "Did you talk to the writers?" I said, "Nobody was home. They're all out to dinner." He says, "Dinner?! If it wasn't for me, they couldn't eat!"

Would each team write a complete script?

No. We usually wrote spots for the Cantor show. We'd write the

Mad Russian spot. You'd get a premise, whatever little premise you needed — Quillan and Elinson and I would get one section, Pierson and White and Rapp would get the other section, and we'd meet on Sunday night at the Warwick. Each would give their hunk of the script to Cantor. One week, the guys weren't finished with the Mad Russian spot. Cantor said, "Boys, we don't need much this week. We're loaded with material. We only need six jokes, boys — six jokes — one, two, three, four, five, six, seven." Got an extra joke out of the writers while he was counting. That's the way those guys were — terrible.

Was Cantor mean-spirited, in the way he treated his writers?

Pretty much so. And also the actors. Joe Quillan is going into the Brown Derby on Vine Street one day, and he sees Bert Gordon, the Mad Russian. He says, "Bert, are you alone? We'll have lunch together." Bert says, "No, I'm waiting for Cantor. Why don't you sit with us? I want to show you how he fucks me." Cantor had been to the studio, and had seen the rushes on a movie — Bert was in the picture with Cantor. They're sitting at the table and Cantor says, "Bert, I just came from the studio. You're the whole picture — you're sensational." They hadn't settled on a price yet...

They hadn't agreed on his salary?

Cantor got Bert to do the movie before they dickered on price, which was crazy. Cantor says, "How much money do you want?" Bert says, "$1250," or something. Cantor says, "What?! For two seconds?" Bert said, "You just said I was the whole picture." Cantor said, "You're in it for about 30 seconds." They haggled back and forth; Cantor wouldn't budge, he wanted to give him $750. And Bert said, "Rather than do it for $750, I'd rather do it for nothing." Cantor got up from the table and said, "You'll never be sorry, it's going to be great for your career" — and walked out. Didn't pay him anything. Bert Gordon turned to Joe Quillan and he said, "Did I tell you, he'd fuck me?" Every year, Bert told me, Cantor used to say, "Bert, you're not only on the show again next season but for the *same money*." Bert said he never got a raise. This stuff makes me laugh, but it's terrible. Professionally, Eddie Cantor wasn't that funny. Off stage, he was very funny, by being a bastard.

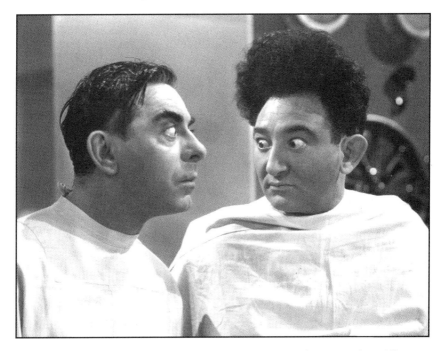

Eddie Cantor has a run-in with Bert Gordon ("How dooo you dooo?"), in the film *Thank Your Lucky Stars.*

What was your salary, by the way?

I finally worked up to about $150 a week. Joe Quillan and Izzy Elinson were getting pretty good money. The big money in radio in those days — it did get bigger — in 1940, I think $300 was the going rate for the top, except a very few. But I think Joe and Izzy each got $350 or $400 a week. That was a lot of money in those days.

I've heard that if Bert Gordon or someone else got the laughs in the show, Cantor would have the script rewritten so he would get the laugh. Any truth to that?

Joan Davis was that way, many of the stars were. With the exception of Fred Allen. Fred always said, "I'll get the credit — the show is funny." Fred Allen hated Eddie Cantor, 'cause Cantor stole material from Allen.

Eddie Cantor (second from the left) with all his wits about him, nameless
servants in radio's laugh factory.

Could you elaborate on that?

One story was that Fred had been in a show in New York on stage,
and it was a flop. He wrote some of his own material. One joke —
this was when zippers were brand new — so-and-so had so many
operations, they didn't use stitches; they put in a zipper. Next thing
Allen heard, Cantor was using this joke somewhere. And Fred got
furious. He had a big meeting with Cantor — he confronted him
with this. Cantor's answer was, "How do you like that? Ida, she
gave me that joke." And he said to his masseuse, "Maurice! Send
Portland [Hoffa, aka Mrs. Allen] a pocketbook." That was it. He
didn't ask if he could keep the joke — "Send her a pocketbook."
And he didn't do that until he was confronted by Allen, for having
stolen the joke. That's the kind of man Cantor was.

What do you think accounted for Eddie Cantor's huge success on radio?

Well, he was a big Broadway star. He was full of enthusiasm and bubbly. He sang; he could tell jokes. They were all rivals — we had Al Jolson on as a guest once. Jolson hadn't been around in a long time, and the show was very successful, a lot of laughs. And the next week Cantor was very upset. What's the matter? Jolson was in the audience. Cantor said, "Get him the hell out of there. Take him upstairs behind the glass — because he'll come running up on the stage and ruin the whole show. He'll take over." 'Cause Jolson had felt results from the week before, when he was on as a guest star and got a lot of laughs.

So there was a real rivalry between Jolson and Cantor.

Oh, yeah. Cantor's answer to Jolson — when he came on the show, the message to the writers was, "You can't give Jolson straight lines 'cause he's got a million dollars. He's rich; you've got to give him the jokes. He'll walk off the show. He doesn't need the money." This was how these people always thought. "He's got a million dollars — well, you've got to give him the jokes."

How long were you with Eddie Cantor?

Just the one season. He didn't pick up my option. Luckily, 'cause I signed a terrible contract, all to his advantage. But anyway it turned out I was very fortunate. I met Paul Henning, and I became his partner. I wrote for Rudy Vallee, Joan Davis and John Barrymore for a couple of years. Paul was on the Vallee show before I was; he and I formed a team.

Rudy Vallee had a high regard for his own talents.

He was funny too, without meaning to be, like Cantor — offstage. But he was a whole different person. Rudy was just tight, really, was what it was. He would do crazy things with money. But he tried to be a good host. He would throw wonderful parties at his house for the writers.

Who were the other writers on the show with you? Was Jess Oppenheimer there?

We had Manny Mannheim, Jess Oppenheimer and Dick Chevillat on the Vallee show. Paul and I were a team, Jess and Manny were kind of a team, and Dick kind of floated around. The three of them usually worked together; Paul and I did our part by ourselves.

Would the producer edit the script, or did Vallee participate in that?

Oh, no, Rudy was never around. We would go down to the building at Hollywood and Vine. Dick Mack was the producer. We'd go and read him the script, and he would accept it, and give us comments. *The Rudy Vallee Show* was on 52 weeks a year; we used to sneak a week's vacation here and there, the writers, without telling anyone. When they went to read the script in downtown Hollywood to the producer, we'd all show up.

Vallee has been described to me as a man with virtually no talent.

Yeah, he got a lot of mileage of out very little talent; it's quite true. He had a great producer. Ed Gardner was the producer of the show, just before I was on. Gardner got John Barrymore to come on the show — that was a big, big plus. 'Cause Barrymore was a great performer.

How would you describe John Barrymore's work habits?

Probably not very good. Once in a great while — before I got there, I heard — he showed up kind of drunk, but they got him sobered up quick before he went on. Once he tried to seduce his own daughter; he didn't know who the hell it was. That was in the dressing room before the show.

Much of the humor on that show was at Barrymore's expense.

Barrymore was wonderful. He was having a good time; he used to laugh like hell when he read the script. I wrote a thing once with Charles Laughton as the guest. He had just finished filming *Rembrandt* or something. And the joke went — John said, "You like to do biographies, Charles. Who's your next biography?" 'Cause he did *Henry VIII*, et cetera. Laughton said, " I would like to relive the life of John Barrymore." That was a big laugh. Rudy said, "So would

I." That's a bigger laugh. And John said, "Me too, brother." The people screamed. Joan Davis said, "I had to be a woman..." In four lines, there were four huge laughs.

Did Barrymore ever take offense at the parody of his image?

No, he enjoyed it. He was a multi-talented fellow. He used to sit at a table — he wasn't physically too well at the time — and he'd noodle and doodle. He'd have some wonderful drawings on his script at the end of the show. He would sit and follow the script.

Did Joan Davis contribute at all to the script?

Not really. She was a difficult lady. Paul Henning got $100 extra, I think, for Joan Davis — she used to do a song. She'd sing a couple of bars, then do about six jokes, then finish the end of the song. The jokes would have to do with the song. "Jim didn't send me pretty flowers... Jim was so-and-so..." I went with Paul one night — we were there all night to get six jokes. 'Cause she would laugh like hell; two minutes later she'd say, "I think we can do better than that." Drove me crazy.

I believe you left Rudy Vallee to work for Fred Allen. How did that come about?

They wanted Paul and I — they wanted us as a team to go with George Burns and Gracie Allen. I said, "Paul, you take *Burns and Allen,* 'cause I'm not going to stay out here." That was in '42. That's when Paul and I split. Our careers would have continued together — it worked fine until the war happened, and the evacuation thing with the Japanese. I was married to a Japanese girl I had met at the University of Chicago; she would have had to go to one of those camps. I said, "To hell with that." I didn't want to foul up my marriage; I'd been married one year. I wanted to work in New York, where we could be together...

Your wife would have forced to go into a relocation camp?

Yeah. They were under the jurisdiction of the U.S. Army. So I got her the hell out of California. We sat up all night packing, and I took Eileen on the train to Chicago, then came back. We were separated for about six months while I was working out here on *The Rudy Vallee Show*. Then I went East. I had a long run in New York with Fred Allen, nine years.

How did you get the job with Allen?

What happened was, one of Fred's writers, Roland Fibbee, became a flight instructor — Roland was a pilot, so he got drafted. So Fred was looking for a writer. He wrote to a friend of his named Harry Tugend, who had been a writer for Fred and became a big shot screenwriter — he was head of Paramount at the time. Harry didn't know anyone, but down the hall were Panama and Frank, who had just come from radio. They knew I wanted to get a job in the East, get the hell out of here and be with my wife. They recommended me to Tugend; he recommended me to Fred Allen.

You couldn't have found a better job in radio.

I think the deal was 13 weeks to see how it was going to work out. It worked out fine, obviously. Fred and I and Eileen and Portland became very friendly and went out to dinner a lot, socialized some-what. It's hard to socialize with the boss — as good as the relation-ship is, it's far from perfect. It was fun; I really had a wonderful nine years on that show. Writing for Allen was a very prestigious thing.

Do you recall your first meeting with Fred Allen?

I was told, "Okay, you've got the job." Then we had a meeting and came up with a premise and were assigned a portion of the show. I went home to a little hotel on 57th Street in New York, and wrote this thing and handed it in, to Allen at his home. I didn't see him, I just left it there. I didn't hear, so I didn't know if it was good, bad, if he hated it. And I spoke to Nat Hiken, who had been on the show; he was a veteran by then. Nat says, "You won't hear anything. Fred won't tell you one way or another. The only way you can tell is when you see the script, how much of your stuff is left in there." There was a reasonable amount; it just happened to work, so I was delighted.

You started with Allen in 1942?

September '42. When the show became a half hour. It used to be an hour show, when I listened to it as a kid in college.

Was Allen a particular favorite then?

Oh yeah. Allen was a favorite of all the guys who subsequently became writers — of that ilk, he was the favorite. He had a great listening audience. Robert Benchley was on the show once, and he was a great Fred Allen fan. One week we did a burlesque of a thing called *Mr. Anthony.* So, Charlie Cantor played a guy with amnesia — he didn't know who he was. The signing off thing was, "If any of you know who this man is, please call NBC..." Fred came down into the dressing room, laughing and waving a telegram. It was from Robert Benchley. Benchley said, "You darn fool. The amnesiac was Charlie Cantor." Guys like that would listen to the show all the time.

Allen worked day and night on the show.

Well, Fred was a nighthawk. He'd say to the guests, "I was up all night." Once Portland said — this is a quote — "He's full of shit. I walked in his studio at 9:30, he was sound asleep." He could tell how much you had written, how much Nat Hiken had written — some weeks he would contribute more than others. We all did Allen's Alley in concert, on Wednesday afternoon. Nat and I, and later a couple of other writers, and Fred. Every week, that was a weekly thing.

Do you recall how much you were paid on The Fred Allen Show?

I started at $250, in 1942. Fred had a bad contract; he signed a bad deal. After the war, the deal was over so he got a new deal. I was getting I think $750 when I went in the army. When I left, I was getting $1150 — I think it wound up close to $1250.

Were you there when he started the Allen's Alley segment?

We used to do The News of the Week. And Fred complained —

Fred Allen polls Senator Claghorn (Kenny Delmar), as Mrs. Nussbaum (Minerva Pious) and Ajax Cassidy (Peter Donald) look on.

there was no carry-over. The actors played various people, depending on what the news was. One week Minerva Pious was a Brooklyn housewife; one week she'd be a society lady. The four people he had in those days were wonderful at doing various voices — that's the reason they were hired. He had 50 characters. Minerva Pious, Alan Reed, John Brown and Charlie Cantor were the originals.

Allen's Alley is so well remembered, I was curious just how the concept came about...

Fred wanted a carry-over character. So we were in a Chinese restaurant one night, and decided we'd do Allen's Alley, have Fred walk down the street as an inquiring reporter, which was a thing in journalism in those days. The actors played the same characters every week. John Brown was first; he was one of these brusque guys, John Doe. Charlie Cantor played the dope, Socrates Mulligan. Minerva Pious was Mrs. Nussbaum. Alan Reed played Falstaff, the poet. Fred wrote all the poems.

How did these characters develop?

Well, Minnie Pious used to do a very funny Jewish dialect, for example. Alan Reed did an arrogant Shakespearean type. Kenny Delmar did the Southern thing, which worked out fine. A guy picked him up once — he was hitchhiking — the guy talked like that, and Kenny remembered that. That's how Senator Claghorn happened. The guy kept repeating, "I say, it's a nice day..." or whatever. Kenny picked up those little things. Fred always wanted to do a Southern senator [on his show]. He did a senator before with a big heavy guy, Jack Smart. Fred called him Senator Bloat. He just did various bills and stuff. You had the extra, the Southern dialect, with Kenny.

The Allen's Alley characters were conceived with the actors in mind, though.

Yeah, 'cause they played those parts. These people had been on *The Fred Allen Show* for years, long before I came in. There were a bunch of people hanging around Greenwich Village, they acted at parties. Harry Tugend, who wrote for Fred, knew most of these people and that's how they got to work on the show. Minnie — Minerva Pious — was one of the people Harry Tugend knew, from acting around at parties in the Village. Minnie could do a million things...

She was on the Allen show as early as 1932, when Lionel Stander was in the cast.

Fred liked to say that Lionel Stander was always late for the show because he was a radical — that he was working on a printing press in the basement, so he couldn't get to the studio on time.

What was Minerva Pious like off the air?

Nice lady. She had a physical affliction — she had a bad hip, a severe limp. She was very concerned about television; she never worked very much. But radio was fine. That's how Fred was. Fred was a terrible actor, but he was a great *vocal* actor. He could act with his voice.

What do you think made Fred Allen the great radio comedian?

He had that distinctive nasal quality in his voice. And he had a great sense of humor — it caught on. Fred was the comedian's comedian. No one has a bad word to say about Allen. They won't knock him. People had great respect and admiration for him. For example, we had a somewhat limited budget for guest stars — Humphrey Bogart wanted to come on. Fred said, "We can't afford Bogart — Chrissake, no way." Somehow they got in touch, Bogart called. He says, "Forget the money, I want to do the show."

Whereas ordinarily, Bogart would have been out of range.

We had a big meeting with Bogart; he was newly married to Lauren Bacall. She said, "I want to meet Fred." They were up at the Gotham Hotel in New York. We had our meeting, told Bogey what we were gonna do. As we walked back to the elevator Bogart waved and said, "Be funny, guys." So we did the show. Bogart said after the show, "You were." So you had guests like that; they all had to come on the show. Money was secondary. 'Cause they knew, it was a plum to be on the Allen show. It was such a prestigious show in those days, because all the stars wanted to be on. The first guest we had was Orson Welles, which was a great show.

Did you write for Welles when he was on Allen's show?

Yeah. I wrote the sketch in those days. Later on, Nat Hiken used to write the sketches and I wrote the interview jokes. We did Jean Valjean [*Les Misérables*] with Orson. The script goes, Orson wanted somebody to share the credit with, because it was "directed by, produced by, starring Orson Welles." And we did three little segments. Orson did all the emoting; Allen played Javert. The episode went where Welles did all the talking at the end; there's a police whistle, and then that's it. And Fred said, "Wait a minute. Hold it! Hold it, Orson! You're supposed to share this." And Orson said, "But the way you blew that whistle, Fred. I've never heard a whistle blown like that." We did three segments; it had some great jokes with Orson.

Would you work with the guest — Welles for instance — on the sketch?

Hardly ever. We would meet the guests and talk and tell them what we had in mind. The great thing about Fred Allen, and Welles was a perfect example — Welles was a pretty important guy in the theater in those days — they had such respect and admiration for Allen. If Fred said, "Here's what we're going to do, Orson, what do you think?" Invariably the answer was, "If you think it's good, Fred, that's it." They all trusted him, and they were right. Basil Rathbone was a good guest because he always played Sherlock Holmes and Fred would play One Long Pan. And once during rehearsal, Basil broke up during the middle of the thing — he yelled out, "Oh, *shit*, this is funny."

You knew you were going to have certain guests ahead of time.

Yeah, but not much ahead of time. We had George Jessel a lot. George was kind of funny, but a pain in the ass. He made Fred laugh for some reason; Fred liked him. George Jessel and Jack Haley were doing a vaudeville show in New York and they were available Sundays, so we had Jessel half a dozen times. He'd come right over from the theater. One time he came over, and he had the damn script in his coat pocket — Fred used to call it "the landlord coat" 'cause it had a fur collar on it — Jessel forgot he had the script and he threw his coat off with the script in the pocket. So we quick rushed down another script...

A lot of Allen's guest were movie stars unaccustomed to radio.

Yeah, but they could do fine reading a script. The great time when Welles was on, they had about four guys played by Charlie Cantor, John Brown, and so on — one was Mr. Welles' personal "acoustician" — so they did a routine of blowing into the mike, "1-2-3. Woof! Woof! Hello, Max..." And Fred is standing there, "Mr. Welles, that's an acoustician." The audience was screaming; it was wonderful. We did about five, six, seven minutes before Orson came on.

Do you have a particular favorite among the shows you did with Allen?

Well, there's so many. The Orson Welles show, the Rodgers and Hammerstein parodies, one or two of the Beatrice Lillie shows. Monty Woolley we had on; he was wonderful. Tallulah Bankhead was wonderful, in the "Mr. and Mrs." sketch.

That sketch was later reworked for a movie called We're Not Married.

Nat Hiken wrote that sketch. And Fred got upset with Nat about something after that. One day I got an extra check in the mail or something, and I said, "What the hell is this?" And Fred says, "Well, I can't keep the money anyway — that sketch in the movie, you know." He didn't send Nat any money. See, he owned all the material in those days. He sent me a check, and the other writer, Harry Bailey — but he didn't send Nat one, 'cause he was upset at Nat for something.

The sketch didn't work in the picture, with Ginger Rogers playing opposite Fred.

That's right. But Tallulah was wonderful. Tallulah was like a female Allen almost — the character — and she could do it. She was great.

I think the Rodgers and Hammerstein parodies are among everyone's favorite shows.

You couldn't fool with Rodgers and Hammerstein. Except Fred Allen. *Oklahoma!* opened and we wanted to burlesque it. They got permission to do it, no problem. We did "North Dakota!" first with Oscar Levant. Rodgers and Hammerstein came on the show, the very next week, playing themselves in a crazy "court case." They were going to sue him for stealing *Oklahoma!* That was the follow up. Then later — probably the next season — we did the English version, "Piccadilly!" with Bea Lillie.

Jimmy Wallington was the announcer on Allen's show during your tenure.

Fred had a great description of Wallington. He said, "When Jimmy Wallington opens his mouth, the words come out lying in state."

You'd try and give Jimmy jokes and stuff — the jokes would lay there.

What was the routine? How did you put the show together?

After the show, every Sunday night, we went to the House of Chan, a Chinese restaurant at 52nd Street and 7th Avenue. We ate Chinese food and discussed next week's show...

The House of Chan sounds like something Fred Allen would have made up.

Like One Long Pan. But the House of Chan was a restaurant; Fred loved it. We went there every Sunday night. That was the ritual. Fred was a man of ritual. He went to church on Sunday mornings and went to the House of Chan Sunday nights after the show. This is a typical Allen story — they had a big fire at the House of Chan. The place burned down; it was closed for five or six months. Fred would break his neck for people like that. Soo Chan, the owner, asked Fred to write a little thing, they were going to have the re-opening next week. So Fred stayed up half the night writing a thing for the Chinese restaurant. And when he came in the following Wednesday, he was furious. The little thing he wrote was in the window; there were only about two lines left. So he went in to complain. Soo Chan said, "It was too long; we had to cut it."

So you started on Sunday night at the restaurant, discussing next week's show...

Invariably on Sunday afternoon, we'd get through rehearsal around 2 or 3 o'clock. Fred's habit was to go home and meet Portland; they would eat later, then we'd have to do the show. On the following Saturday afternoon, by 1 o'clock we'd meet at Fred's house. With our pads and pencils. We'd get the premise lined up, because Sunday was the show. We took Mondays off. Tuesday, we started to work on the show we discussed on Saturday, for the following week. In other words, Saturday was next week's show. Not tomorrow's show, a week from tomorrow. "We've got this, then we're going to do this with Orson Welles, and so on..." So it was all set. Sunday we did *this* show. Tuesday, we'd all start to write — now I'm writing for next Sunday's show that we had discussed Saturday.

Most people didn't realize all the work that went into actually writing a weekly show.

Fred said it first: "Nobody's here on Monday when the paper's blank." Everyone has ideas, after you've written it. To this day, that's true.

Once the premise had been worked out, you and Nat Hiken would more or less work out the script and then...

Yeah. Nat would do a part, and I would do a part. And we'd turn it in to Fred, and he would look over the script and put it together. The ritual was, Fred actually participated in the premise. We all met at his house. As a matter of fact, I would say the majority of the time, the premise came from him. Even though we would throw ideas back and forth.

The premise would generally be supplied by Allen?

Well, to a great extent. He was certainly a big contributing factor in the premise. Most of the time there was Fred and I and Nat Hiken, in my career with the show. Fred finally said, "Jeez, we're all gettin' stale. Don't you think we ought to get some other writers?" So we hired Terry Ryan and Harry Bailey. They were with Fred and me and Nat for the last three or four years. Then Nat quit; he made a deal to do Milton Berle's show. And there was just myself, Harry Bailey, Terry Ryan for a couple years. When Nat Hiken and I were in the army Fred wrote a lot of the shows by himself, although he did do a couple of repeats.

How long were you "on hiatus" in the army?

One season. Then Nat and I had to come out here to do the film, *Winged Victory.* Even though Fred was an ardent Catholic, he got a letter from a bishop in Boston, commenting, "I've noticed you're doing a lot of repeats lately." So Fred wrote a letter to the bishop: "Caught your sermon. You're repeating a lot from the Bible lately."

Apart from the time you were in the army, would Allen write quite a bit of the show himself?

Yeah. Certain weeks he did more than others. We all did Allen's Alley together. Nat would write the sketch, I would write the interview spot, and then Fred would go over the interview spot. We had the Alley, 'cause that was done on that Wednesday. By the end of the day, usually it was pretty much lined up. Fred just actually put it together. And then he would read our two spots, and if he liked most of them he wouldn't have much work to do on it. If he didn't like something, he would fix it. That was a great thing, 'cause you never got called to stay up late at night. We'd give the stuff to Fred, work during the day. He liked to work at night, but he didn't work that late 'cause he had good writing. He always used to say, "If you have to stay up all night writing, then you've got the wrong writers." And he was right. The way they work television today, they're up most of the night. It's ridiculous.

Once Allen put the script together...

Then we had the rehearsal on Friday with the guest. Then there was some more fixing. The guest would go home. Friday we would meet, let's say noon, until 2 o'clock or 3... then Fred and Nat and I would go down to a room at NBC and go over the script some more. "That didn't work too well, this was great..." And then Saturday was talking about next week. Then Sunday, that was it. We did the show from this fixed-up script from Friday. You didn't have to write it 58 times.

Would Allen write his own monologue?

He didn't really do one; he'd have some funny stories he would tell in the warm-up. He was a genius at telling long stories, working up to one laugh. Fred used to tell a story about how a guy left home — the kid ran away from home, his mother was distraught — the story took seven or eight minutes, nobody knew what was going on. The mother is overcome with grief, she leaves a little light burning in the window... finally seven years later, the kid shows up. The mother throws her arms around the son — and hands him a bill for $4800 from Con Edison. That was the joke. But for six minutes, nobody knew what the hell was going on with this. Fred was a genius at that.

Allen wouldn't do any blue material during the audience warm-up, would he?

No, he wouldn't. That wasn't his way of performing. He used to tell different stories. Every now and then he used to say, "Jeez, we could use a new warm-up..." He'd have certain jokes that were wonderful. He used to have a joke on St. Patrick's day, a real New York joke: "How do you cross Fifth Avenue on St. Patrick's Day?" (They always had a parade). The joke was, "You can join the Ancient Order of Hibernians and march six blocks at an angle." We'd say, "You're not going to get a funnier joke than that." So every year he'd tell the same joke, and every year he'd say, "Jeez, we ought to get a new joke."

Did you learn much about the craft of comedy writing from working with Fred Allen?

I'd say yes, but I really don't know what there is to learn about comedy writing. As Ed Gardner once said, "Comedy is thinking crooked." That's the way he defined it. You either thought funny, or you didn't. There are certain things you can learn from comedy but not a great deal, I don't think. It's an old cliché, but I think it's true — 'cause most clichés are true — if you want to be a writer, you've got to write. That's it. There are a few rules, but they're not going to make you that much better or that much worse.

I guess you got accustomed to writing Allenisms after a while.

Oh, yeah. I would have a joke occasionally that I couldn't use someplace, and I'd tell it, and Fred would laugh. I had a joke once — "Do you know why the White Cliffs of Dover are white?" "Why?" "Because all those bluebirds flying over, naturally they'd be white." Fred loved that joke, but you couldn't tell it on the air in those days. But he told it at a luncheon someplace. He used to call me and ask me, could he use that joke. Of course.

Speaking of which, were you there when Mr. Ramshaw, the eagle, was on the show?

I think I was there the second time. The eagle got blinded by the lights, and flew up to the rafters; they couldn't get him down. He was crapping like mad, all over the stage. I remember I heard the show — you couldn't hear anything but laughter. They went out and got chicken heads for the eagle — that's what he ate — to try to get him to come down.

Undoubtedly one of the funniest shows Allen ever did — even if most of the laughs were unintentional.

There were a couple of other funny incidents with a bird. There was a talking mynah bird that got loose. This bird was English, with an English accent. He would say, "Have a baaath?" The bird had traveled in Europe [with his owner]; he met Stalin. "What did you say to Mr. Stalin?" The bird was supposed to say, "Hello, Joe." So on the show, the bird got panicky. They said, "What did you say when you met Mr. Stalin?" And the bird said, "Have a baaath?" The audience screamed.

Was Fred Allen much of an ad-libber?

Oh, yeah. If something happened, he would say something funny. Fred used to drive the producer crazy, because if he went over, with his spread, with jokes and ad-libs — 'cause Fred really did ad-lib — he was one of the few guys I know who could ad-lib and be funny in his ad-lib...

Certainly Eddie Cantor or Rudy Vallee didn't have the ability.

Oh, no. Some of them ad-libbed, like Groucho Marx and Bob Hope. You'd have a bunch of jokes handy that fit; it would sound like an ad-lib. But Fred would do it on the spur of the moment, 'cause it really fit the situation. It wasn't a joke that he used for ad-libs all the time, like Hope and these other guys used to do. Fred was the only one who could really ad-lib. I saw Fred once — the first couple of pages of material just laid there, there wasn't a laugh — and Fred stopped the show and said, "Portland, I don't know if I warmed up the audience or cremated them." I thought, "Jeez, that's a dumb thing to say." But they screamed. And he just made that up, on the spur of the moment.

Did any of Allen's guests ad-lib?

No, they wouldn't. Jack Benny once in a while would ad-lib some dumb thing. In the middle of a thing, he'd say, "Boy, he'll have a crowd here tonight." People would laugh. We'd say to Fred, "What the... ?" The script goes in the toilet if you're going to start ad-libbing, fooling around — he didn't want that to happen. So Fred would stick to the script.

The Fred Allen-Jack Benny rivalry was strictly for a gag.

Oh, sure. They were quite friendly. Fred used to laugh — Benny did 35 shows a season, and Allen did 39. And Fred used to come in laughing, waving the telegram. "Benny's in the 36th week, and he's getting restless already. He's off one week, can he come on the show?" Of course he came on — he was a great guest for Allen.

They were always playing off of each other's shows...

On account of the time change, we'd listen to the Benny show. Benny used to do a show at 5 o'clock in the afternoon. Then we'd have jokes on the show. Allen would say, "Did you hear Jack Benny tonight?" Our show was all done, the script was ready to go on. Sometimes we couldn't get much out of the show; occasionally, we'd get two or three good jokes out of what Benny did. Once Fred said, "How do you like that? Benny gets bigger laughs on our show than he does on his own."

So it was part of the ritual to listen to Benny's show?

Yeah, pretty much. It would be a riot. People just heard Benny an hour or two ago, and Allen's got jokes about him. Those were the fun days.

Jack Benny was a sure-fire subject for a joke.

Fred used to do Benny jokes during the war. He was driving and the cop stopped him, and he wanted to know, what's Fred doing with the gas coupon? And he said, he was going to *The Jack Benny Show.* The cop says, "Oh, okay. As long as you're not driving for pleasure."

Would Benny bring his writers when he came on the show?

Mary Martin is caught in the middle as Jack Benny throttles Fred Allen, in the 1940 film *Love Thy Neighbor.*

No. We did that. I think we had better shows with Benny — Benny was a pretty good guest star, better than most. People would scalp tickets. There was bedlam. People'd scream and hang from the rafters; the fire people would be there because they used to try to overload the theater. It was a big draw, Benny and Allen.

The studio audience could get out of hand.

Eddie Cantor was the first guy who wanted an audience in the studio. Radio really wasn't meant for — it got out of hand with the comics. Two hundred people sitting in the room determined your material. Never mind that three million maybe thought it was funny, sitting in their apartments listening to the radio. You went by what the studio audience thought, and that wasn't necessarily...

They didn't necessarily know what was funny.

Fred once was a guest star on Ed Gardner's show, *Duffy's Tavern.*
They did the preview — the writers had been up all night, he had
just sent them home. It's raining, a bunch of fat ladies — they're
soaking wet — they're in there listening. They didn't laugh.
Gardner got panicky and started to call the writers back. And Fred
said to him, "I thought the show was funny. Just because the fat
ladies were angry, and they're wet, and didn't laugh..." Gardner
said, "Jesus, you think so, Fred?" He said, "Of course." From then
on, the show was fine. If it hadn't been Fred Allen as the guest, the
writers would've come back, they would've thrown the whole
script out and done God knows what.

Allen didn't like studio audiences.

No, because he felt they didn't belong in a radio show. But that was
the custom, they all insisted on it. Fred would say, "Sure, you're
nicely at home while I'm sitting with those cretins in the front row."

Were you generally at home or were you in the audience for the broadcast?

Well, I gotta tell you. Nat Hiken was a lovely guy, and we had a lot
of laughs together; we were very friendly. But Nat was like a lot of
writers I know — terribly insecure. Wanted to be the boss. You
wouldn't get this out of him, but it was true. And Fred knew it. And
when Nat left the show to do this Berle thing on Sunday night —
this was Sunday afternoon — I said to Fred, "See you tonight." He
said, "For what?" I said, "Well, Jesus, Nat used to come down to the
show; you need someone there." His answer was, "You know why
Nat used to come down? So he could walk into Toots Shor's and
take credit for writing the show." And Fred just let him do it. So I
never went down on Sunday night. And there was no need to go
down there; the show was done. Sometimes it would not be as great
as we thought it would; most of the time it was fine.

Of course Hiken had great success later in TV with The Phil Silvers Show.

He was a good writer. But he used to say, "Jeez, you guys, I have to
go down there every Sunday." It was bullshit. He didn't have to go

down; he wanted to go down.

Other than resorting to something like that, you didn't get any credit. There were no on-the-air credits for writers then.

No. Actually, people used to say that Fred Allen wrote all his own material. That used to be the one thing that got to Fred. In actuality, Fred was better — kinder and more liberal and generous — with writers than anyone else that I worked for. Even though publicly he used to complain about them. Fred really respected writers. He had an argument once with John Reber, who was head of radio for J. Walter Thompson, and Nat and I were standing there. And Fred got angry at him. He said to John Reber, "If it wasn't for boys like this, you wouldn't have a job" — pointing to me and Nat Hiken. Things of that nature.

What do you recall about Allen's frequent battles with network executives?

Those were kind of just good-natured, actually. Fred got cut off the air a couple of times. He would make a joke — he was long one night, they cut him off. They do that to anyone if you're long. Next week he wrote a thing — Portland says, "What happens to that time when you get cut off?" He said, "They save up the time. They take a two-week vacation with your time." One of the network executives got aggravated by that and upset, and made some remark. The guy got fired. Fred felt guilty as hell. He said, "Jesus, I didn't get him fired, did I?"

This executive actually got fired?

The guy did, yeah. I don't know how much that had to do with it. Fred called me one day, he said, "You want to do me a favor?" Some executive invited him to "21" Club for lunch. He said, "I really don't want to stay there. If you'll come with me, I can say, 'Bye bye, I have to work.' " So I got a free lunch at "21," and sure enough, we got out of there. Those things would drive Fred crazy; he didn't like to be with those people. He'd see a celebrity on the street, he'd cross the street, ignore them. But some lady with a shopping bag, he'd stop and talk 15 minutes. It would drive you crazy. Nat and I used to watch — "Christ, we'll be here 15 minutes now."

Did Fred Allen get a lot of flak from his sponsors?

Only a little. Because — it's the old story — if you're doing well, no one's going to give you too much trouble. He got a little flak from the network, when he said the executives were saving up time to take a vacation, stuff like that. The sponsors were always — the shows were paying for themselves in terms of the sponsorship — they were successful. They didn't give you any trouble. We were on the air for Ford during the war — he would have a wonderful line after the show was over. Nobody had any goddamn cars in those days. Fred used to say to the studio audience, "Do me a little favor. If you enjoyed the show tonight, on the way home, if you pass your Ford dealer, for God's sake, go in and sit with the man."

You didn't write for Fred Allen in television, did you?

No. Fred was on radio through June 1949. When he went off the air and started in television, he didn't work too well. I was associated with him, and I got a lot of the blame, which was kind of silly.

Allen blamed you for his failure in TV?

He didn't, but the public did. In terms of hiring me for future shows — "he was great for radio, but he can't write for television." Fred didn't like TV, you know. He was afraid of it. It turned out, he didn't do enough.

Of course, Allen once said the reason television was called a medium was that "nothing on it is ever well done."

Fred did a variety show which was quite good. He had an opening once: "Good evening, ladies and gentlemen. Usually when a television show starts they have six dancing girls. But it costs $100,000 to do a number like that," he says. "You've all seen dancing girls. How many people have seen $100,000?" Two guys dressed as bank guards come out with a box, they open it and show $100,000. It was a good laugh.

You Bet Your Life *would've been a great vehicle for Fred Allen. If he'd found a vehicle that fit him as well as that fit Groucho Marx...*

That's right. Groucho thanked him once that he got *You Bet Your Life* instead of Fred. Groucho told him, "This would've been perfect for you." It's true. But Fred didn't give television a chance.

You feel that if he had persevered, Allen could have found success on TV?

He'd have been more successful, if he stuck to it. He hired Davey Burns on this show — Davey was going to play his television consultant. On one show, they had a thing where they were going to throw pies. Fred figured out the anticipation of throwing the pie is much funnier than actually throwing it. The audience screamed just when you aimed the pie. Fred wrote a line — they screamed at one pie, and Davey Burns said, "There you are, Allen. This pie doesn't need you. It could have its own show." Funny stuff.

What other comedians do you think radio captured better than TV?

Burns and Allen. They were good in television, too, of course. They had a director [Ralph Levy] who was very shrewd. Instead of just Gracie telling jokes — she was not only telling jokes, but she was shelling peas, getting ready for dinner. So it made it look visual. But by and large, it was what they said. Burns and Allen were really radio comedians. You can't tell me anything funny Gracie *did*, or George *did*. It was what they said that was funny.

Jack Benny was more of a visual comedian than Fred Allen. In fact, most of the best comedy on radio was visual...

It seemed all the time, "Jeez, if we could only see this, it would be funny." Then you get to television, you have to see everything, it's a pain in the ass. Jack Benny had that voice — when he did "Your money or your life?" you saw your own picture of the guy hiding in the bushes, and Jack — that was the beauty of radio. You made your own pictures; you didn't have to show everything. When we had Jack on Fred's show as a guest, we had a quiz show where he lost his clothes — he had "LSMFT" on his shorts, which was a big scream. It was all visual.

Before you got into television, you also wrote a radio show for Perry Como — a show called The Chesterfield Supper Club.

Terrible man. He was scared, really. Como was doing a 15-minute TV show, and a half-hour radio show, and he wanted to be another Bing Crosby. He wanted to be like Crosby on the radio show; he'd sing a number and then do a sketch. Como did some funny shows. I wrote them myself, and they were tough to write.

It was a typical musical-variety show with guest stars.

I got Fred Allen to go on as a guest; he wouldn't do it, except for me. I had quit; I came back and wrote the show. I wrote a premise for Fred — he looked at it, we fooled around with it a little bit — he said OK and I went ahead and wrote it. We now go to see Como. Fred and I walked in like two schmucky writers with hat in hand; Como, the dumb ass, doesn't know Fred has read the script. He reads it, the big executive at his desk, and literally throws the script across the room and says, "This is shit." I thought Fred was going to turn all colors of the rainbow. He said, "Now I see why you quit." Somehow we got it calmed down with the producer and Mr. Como backed off. And of course the show was sensational; they wanted Fred to go on again. I said, "You can get someone else to write it, 'cause I ain't gonna do it." That was one incident with Como.

It doesn't sound like a very pleasant association.

We did a special with Arthur Godfrey, Bob Hope and Perry Como — there was a new factory opening. Hope did a monologue and Como blew his stack: "I'm not going to stand there while Hope tells jokes." I said, "Why don't you ask him to let you tell some of the jokes?" That's why I quit. The only decent guy was Hope; he came up and thanked me. They were all funny, but they were all arrogant and insecure.

Do you recall having any trouble with censors in radio?

Occasionally, but it was minor. The sponsors and the advertising agencies, those were the ones that gave you the trouble. What happened was, you got protected by the stars. We did a great show with Mae West, who got banned from radio for doing a dirty show once, and this was like three years later — on Perry Como's show. They finally allowed her to come back. The script was fairly dirty. One of the hot songs at the time was, "I want to go home with you/Nobody one else will do..." Como sang, "I want to go home with you," and she said, "Anytime," or something like that. Then he sang, "Nobody one else will do..." And she said, "Do what..." Then they wanted to do another show. I said, "Hire someone else, 'cause I ain't gonna write it. It'll get too dirty and I'm not interested."

Did you work on other any other radio shows?

Not really for any length of time. A show here and there, a script here and there. Then television happened. I had a couple of lean years. There weren't very many shows in New York. I loved the East — but things began to peter out, and more and more it moved out to Los Angeles. So we came back here in '53.

How did you come to team up with Bob Schiller?

We didn't know where to send our kids to school. We didn't know how half-Japanese kids would function out here. We heard about UCLA Elementary School; we asked a friend if there was any way we could find out about the school. She put us in touch with Bob Schiller's wife — he happened to be a comedy writer. I was looking for a partner, 'cause I had a commitment for the Danny Thomas television show. I did a couple of scripts myself, but it was more fun working with a partner.

All of your radio work was done apart from Schiller?

Yeah, virtually all of it. We did a radio script for *Our Miss Brooks,* when Bob and I first started working together. We did only one script for the show. The reason I got out here was on account of television. Danny Thomas read something I wrote. I got a deal to do six scripts for *Make Room for Daddy.* I did two or three by myself; I really didn't like working alone. This guy Schiller seemed like a pleasant guy, so I called him up.

Why only one script for Our Miss Brooks?

There was not much left in radio. After I started working with Bob Schiller we kicked around a lot. Bob and I wrote one or two left over from my assignment with Danny Thomas. The first real show we had together of any consequence was *I Love Lucy.*

How did you get the job?

A friend of ours, a writer, got his own show; he liked our work, we had three or four scripts with him. He was very honest; he said, "Look, guys, I've got my 13 scripts, now I'm going to be tough." And by Christ he was; we couldn't clear a premise with him after that. It was so easy before. We were in his office at General Service Studios — we weren't getting anywhere — I looked out the window, and I saw Jess Oppenheimer coming in. He says, "Hey, I'm looking for two writers for *I Love Lucy* but I read in the trades you were working for so-and-so." I said, "That was a mistake. Get us off this thing; it's a pain in the ass."

You had worked with Jess Oppenheimer on The Rudy Vallee Show.

Yeah, Jess and I worked together for six or seven months. When I took my wife to Chicago to be with her parents [in 1942], Jess was single at the time — so we took an apartment together in Hollywood and became very friendly. When Jess saw me at the studio [in 1953], he was looking for a couple of writers — he thought Schiller and I were busy because *Variety* had mistakenly printed something about us. I said, "No, we're available." That's how we got with *Lucy* — and it worked out great.

How did you adapt to writing for a visual medium?

It really wasn't that different. It's somewhat different. Because even when you write radio, and you do sketches and things, you think in your mind — you have a picture. Radio and TV are both tough. To get people to laugh is tough. Writing's hard — which is why nobody's there when the paper's blank.

Was it more difficult writing comedy by yourself, as opposed to collaborating?

Yeah, I think so. 'Cause you bounce off each other, back and forth. By and large, the most successful comedy writers have been the teams, but there have been a lot of individuals who have been successful. I like working with a partner better. Most of the time on *The Fred Allen show,* we worked alone — our own spots — and then with Fred.

Did you enjoy writing for radio moreso than TV?

Well, when you wrote for Lucille Ball, who was a very visual comedienne, you got satisfaction. But I've gotten great satisfaction out of my career, making people laugh. Lucille Ball gave me a lot of satisfaction. Carroll O'Connor gave me a lot of satisfaction, and Jean Stapleton — they're good performers, even though they're not comics. Carroll knew how to play that part [Archie Bunker on *All in the Family*]. I gotta give him credit, 'cause he's not a comedian. But when you were in radio, you worked for a comic — Fred Allen, George Burns, Jack Benny. And the funnier the people, the better off you are for the writing.

CREDITS

Radio (without Bob Schiller, except as noted): *The Bob Hope Show, The Eddie Cantor Show, The Rudy Vallee Show, The Fred Allen Show, The Chesterfield Supper Club, Our Miss Brooks* (with Schiller).

TV (in collaboration with Schiller): *Make Room for Daddy, Bob Cummings Show* (one script), *That's My Boy, Professional Father, It's Always Jan, I Love Lucy, My Favorite Husband* (one script),*The Lucy-Desi Comedy Hour, The Ann Sothern Show* (also co-creator), *Guestward Ho, Pete and Gladys, The Lucy Show, The Red Skelton Show, The Good Guys* (also co-producer), *The Phyllis Diller Show, The Carol Burnett Show, The Flip Wilson Show, Maude* (also co-producer), *All's Fair* (also co-creator-producer), *All in the Family, Archie Bunker's Place, W*A*L*T*E*R* (pilot), *Living in Paradise, The Boys.*

Film (without Schiller): *Winged Victory.*

Theater (with Schiller): *So Long, Stanley.*

BOB SCHILLER

"A sense of humor is something you're born with — either you got it or you ain't. It's kind of a silly thing, to have a gift for that. You spend your life being a child — there's nothing terribly intellectual about writing a joke," observes Bob Schiller. "There are no good comedy writers, only bad parents. You've got to be born with it."

Schiller was born with it in San Francisco on November 8, 1918. He earned his B.A. in Economics at UCLA, where he has returned to lecture on writing for radio and television — at which he earned a living for 45 years. "People always ask, 'How do you break in?' You cannot teach a person to be funny. You can teach 'em the elements of a joke, but I don't think you can teach comedy writing," he says.

An innate penchant for off-the-wall humor, and an unrelenting appetite for jokes, led young Schiller to a regular byline in school newspapers. Following World War II, he parlayed his articles for *Stars and Stripes* into a one-week tryout on *Duffy's Tavern.* Despite a precarious apprenticeship on radio — during which he was repeatedly fired — Schiller eventually found his talents in demand. After writing for such radio shows as *Abbott and Costello, The Adventures of Ozzie and Harriet* and *The Mel Blanc Show,* he graduated to television, where he achieved far greater success.

In tandem with Bob Weiskopf — with whom he teamed shortly after his TV debut on *Four Star Revue* with Danny Thomas — Schiller worked on *I Love Lucy* during the show's last two seasons (1955-56), co-writing "some of the so-called classics." They continued their relationship with Lucille Ball on *The Lucy Show.*

Schiller and Weiskopf served as Red Skelton's head writers for three years before moving on to *The Carol Burnett Show, The Flip Wilson Show* (which earned them their first Emmy), four years on *Maude* and two years on *All in the Family.* The latter resulted in a second Emmy; the team also won two Peabody Awards and a Golden Globe during their long collaboration. "We were bound to each other, whether we liked it or not," noted Schiller.

The writers retired in 1990. "The last thing we did — Weiskopf looked at me, we were working late at night. He said, 'What are we doing this for? We're not poor enough, and we're not young enough.' So we quit," says Schiller. "The humor that's going down today — if *Married With Children* is an example of comedy, I just don't want to be involved. I don't want to have anything to do with it. And to have people who are employing you who are younger — who are telling you how to do it — they learned from us. I don't need that."

Although he depended on TV for his livelihood for many years, Schiller is not enthralled by the medium. "I blame television for the demise of America," he noted. However, it is a family affair. His son, Tom Schiller, has followed in his footsteps, writing for a new generation of comedians on *Saturday Night Live;* his second wife, one-time actress Sabrina Scharf, appeared in a classic episode of *Star Trek.*

Schiller, who peppers his conversation with self-deprecating wit and gallows humor — "Excuse me, I gotta call a casket company and get a reservation" — invited the author to lunch at a West Los Angeles country club when asked to discuss his career. As the setting was not conducive to serious talk about comedy writing, Schiller was asked to hold off on the topic until the post-lunch interview. "In that case, let me tell you some stories about my partner," he chirped, and proceeded to regale me with anecdotes about Bob Weiskopf. Some of which may have been true.

I believe you started by writing for Stars and Stripes.

I always wanted to write — I thought I could write funny. When I came down from San Francisco to Los Angeles, I was a stranger here; I had no friends, and I found out that if I wrote, I could gain some kind of access and popularity. So I wrote for the junior high school paper — I had a humor column, in the sense of — in those days it would be Robert Benchley, today it would be Art Buchwald. I wrote for the high school and college newspapers, and newspapers in the army — one in Fort MacArthur, and one in Charleston, South Carolina. I've always written. I was blessed with having a cousin who was funny, and was interested in humor. We would write funny letters to each other. He introduced me to Benchley, and things like *The California Pelican,* a humor magazine at the University of California.

Were you an avid radio listener?

Oh, yeah. It was exciting. It's still exciting — I'd much rather listen to radio than watch television. When I first moved out here, we got a short wave radio. In those days, you could get New York. And I used to pick up the first *Fred Allen Show*, before it was rebroadcast [to the West Coast]. They did two broadcasts. I'd listen to the early show and memorize some of the jokes, and I'd work them into the conversation at dinner. Then my family and I would sit around listening to the second show. "Robert, they just said your joke." They couldn't get over the fact that some of the things that I said were on that show.

Did you aspire toward writing for radio?

No. I didn't know what I wanted to do. I would write anything I could — I would write these columns and so forth. Every now and then I'd get things published here and there, and I got a lot of encouragement, for example, from Matt Weinstock, who had a column in the *Daily News*. When I got out of the army, I went to Matt and I said, "How about a job?" He said, "Go out there — there's no money here." He meant Hollywood.

How did you get your first job in radio?

I had a friend who knew Ed Gardner's agent, the agent for *Duffy's Tavern*. And he knew that Ed Gardner would hire anybody for a week. And if he had any promise, Gardner would give 'em $50 for the week. You know, $50 was a lot of money in those days — so I wanted to do it for the week, 'cause you'd make $50. I was really green, 'cause I didn't know how to write jokes. There's a major difference, as you know, between writing to be read and writing to be said. Writing to be said, you have to have a strong enough — it's a technique — a punchline that's got enough muscle, that will arouse a laugh in an audience. You just can't do whimsy, the kind of stuff you do in columns. You have to have *whamsy*, really.

That's a good distinction between writing for the two media.

I stayed up for two or three nights writing this spot for *Duffy's Tavern* — I didn't think I could ever write again — it was so goddamned difficult, to write a joke. I went in to the head writers — one of whom was Bill Manhoff, the guy who wrote *The Owl and the Pussycat,* and the other was a guy by the name of "Fat" Larry Marks. And they read the stuff and liked it. So they called Ed Gardner, who was a tyrant — he owned the show — they said, "We've got a guy here who seems to be okay..." I'm really green, I don't know anything at all about the business. They said, "We go out every Sunday, to Ed's house. How are you at pitching?" I said, "I used to play first base." And they laughed; they thought I was making a joke. I was serious — I thought they played baseball on Sundays. They laughed; they told Gardner. Gardner says, "Hire him."

How long did you work on the show?

Gardner doubled my salary to $100. I made $100 a week for about four or five weeks, and then I was fired — I think it was seven weeks. I was fired four times from *Duffy's Tavern,* which was the norm. He would hire people and fire them, at will. The last two years that I was on *Duffy's Tavern,* I had a contract; that was 1946 on. I think I made $150 a week, which was pretty good dough in those days. But after he fired me the first time, I went to work with Parke Levy on *Abbott and Costello.* In order to get ahead on the show, we started out in the summertime. We wrote I think seven scripts, and after about the third week it was on the air, Abbott and Costello didn't like it, and MCA didn't like it — they were the agency of record, they ran the show — so we were all fired. So I got fired from the first job, I got fired from the second job — then I went to a show called *Sweeney and March* — I did three scripts for them, and Manny Mannheim, the producer, called me and said, "Get out of the business, you'll never make it."

Was he ever wrong.

"You're too nice" is what he said — translation, "You can't write." I asked him once, after Bob Weiskopf and I won the [Writers Guild of America] Laurel Award, "You still think I ought to get out of the business?" He said, "Probably."

Good thing you didn't take his advice.

I thanked him — and didn't get out of the business, but I got a job with one of the original writers of *Duffy's Tavern*, Mac Benoff, on *The Mel Blanc Show*. And I had a partner there by the name of Stanley Adams, who knifed me. We were writing together, and he walked into Benoff, he said, "Look, I've got a wife and children, and I don't want to work with him; he can't write." This is my partner. So I got fired. It was a particularly painful thing for me.

I would think so.

So my first four jobs, I got fired. There's hardly a show that I wasn't fired from. It's hard to believe that we ever did anything well. I went back on *Duffy's Tavern*, lasted the season there. They fired me at the end of the season, hired me at the beginning of the next season — Ed Gardner would do that to keep your money down, among other things. There's an apocryphal story — Gardner would say, "Okay, Jack, you work with Jim; George, you work with Harry; Charlie, you work with Matt; and Sol — nobody for you to work with — you're fired." He did things on a whim. We were fired a lot in those days.

Just on the spur of the moment.

We were serfs. We were slaves. Listen, they owned you. The image that comes to me is, guys on a slave ship. "More steam!" *Smack!* When the comedians paid you, they figured they were giving you an allowance, like you were their children. They owned your life — literally. "My writers." They all bragged to each other about their writers — "I've got..." Never on the air. They rarely ever talked about writers. Fred Allen never talked about his writers. There's an apocryphal story about Nat Hiken, who wrote for Fred. He was coming cross country — he had his own plane — and he was forced down in Arizona. An Indian tribe rescued him and took him to the chief. They were waiting for the repairman; the chief said, "What do you do?" Hiken says, "I write for Fred Allen." The chief says, "Ugh. Fred Allen. Write own material."

Getting back to Ed Gardner — he sounds like a wild man.

Gardner was a terrible chaser. He was constantly bragging about his sexual organ; he and Milton Berle. They used to measure them.

Which was bigger, their egos or...

I think probably the egos, although the sexual organs were bandied about. As was Forrest Tucker's, and one of the Dead End Kids [Huntz Hall]. But they had a measuring contest at Lakeside Country Club, and they put money on the table. So Berle puts his out, and Gardner puts his out, and [Hall] says, "How much do I have to show?"

Rudy Vallee said Gardner had "a strange streak of irrationality."

He did. He was a strange, erratic man. And he had a cruel streak, too. The cruel streak was that he kept us all in — I was a beginner — and we would work around the clock. There was a wonderful line by one of the writers, Larry Rhine, who said, "If we were horses, they'd arrest Gardner." He used to come in on Sunday morning, and we would work — I was a newlywed then — I'd go to work Friday morning, and we wouldn't come out until Monday morning. We would sleep there. We were all afraid to go home, because somebody would get ahead of us. We were all kind of beginners. And really afraid to let anybody else have more time. Ed knew this — he had us all in competition with each other.

He was a shrewd character...

I had two guys on the show who were ex-druggists — Gardner used to call them, "The pharmacist and his mate" — Bill and Morris Friedman. They thought my stuff was great — 'cause I wasn't writing those kinds of jokes that — I would write different kinds of jokes. One of the brothers said, "Ed, you have to understand, he's got the Dickens touch." Ed says, "Dickens, shit. He couldn't last a week on *Duffy's Tavern.*"

So much for literature.

Al Johanson — he was a terrible writer — he used to bring in thick sheaths of jokes, but one word would be changed in each line, it as if it were a new joke: "Who was that lady I saw you with last night? I don't think that was any lady, that was my mate." That kind of thing. I'm exaggerating, but he'd change just a little — he'd bring the material in, and we'd all be given a couple of pages. Gardner once looked it, he said, "What are you trying to do, Al? Win the Underwood Speedwriting Championship?"

As long as you could convince someone you were a writer...

I later worked with Al Johanson on Ed Wynn's television show. He was one of these officious putzes — he would do everything but write — and what he would do, he would arrange things. When Ed came in, Al would take out his script. When Johanson walked out of the room one day, Wynn said, "He's the most expensive pencil sharpener I've ever had."

Did Ed Gardner contribute much to the writing on Duffy's Tavern?

Yes. Gardner okayed the stories — this is later on. The show started in New York. When they brought it [to Los Angeles], he and Abe Burrows split. Burrows was off the show by the time I got there. Larry Marks and Bill Manhoff were the head writers. Then — you have to dissolve for the next season — by that time, they were off. Gardner had fired them. Vinnie Bogert was the head writer. When we got all our roughs together — after Vinnie put 'em all together, with all the jokes and stuff — then it would go through Ed's fingers. We would all sit there with him while he did it. And it was always — very tense. We all had to sit around while he was "creating" off of our stuff.

Would Gardner mainly act as an editor?

Yes, but the head writer also acted as an editor, and by the time it got to Gardner, it was pretty well refined. Then Gardner would just put his mark on it. Sometimes he'd rewrite a lot, and sometimes he wouldn't. Depending on how much time he had — whether he had a date — they all think they can, and they rarely do.

They really took advantage of you.

Those were strange days. The writers used to have to sit in the audience and laugh. I just hated that, 'cause it's nervous enough without having to force a laugh. You know all the jokes anyway. So we'd have to sit under microphones. Once he called us all — we'd always have a post-mortem in the halls of NBC, at the corner of Sunset and Vine — we'd all stand out there like peasants while the king gave his opinion. We were all very competitive; he made us compete with each other. You'd count how many jokes you had in the show; if you had X number of jokes, you were safe for another week. Gardner said, "Schiller, I looked down, and I saw you weren't laughing." I said, "Well, Ed, that was probably the one joke I didn't write." Gardner used to call me Peck's Bad Boy, 'cause I had no respect for him.

The things a writer has to do to earn a living...

Ed Gardner was notoriously poor paying. They had a strike in the Radio Writers Guild — I don't know whether it ever got to be a strike, but they had a big meeting in Hollywood. After they voted to strike, they said, "We need a strike fund." So a guy would get up and say, "My name is Don Quinn, and I write *Fibber McGee and Molly*, and I pledge $1,000." "My name is Reuben Ship, I write *The Life of Riley*, and I pledge $1,000." "My name is Abe Burrows, and I write *The Dinah Shore Show*, and I pledge $1,000." It was a great straight line — I said, "My name is Bob Schiller, I write *Duffy's Tavern*, I pledge my week's salary, $25." So the next week, we're all standing out there [in the hallway at NBC], and the Pope is making his comments. He says, "I heard about the remark — I don't know which one of you said it, but you better write big goddamn jokes next week." So I called him, I said, "Ed, I know that you know who it was. It was I." I said, "But I gotta tell you, if you had been in my situation, with a straight line like that, you couldn't ignore it." He said, "You're probably right, Bob." He couldn't fire me as a result of that — he'd really be a shit if he fired a guy for...

He wanted to, though.

Sure. There was a guy by the name of Seymour Kapitansky. He came from Detroit; he was on *Variety* or something. He came out here and gave Ed a joke; he got a job, as a result. Kapitansky is downstairs, he's sitting there typing as fast as he can — we'd tell him, "Hey, Seymour, this isn't it. You gotta sit down and refine these things. A joke isn't something you can just type like a letter."

Gardner never bothered to look at his roughs, because he was at that time very much concerned with moving to Puerto Rico; he had a deal where he could move to Puerto Rico and save taxes. So one day, Gardner reads Kapitansky's roughs — the first time — the guy's been on the show for four weeks and hasn't contributed a word. "What the hell is this shit?" Ed's furious — he's more furious with himself than anything, he hasn't paid any attention to the stuff. He goes downstairs and storms into the room, where Kapitansky had a little corner, because he wouldn't write with any of us. He's about to fire the guy, and Kapitansky says, "Ed! Would you stand over there?" He pulls out a camera. He says, "My family back in Detroit don't believe that I'm working for you." He takes a picture of him — Ed had this shit-eating grin — and the guy got another week. He couldn't fire him.

Duffy's Tavern *was considered a prestigious show to write for, according to Sol Saks.*

Oh, *Duffy's Tavern* was prestigious. An awful lot of writers cut their teeth on *Duffy's Tavern.* I learned an awful lot, being a junior writer. It was a wonderful show — great jokes. Archie [Gardner] would say, "I went to the ballet last night, Duffy..." You never heard Duffy — it was a monologue. He says, "What do you mean, did I like it? It's silly. A bunch of dames dancing around on their tippy-toes. Why don't they just get taller dames?"

You once pointed out the resemblance between Archie on Duffy's Tavern, *and Archie Bunker on* All in the Family.

On *Duffy's,* Archie was a know-it-all —he thought he knew everything. He'd say, "Hello, Duffy's Tavern, where the elite meet to eat. Archie the manager speaking. Duffy ain't here... Oh, hello, Duffy. How's the fatuous Mrs. Duffy? Fatuous, Duffy, overweightuous." That's a brilliant malaprop. The ego of a character that is explaining something, and is wrong, is what Archie Bunker did. Ed Gardner did malaprops much better, by the way, than Carroll O'Connor.

Duffy's Tavern *bears a similarity to* Cheers, *but they're different...*

Cheers is really more about sex than anything else. *Duffy's* wasn't.

Miss Duffy was laughed at. She went out with a guy who was a bat-tleship painter — he always tired because he had to run in and out with the tide. The show had good characters, like Clancy the Cop. I wrote a joke once [for Clancy]: "I hate my wife, but I'll always be grateful to her for one thing. She drove me to drink."

Would you write specifically for the actors on a show like that?

You had to. For example, Charlie Cantor — he was a wonderful radio actor. Charlie was Clifton Finnegan on *Duffy's Tavern*, named after Clifton Fadiman, the host of *Information Please*. Of course, Finnegan was the direct opposite — he was an idiot. "I went to the beach and, uh, a lobster bit off one of my toes." Gardner says, "No kiddin'? Which one?" "Duh, I don't know, all them lobsters look alike." That was a typical joke. *Duffy's* was not a sitcom. It was a bunch of jokes put together with a little story.

Was there a type of joke you specialized in, compared to the other writers?

No. You wrote what you could.

And everyone wanted to write for that show.

Duffy's Tavern, in the early years before I was on it, was absolutely a classic show. Brilliant. All the intellectuals — particularly in New York — who wouldn't listen to the radio, listened to *Duffy's*. And *Fred Allen*. They were two most prestigious shows to write for. But over a period of years, I'm sure over 100 writers wrote for *Duffy's Tavern*. Dick Martin [of Rowan and Martin] was on for one week — I know he always claimed that.

Was there any problem with censorship on the show?

Yeah, every now and then you'd have some problem. But compared to what goes down today — today it's just a race to who can say "fuck" first. You do everything but say it. It's a lot easier to write dirty than it is to write clean.

Do you recall any specific instances with censors, where you couldn't do something on Duffy's *or another show?*

We had a line once: "Happier than a sparrow on a lark." And the censor wanted to take it out. He said, "What is that?" There was this kind of crap — they've got to earn their money somehow. We got it in. It didn't get a laugh, though.

That's a funny line.

Of course it's a funny line. But you have to think about it. If you have to think about it, you're past it. That's one of the tenets of radio comedy — you don't have time to think. That's why subtlety was not one of the hallmarks of radio comedy. You've gotta be right on the nose.

Duffy's Tavern *was a sophisticated show.*

Ed Gardner was pretty fast. He was a fast man. After I worked for him, some years later, we used to play golf together. I called him one morning, ánd started talking to him about arranging a golf thing. It was about 9:00 a.m. He and his wife had separate bedrooms. She was a French woman; he used to carry naked pictures of her. So I'm talking, and all of a sudden the other phone — apparently the extension — comes on. Without saying "Excuse me" or anything, she says, "Honey, would you tell the cook that I would like my breakfast now?" "Yeah sure, honey." "And when you get off the phone, why don't you come on in?" "Yeah, I'll do that, honey." She hangs up. I said, "Ed, does she always sound that sexy in the morning?" He says, "Well, Bob, that's the difference between radio and television."

After you were fired from Duffy's *the first time you went to* The Abbott and Costello Show.

That was an unhappy experience. We all got fired. They weren't too happy — I guess the ratings weren't good. Parke Levy — whose reputation was quite enormous because of his being one of the original writers of *Duffy's Tavern* — was the head writer. He did all the fronting for us. We were not allowed to even meet them.

You never met Abbott and Costello, all the time you were working with them?

Never met them. We wrote seven shows, and we got paid for three. And I really got pissed off. I went to MCA and complained. Parke wouldn't go; I think he probably got paid. I went, representing the other writers on the show, and we got some kind of a settlement, but we would not have gotten it if I hadn't complained. They're always threatening you, "You'll never work in this town again," that kind of thing. I said, "I don't care, I'm not that well established." I said, "We were told that we were going to get paid, and now you're reneging on us. I can't put MCA out of business, but you can put me out of business. You want to do that, fine. Fair is fair." They gave us half of what we should've gotten.

Lou Costello reportedly demanded two of the show's writers be fired so he could replace them with his brother, Pat.

That's probably true. A lot of these guys had people in the closet writing too, that none of us ever knew about. A lot of the times, the stars were so nervous and insecure, they'd have their own pets punch up things. Joe Conlon, who was a prick — he knew Abbott and Costello, and they put him on the show. I think he was the guy that blew the whistle on us, and said all of us couldn't cut the mustard. He stayed on. There was a lot of knifing in those days.

After Abbott and Costello, *you worked on* Sweeney and March — *Bob Sweeney and Hal March — I had been under the impression they wrote their own show.*

Nope. They may have written some of it, but they had two awfully good writers by the name of Bill Davenport and Frank Fox. *Sweeney and March* was on CBS [in Los Angeles], and it never got a sponsor. It was a cult show. People who heard it loved it. It was quite different. It was really interesting stuff, kind of like Stoopnagle and Budd. Three weeks, and I got fired from that. Bill and Frank were just wonderful writers. They were really very sweet, naïve kids — they wanted to defer their salaries and help pay for the show — take out ads, so it would be sustaining. They liked my stuff, but the producer obviously didn't, because he got rid of me. I then went to *The Mel Blanc Show.*

Did Blanc ad-lib at all? Was he much of an ad-libber?

Mel? No. That was a terrible show, by the way. I got fired from that, then I went back to *Duffy's Tavern* — I was on four seasons on *Duffy's*. When Ed Gardner quit, I went on *The Adventures of Ozzie and Harriet* for 13 weeks, with Bill Davenport and Frank Fox; they recommended me, from the old *Sweeney and March* days. That was an interesting experience, the way it was done. I had a lot of respect for Ozzie Nelson. Like Desi Arnaz he was a bandleader, and learned everything there was to know about the business. He knew editing, he knew scriptwriting, he knew producing. Desi was a wonderful producer; so was Ozzie. He's underrated.

Ozzie would participate moreso than most, in working with the writers?

We would meet on a certain night at Ozzie's house, and work until we had gotten a story. It was like *Father Knows Best*; it was that kind of a milieu. We would go there, and at midnight Harriet would bring in a tray of ice cream and homemade cookies. It was all so American.

It was Ozzie and Harriet, after all.

It was. And we would continue — the toughest part was the story. Then we would all go home and write an act, and then turn it into the head writer, who put it together. We'd bring the final script to Ozzie; he would then do the same thing Ed Gardner would do. Ozzie was a strange bird. Sol Saks once called him after a show — we didn't go to the shows — he once called him right after the show, and Ozzie said, "What'd you think, Sol?" He says, "I didn't like it." Ozzie said, "I don't want to hear this. Now call me back and tell me you liked it." Sol hangs up, calls back. "What'd you think, Sol?" "I liked it." Ozzie said, "That's better."

How did you write for Ozzie and Harriet, since they weren't really comedians?

The *Ozzie and Harriet* radio show was one of the best situation comedies around. It came out of the same genre as *The Aldrich Family*. It was a wonderfully crafted show. Good solid stories — and good characters. There weren't a lot of sitcoms. *The Jack Benny Show* wasn't a sitcom. *Fred Allen* certainly wasn't a sitcom — it was a bunch of little sketches. So sitcoms on the air were very rare. The original

Ozzie and Harriet shows were written by John P. Medbury and Jack Douglas, and they were just brilliant. Medbury was a humorist like Robert Benchley. They did some wonderful stuff that's probably lost forever.

Jack Douglas seems to be a favorite among other comedy writers.

He was a legend. I worked with him on the first show I did on television, *Four Star Revue*. He had a great reputation. He was a wild man, but he could be harnessed. He wrote a joke about the way to cure baldness — "every night before you go to bed, drink a tall glass of warm hair." Douglas was a great joke writer. He said, "I went to the movies last night, I sat in back of one of those women with a picture hat. It was a great movie." "How did you see it?" "Fortunately, she had pierced ears."

Ozzie and Harriet *wasn't much of a TV show, but I hear it was different on radio.*

It was a much better radio show than it was a television show. If I had to name a sitcom that I thought was a classic, I'd say it was *Ozzie and Harriet*. It was terribly underrated — from a writing standpoint, from a performing standpoint. And Ozzie was a very good editor. They had solid stories, partially due to Ben Gershman. He was a droll man. Ben did all the stories, that was his job — that was the only show I ever worked on that had one guy doing stories. And that was great, because he'd spend the whole week just doing the story, then he'd bring 'em in and we'd all kick 'em around.

And you were fired after 13 weeks on the show?

I was fired, and I asked why — you can tell whether you're doing work that's pleasing, by the amount of your material that gets into a script. Ozzie said, "Well, Harriet feels we should have the woman's viewpoint on the show." I said, "Who are you hiring?" He said, "Selma Diamond." I said, "You hired the wrong man." So Selma replaced me.

Selma Diamond was one of the few female comedy writers at that time.

The jury is still out on whether Selma was a comedy writer. She was really a very interesting character — salty, and she was — exactly what you saw on camera is what she was. I first encountered her on *Duffy's Tavern*. I came in just afterwards, and I heard all the stories about her.

What kind of stories?

It was always, "Selma, make tea." She was on *The Big Show*, with Tallulah Bankhead, and we could never understand how she kept working on it. Goodman Ace ran that show; he was a superb comedy writer. Somebody said, "How do you suppose Selma keeps her job?" Turns out she and Goody were having an affair. I said, "She has an Ace in the hole."

After Ozzie and Harriet *you wrote for Jimmy Durante.*

It was Durante's last radio show. I worked for Morris Friedman; Phil Cohan was the producer. We did the last 13 weeks of the show. There wasn't a helluva lot of interest in the show. In those days, as in the early days of television, the shows were pretty much run by the advertising agencies — as a matter of fact, we used to work at J. Walter Thompson, on the Durante show. That's where our offices were. Then along came the quiz scandals and knocked that out — the networks took over the control.

How much of the malaprop comedy was written, and how much of it was Durante?

Most of it was written. But sometimes he really had trouble with words. And by that time he was tired of the [radio] show, and television was coming in.

Would Durante involve himself in the writing very much?

Never. Durante was given a script and did it. He was a very decent guy. So was Garry Moore, by the way. Durante was no problem. He was a very sweet, cooperative man who knew what he was doing, and didn't give anybody any trouble, as far as I know. He was pleasant; it was nice to work for Durante. Although my connection

with him consisted of being at the readings — that was it. I wasn't
at the shows; I listened to them. They were not masterpieces of
humor.

You would be at the readings, though...

When they read it the first time — in case there was a rewrite. All
this time I was still learning writing. Even though I'd been fired
from every show I did — except the Durante show, because it went
off the air — I'm learning, and I'm getting credits. *Duffy's Tavern*
went to Puerto Rico, and Ed Gardner invited me to join him — I
didn't want to go — the sanitary conditions were not very good
then, and I didn't want to move. I went back East, because my
father-in-law had died — he was the West Coast representative for a
company that made housecoats; I was going to take over his job. My
agent was a fellow by the name of Harvey Orkin — one of the funniest men who ever lived.

Yes. Orkin was the basis for the character in Bernard Slade's play, Tribute.

Harvey was a dear friend. He said, "You sure you're not going to go
back in the business?" I said, "I haven't changed my mind, but in
case anything should show up that's really terrific, I'd consider it."
He said, "Let me take care of that." The next day, he goes to the
William Morris office — this was the end of 1950 — and it was
chaos. The only thing that was really doing well on the air was
Milton Berle. And they had Berle. And they had the *Four Star Revue.*
Harvey opened the door — there were a bunch of agents trying to
fix this show. And Harvey said, "If we could only get Schiller." He
closed the door, and took two steps. "Why can't we get Schiller?"
He said, "Haven't you heard, he's getting out of the business." They
said, "You call yourself an agent, for Chrissake. We need him." They
didn't know who I was — they didn't know my first name — but I
had all these credits. They didn't know I was fired from everything.
The end of the day, I had three [television] shows — Danny Thomas,
Ed Wynn and Garry Moore. So we moved back to New York.

This was Danny Thomas' first TV show, Four Star Revue.

That's right. The four stars were Danny Thomas, Jimmy Durante,

Jack Carson and Ed Wynn. I eventually wound up doing both Thomas and Wynn. I replaced Ed Simmons and Norman Lear on Danny's show. That lasted for three years; it was never a big success. But that's how I got my start in television.

Did you have any trouble making the transition from radio to television?

No, I was equally bad. No, actually writing radio was tougher than writing TV. You're writing more for the imagination — you have to paint a picture. Which is a little more difficult to do than if you've got somebody looking at it. Norman Corwin told a story about a kid who was asked, "Do you like radio or television better?" He says, "Radio." "Why?" "The pictures are better."

You were sort of inventing the medium when you began in TV.

More or less. It was 1950 or '51. It's actually a little different technique. But a joke's a joke. I was the head writer for Danny Thomas — having come off of all my failures in radio. Danny did a lot of his nightclub stuff. That was his major complaint; he said, "I'm using all the material that I use in nightclubs, I don't want to do that." His dear friend, Abe Lastfogel, who was head of the William Morris office, kept encouraging him to do it. Well, he lasted a helluva long time. But Danny never cared too much for that hour once-a-week show; he wasn't too happy with it. You're treading new water there, and you don't know how to go; you don't know who likes what, and so forth. It was a different ballgame. There were only three writers on that show. You stop and think, on the Sid Caesar show there were great sketches, dancing, singing, amusing stuff. He started out with two writers on *Your Show of Shows*, Mel Tolkin and Lucille Kallen. Then Mel Brooks came along and amused him. And for a long time there was only the three of them.

In the beginning TV was pictures of people telling jokes, to a large extent.

No, no. They had situation comedy. It wasn't just a matter of telling jokes — although there were — the bellwether was Milton Berle, he was telling jokes but he was doing sketches.

Did you get your ideas about what TV was supposed to be from watching Berle?

Well, I was never a big fan of Milton's. I loved his gall. I mean, he had chutzpah — he would tell a terrible joke as if it were the funniest thing in the world. He was not bashful about stealing. He amused me because he was so brash. But I never made a point of watching the Berle show.

What association did you have with the producer on Four Star Revue?

I always remember the producer of the show, Leo Morgan. In those days, the William Morris office pretty much controlled television — at least comedy that I know of. So Leo was really out of the Morris office. We would get through in the theater — which is no longer there, on Sixth Avenue — and say, "How did you like it, Leo?" He'd say, "We got off right on time." Good show, bad show — his job was to get it off on time. That was very important.

That was basically the job of the producer in radio, too, to sit there with the watch.

That's right. He never had anything to do with telling the people how to move about. Ezra Stone directed the first television show that I ever wrote. Danny's show. It was wonderful to have Ezra, because with his Broadway background, he would refer to the writers as "authors." I've never referred to before or since as an author.

Suddenly you had a new status. So it was the first time you had a director of any...

That's right. In radio, the producer directed. And generally speaking, in radio the star would also direct.

Was Ed Wynn difficult to write for?

No, no. I used to love Ed Wynn, when I was a kid. I adored him. He was one of my heroes. When I was a little boy, when radio first came in, he was a big star — the Fire Chief, and all that. "I've been there, Graham!" Graham McNamee was his announcer; no matter where he mentioned, Wynn would say, "I've been there," and tell a story — that was his radio show.

Wynn didn't participate in the writing of his TV show, did he?

Ed? No. He was a dear man. Like everyone else, an enormous ego. Ed claimed that he discovered everybody in show business. But he was such a cute fellow. It was very difficult not to like Ed; he was a sweet old man who had this wonderful reincarnation thanks to television. By the time I knew him he was pretty old. You can't really relate to Ed Wynn because he's not a person — he's a clown — any more than you can relate to Jimmy Durante or Bert Lahr.

So you even saw Wynn as that personality off the air?

When Ed talked, the head shook from right to left. The producer was a man named Dick Mack. His head shook — he had a tick — he shook up and down. One wonderful day Ed was saying, "I like it," and shaking his head no [right to left], and Dick Mack was saying, "I don't like it at all," and shaking his head yes [up and down]. It was a classic moment.

Where did you go from there?

Four Star Revue was canceled, then I came back here [Los Angeles] and did *December Bride* on radio. That I did a full season on, and I didn't get fired. So after writing for Danny Thomas and Ed Wynn, I went back to radio for a year. Then I went to *The Red Buttons Show* for eight weeks.

Eight weeks?

Everybody got fired on that show except Larry Gelbart. I think Red Buttons had 40 or 50 writers. I was the first in a long line of writers who came and went in [a few] weeks. In later years, I saw him under different circumstances, and he apologized. He said, "I was crazy." He'd gone through analysis, and so forth. It was sudden fame — he was one of those guys who...

He couldn't handle it.

Well, the country couldn't handle it either. The first year Buttons was a major sensation. The second year, he went right down the tubes. The public is not too faithful. They learned all his tricks. He had a bag of tricks. He did them, and they got boring after a while; he didn't do anything different. "Ho, ho, ho..." — how often can you listen to that? A lot of the comics in those days would go on for a year, make a big splash, and fade. Alan Young was a big sensation for a year, then he became second banana to an equine.

Red Buttons didn't vary his material very much?

That's right. One of the things — the story is told about the guys who wrote the first Red Buttons show — Joe Stein, who wrote *Fiddler on the Roof,* and his partner, Will Glickman — it was on live in New York, and it was an enormous success. They were getting into a taxi. One said to the other, "Jesus, this is really great." And the other one said, "Wait 'til he gets that shit-eating grin." They go into rehearsal for the second week, and the first thing Red says is, "This isn't me." And the two guys walked out. That was the last show they did. They were independent enough not to have to take any crap from him. He was nutsy. From nowhere he became a major star, and then he fizzled like 4th of July firecrackers.

Were you on the show the first year?

No, the start of the second year. I went back there [New York] with Larry Gelbart, who was a friend. I think I was getting $250 a week. I had an eight-week deal. At the end of the sixth week — they had to give me two weeks notice — they said they weren't picking me up. I said, "Why? You have no idea whether I'm one of the great sketch writers in America, because I've working with other people." They had never seen anything I had done alone. Gelbart worked with a fellow named Hal Collins, who was one of Milton Berle's flunkies for many years. Woody Kling and Buddy Arnold and I worked in a different location, and just sent in sketch jokes — they didn't know which. They didn't know whether I could write or not. And Buttons' agent said, "It doesn't matter whether you're the best sketch writer in the world, we can't afford you." I said, "$250 a week?" He said, "Red only gets $1250 a week and he's got to take money from the writer's budget, so we've got to get somebody less expensive." I said, "You're in trouble."

That second year was just writers going through the revolving door.

That's all I know about. I had eight weeks of it. I came back home to California. I wasn't fired, but my option wasn't picked up, which is a nicer way of saying it I suppose. Less harsh — and his band of renown.

According to Steve Allen, Buttons was unable to resist reworking the script.

We never went to rehearsals. Gelbart would go; he was the head writer. He would call us and tell us what he needed. I may have gone to rehearsals and blocked it out; to be honest, I don't remember. I wasn't working with Larry directly. I was sitting in a room with two other guys, working on jokes and ideas for sketches. It was frustrating. There was no chance for any kind of individuality.

Did you work directly with Red Buttons at all on his show?

No. Well, we saw him, and he knew us. But he was suddenly rich. Nouveau riche. When we came to his apartment — there were a few sessions there — we had to sign in, so he could deduct us for tax purposes. You know you've made it when it you have a tax advisor.

Did he seem to have a good sense of material?

Oh, yeah. Buttons pretty well knew his characters. Most comics know their characters; after all, they've worked with them for years. It's not easy to create a new comedy character, and these were characters that he knew. Same thing with Red Skelton. He had this list of characters that never varied; he had a bunch of 'em, so it didn't seem like the same show every week. But there's a big similarity between Buttons and Skelton. Why would Skelton last for umpteen years, and Buttons fizzle?

Had you worked with Larry Gelbart before?

He was a kid when I first met him. I don't remember whether we overlapped on *Duffy's Tavern* or not. But he was working with Sid Dorfman on *The Eddie Cantor Show,* and they called me over to help them — Sid was sick or something. They were working at a little bungalow in Hollywood; it was one of those typical *Day of the Locust* bungalows. There was a very small group of comedy writers then. We all knew each other socially. In those days, we used to have Saturday night parties at each other's homes. We all went to the beach together — and rapped other comedy writers.

You teamed up with Bob Weiskopf, after The Red Buttons Show. *Exactly how did your collaboration come about?*

I got canned from that show, and I was coming back after eight weeks — in those days they had teletypes — the William Morris office teletyped from New York that I was coming back, and looking for work. And by coincidence at that moment, Weiskopf was in the Morris office; we had the same agent. Bob had a deal to do *Make Room for Daddy,* to do four of them; he had done three and he was tired of working alone. He was used to working with a partner. He called the agent and wondered if there was anybody available — and almost at that moment the teletype came through, and he said, "How about Schiller?" We had met prior to my going to New York on the Buttons show; he came over to my house and we spent an evening together. And that's how we got together. I came back and we did a *Make Room for Daddy.* We did one show for *Our Miss Brooks.* We struggled for a year.

But you preferred working with a partner to working alone?

Much. It was strange — most partnerships are opposites. We're very much alike, so we understand each other. We're both kind of lazy — we worked like dogs, and we're both still kind of lazy. Somebody said, "How do you become a successful comedy writer?" I said, "It's very simple. You learn how to type and find a funny partner."

And that's what you did.

That's what I did. Ed Gardner was asked, "Where do you find writers?" He said, "I look for people who think crooked." And that's exactly right. When I first said hello to Bob Weiskopf, he said,

"That's what you think."

The first time you met him?

That's right. That's thinking crooked, not in a straight line. There's people who cannot — it's almost psychotic with some comedy writers — who cannot say anything straight. It's awful, because — if you examine it from a psychological standpoint, it's pushing people away, really — you don't let anybody get close to you.

Were you familiar with Lucille Ball's radio show, My Favorite Husband, *before you starting writing for* I Love Lucy?

Sure. It wasn't a very popular show. Lucy wasn't the knockabout comedienne that came along later. She didn't start getting her reputation until she was 40 years old. Sol Saks wrote a very good television show with Nate Monaster called *My Favorite Husband*. It was quite different though; I think they just took the name. It was a lovely show, but it didn't work — there's nothing funny about Joan Caulfield. She couldn't get a laugh if she slipped on a banana peel.

Lucy was a terrific physical comic, though.

She was really great. She never made a move that wasn't right. There was a wonderful sketch on *The Ed Wynn Show*, a silent sketch where they held up signs, instead of speaking dialogue. It was a very clever sketch — it was the TV first show Lucy was on, and she was wonderful. People started talking about moving her *My Favorite Husband* radio show over to television. That was the first interest there was in Lucy, as a television performer.

At what point did you and Bob Weiskopf start working on I Love Lucy? *You weren't on the show from its inception.*

No. That's one of the miracles of show business. There were only three writers — Bob Carroll Jr., Madelyn Pugh [Davis] and Jess Oppenheimer — for the first four years. Then Bob Weiskopf and I came on the fifth and sixth year. There were never any other writers on *I Love Lucy*. Ever. Not a word was ever written by anybody else.

Would the five of you write together?

We all worked together on story. All five of us. Weiskopf and I would write the first draft. Then Bob and Madelyn and Jess would get together and decide what else was needed, and Bob and Madelyn would do a brush or a rewrite, depending on how badly it was written. And then Jess would turn it in. It all went through Jess.

Jess Oppenheimer was also producing the show.

Jess was wonderful; he was a producer who would turn off the phone and say, "No calls except emergencies." We would sit in the room, and outside of lunch we wouldn't leave that room until we had a story. Jess was only on *I Love Lucy* the first year that we were on. At the end of that season, he quit. They had a big party for him. Desi said, "We haven't lost a producer, we've gained a parking space."

Oppenheimer was pretty much the arbiter of things, your first season there?

Yeah. He pretty much — what he said went. There was always kind of a tension between Desi and Jess. That's one of the reason Jess quit. He and Desi had a hit, obviously, and it was a matter of "Who gets the credit?" I think when you have two strong egos involved...

They kept butting heads.

Yeah. Well, Jess was the best producer I ever worked for. He was organized, he was compartmentalized. It was an enormous task to do a weekly show, particularly in those days when not a helluva lot was known about it. And when you stop and think of it, you're working on a script — most producers are not writing today — he was writing, he was in there — most producers enjoy casting, because it's not nearly as difficult as writing or directing. And Jess was very good — there was a kind of jealousy between the two of them, between Jess and Desi.

How did things change when Oppenheimer left? It was just the four of you then?

When Jess left, Weiskopf and I did the first draft again; it went through Bob and Madelyn, and onto the air. It was relatively easy, in retrospect. We never worked a night; we never worked a weekend. It was quite different from the way things are today. Today they just keep rewriting and rewriting and rewriting. We never did things after the audience went home on *I Love Lucy*; no pickups. Even though William Frawley would often flub — they'd work around it.

You told me that the "secret" of I Love Lucy *was that the characters of Lucy and Ricky were sort of based on Baby Snooks and Daddy.*

Well, they weren't, but we thought it was that. When you stop to think of it, she's trying to put one over on Daddy. Over the years, people have said, "How did you do it?" Once you come up with that thought, you get the picture.

I had never thought of it, until you mentioned it — but you can immediately see the parallels.

Right. Jess did work on *Baby Snooks*. But I never talked to him about it. And I don't know that anyone else ever analyzed it.

Madelyn Davis and Bob Carroll Jr. had written for Lucy's radio show.

Madelyn and Bob and Jess worked on *My Favorite Husband*. Madelyn and Bob were staff writers at CBS originally. Any of the physical things we did [on TV], Madelyn would try them out; if she could do them, we figured Lucy could do them. Some of the things that she couldn't do, Lucy could do. I remember things like stilts. We called Lucy and said, "Can you do stilts?" She said, "I did it when I was a kid; let's try it."

Why do you think there were so few women comedy writers then?

I don't know. I can give you a conjecture. And that is — it goes back to the battle of the sexes, really. Let me back way up and say that one of the things that made Lucy so successful is, she was always feminine. It's not easy for a woman comic to be feminine. Funny is Martha Raye — masculine. Most women when they try to get funny become masculine; it's not terribly attractive. Maybe that trickles down to writing, I don't know. I think it's probably cultural.

Producer Jess Oppenheimer discusses *I Love Lucy* with writers Bob Weiskopf, Madelyn Pugh Davis, Bob Schiller and Bob Carroll Jr. (bearded) at Desilu, 1956.

You continued your association with Madelyn and Bob on The Lucy-Desi Comedy Hour.

Weiskopf and I were the writers on that and Bob and Madelyn were the story editors; they wanted to take it easy. They just came in and did brushes, and overlooked the thing. We did all three years of the *Comedy Hour*. There were no other writers. Oh yes, there was — when Bob and Madelyn retired, briefly, Desi asked us if we wanted anybody to help us. So we got Everett Freeman, with whom I had worked on *That's My Boy*. He came in and we sat around and tried to work out a story together. He got up in the middle of thing and said, "You guys don't need me" — and left. The next we heard of him, he wanted top billing. Weiskopf and I wrote the whole show — he was there for maybe three hours.

Some things never change.

It went on for two more years as *The Lucy Show* — Bob, Madelyn, Weiskopf and I did it the first two years. We used to call "The Dyke Van Dick Show" — it was without the men [Desi and William Frawley].

How much participation did Lucy and Desi have, as far as the writing of the show?

Not a helluva lot. Oh, I can't answer that without splitting it. There's B.D. and A.D. — before Desi left, and after Desi left. Lucy had a lot of faith in her writers. So did Desi — Desi was wonderful with writers. He admired them, and respected them. When he left, Lucy was scared to death, and didn't know really how to deal with people. He was a charmer — I'd do anything for Desi. And Lucy, she'd have to beg me. She did not really know how to ask for things. And she was always afraid — she depended on Desi: "It's okay, honey."

Your contact would've been more with Desi, until they split up.

Yes. One time Desi calls in Jess Oppenheimer and says, "We can't go on like this, we've got to work it out democratically. If you and Lucy agree on something, majority wins, you and Lucy. If Lucy and I agree on something, majority wins, Lucy and I." Jess says, "Fine." As Desi is walking out, Jess says, "What happens if you and I agree on something and Lucy doesn't?" Desi says, "Majority wins — Lucy."

Behind the scenes, Lucy had a definite idea about things.

She was a perfectionist, really. Anybody who ever worked with Lucy, particularly actors, will tell you that she had to know every eye blink. She had to know exactly where — she would never ad-lib. She had to know everything that was going on, where you were standing. Desi kept her from doing that. He kept her from at least being nervous. Lucy depended on him when Jess left. Jess was really — the year that we worked with him — he had the upper hand. Although he didn't sleep with her, didn't go home with her — he

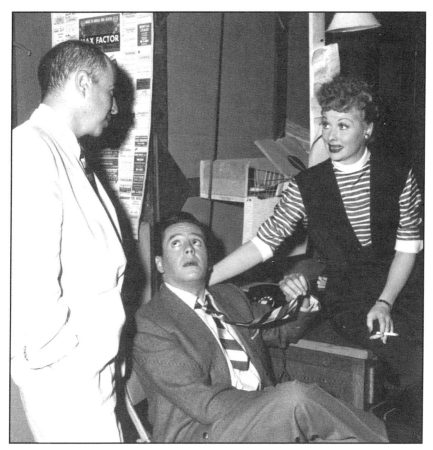

Jess Oppenheimer converses with Lucille Ball and Desi Arnaz on the set of their sitcom.

could see the tension that was created by a man and his wife. Once Desi left, Lucy was — she had a double duty. She thought that she was directing; she was acting, she was the producer, and she also had to run the studio. So she was scared. And it was not a pleasant sight.

Between I Love Lucy *and* The Lucy Show, *you and your partner wrote for* Pete and Gladys, *with Harry Morgan and Cara Williams.*

Cara was pretty good. I remember going down once and watching it. I was watching her do a take on a thing that I had written — and being very undiplomatic, I said, "I think you're not doing that right." Cara was kind of taken aback by it. "Who are you to tell me I'm not doing it right?" she said. "Well," I said, "I used to write a show with an actress [Lucy] who does a great imitation of you."

You also wrote for Red Skelton on TV. Were you familiar with his radio show?

Yes. I first became acquainted with Red when I was in the army. I was going to officer candidate school, and he came and entertained us. Nobody paid any attention to him. It was awful. Embarrassing. Slapabout, knockabout comic. Very childish, very primitive — embarrassingly primitive. I never cared much for Skelton's stuff.

Was he difficult to work for?

Skelton always said, "If I weren't so rich, they'd put me away." He was right — he was crazy. We would do a run-through on Monday night, and then do a rewrite; he'd come and do the show on Tuesday night. But Skelton would bring in a whole bunch of his old jokes — and really ruin it. We had good writers on that show; Bob and I were the head writers. It was disappointing, and heartbreaking, to see a good sketch fucked up with old jokes. Skelton would bring in all his files.

Milton Berle had a habit of doing the same thing.

Weiskopf and I suggested getting Charlie Isaacs when we got fired from the Skelton show, after three years. So Charlie came down. We sent him a script and he read it; he said, "This is funny." We said, "Wait 'til you see what he does with it." By coincidence, that day, Bob and I had given an interview to Hal Humphrey — who was the TV editor at the *Los Angeles Times* — complaining about this. Weiskopf's line was, "Being head writer for Skelton is like going to junior high school. He's good for three years." The story was not very flattering to Skelton. So we always watched up in the producer's office — Seymour Berns. And then we'd do the rewrite, after the run-through on show day. So Skelton read the column and was pissed off...

You'd already gotten the axe.

Berns comes upstairs after the run-through. He's giggling; he says, "You guys should give an interview every week — we were seven minutes over with laughs." Skelton said, "I'll show those sons of bitches. I'll read it the way they wrote it." It went much better than the stuff he would bring in. It was the first time we ever had an example of our work on the air. Naturally, we cut it down. But that was his way of showing us, we didn't know what the hell we were talking about.

CREDITS

Radio (without Bob Weiskopf, except as noted): *Duffy's Tavern, Abbott and Costello, The Adventures of Ozzie and Harriet, The Mel Blanc Show, Sweeney and March, The Jimmy Durante Show, December Bride, Our Miss Brooks* (one script, with Weiskopf).

TV (without Weiskopf): *Four Star Revue* (aka *The Danny Thomas Show, The Ed Wynn Show*), *The Garry Moore Show, The Red Buttons Show.*

TV (in collaboration with Weiskopf): *Make Room for Daddy, The Bob Cummings Show* (one script), *That's My Boy, Professional Father, It's Always Jan, I Love Lucy, My Favorite Husband* (one script), *The Lucy-Desi Comedy Hour, The Ann Sothern Show* (also co-creator), *Guestward Ho, Pete and Gladys, The Lucy Show, The Red Skelton Show, The Good Guys* (also co-producer), *The Phyllis Diller Show, The Carol Burnett Show, The Flip Wilson Show, Maude* (also co-producer), *All's Fair* (also co-creator-producer), *All in the Family, Archie Bunker's Place, W*A*L*T*E*R* (pilot), *Living in Paradise, The Boys.*

Theater (with Weiskopf): *So Long, Stanley.*

HAL KANTER

Leave it to Hal Kanter to introduce himself as no one else could. "I'm the internationally famous writer-director who's known to his barber as 'Next!' " And leave it to Kanter to lighten the mood by introducing himself in such typically irreverent fashion at a memorial service for playwright Robert E. Lee.

The reaction to Kanter's arrival into the world has not been recorded for posterity, but doubtless he knew how to make an entrance even then. He was born December 18, 1918, in Savannah, Georgia. He sold his first article at the ripe old age of 11, and became a newspaper reporter at 16 — by which time he was already selling cartoons. The boy wonder was just shy of 18 when he migrated to California as "a ghost writer for a ghost writer" for a comic strip, and promptly broke into radio.

Kanter wrote jokes anonymously for the likes of Jack Haley and Joe Penner before relocating to New York, where he contributed topical material to Olsen and Johnson's long-running Broadway hit, *Hellzapoppin*. Moving from the ridiculous to the sublime, he took a stab at radio drama; *Grand Central Station*, for which he wrote numerous episodes, gave him his first on-air credit.

During World War II Kanter took an active role in Armed Forces Radio Service, writing, producing and acting in shows on various local stations. He also built radio stations for AFRS in such far-off places as Enewetak, Guam, Iwo Jima and Saipan, before being discharged with the rank of Technical Sergeant late in 1945.

Once out of uniform Kanter wrote for Danny Kaye, then signed on with *Philco Radio Time*, putting words in Bing Crosby's mouth for four years. He also wrote for Don Ameche, Jack Paar, *Amos 'n' Andy* and *The Beulah Show* before making his television debut with *The Ed Wynn Show*.

The '50s found Kanter largely avoiding TV — where he nonetheless scored a hit with his Emmy-winning *George Gobel Show* — in favor of motion pictures. Among the films he worked on during that period were Bob Hope and Bing Crosby's *Road to Bali*, Dean Martin and Jerry Lewis' *Money From Home* and the screen adaptation of Tennessee Williams' *The Rose Tattoo*, which won an Oscar for

Anna Magnani. Kanter took the director's reins on two features: Gobel's *I Married a Woman* and Dan Rowan and Dick Martin's *Once Upon a Horse*.

After tackling such diverse screenwriting assignments as Frank Capra's *Pocketful of Miracles* and Elvis Presley's *Blue Hawaii*, the veteran scribe began shuffling back and forth between a myriad of TV projects. For the home screen Kanter wrote and produced *Valentine's Day, The Jimmy Stewart Show, Chico and the Man* and *All in the Family*. He handled similar responsibilities for a number of specials for Bob Hope, Lucille Ball and other stars.

His most notable achievement in TV may be the ground-breaking *Julia* with Diahann Carroll — the first contemporary sitcom headlined by a black actress. "I wrote it on spec, not knowing if anyone would have the guts to buy it," noted Kanter, who was inspired to create the 1968-71 NBC series after an impassioned plea from the NAACP. "It so happened the timing was right. There was a growth of social consciousness and it met that."

Kanter, who is perhaps best known to the general public for co-writing the annual Academy Awards presentations — 28 times since 1952, when the show was still broadcast on radio — is not above biting the hand that feeds him. As he once observed: "Television has the same function as the old medicine man — to do a jig on the tailgate of a wagon to entertain and sell snake oil."

His lesser known works include the novel, *A Snake in the Glass*. ("It's about writers. Absolute fiction. It's a story about the last of the live television shows.") In recent years he has written and performed in the stage production, *Laughing Matters*, and completed his memoirs, *So Far, So Funny*.

A sought-after speaker and emcee at industry functions, Kanter is every ready with a quip. When asked if there were any photographs available of himself from radio or early television days, Kanter suggested to the author, "Why don't you take the pictures you shot [at a 1992 luncheon] and retouch 'em?"

When did you decide to become a writer? You started out awfully young...

When I was 11 years old I did "Boy Scout News" for the *Miami Herald* in Miami, Florida. I wasn't able to join the scouts, because you had to be 12. So I decided to go to the meetings anyway, and explained that I was going to report it for the *Herald*, and they said fine. And I did. I sent it in and got 50 cents for it. When I became 12, I was eligible to join the scouts. I joined this troop immediately; I became the troop scribe. And one of the official duties of the troop scribe was to send to the *Miami Herald* a report of what they had done. So by joining the Boy Scouts, I lost about $35 in income.

But by then, you knew what you wanted to pursue...

I wanted really to be a writer. And comedy came naturally, because I came from a very amusing family. My father and my mother and my brother and my sister are all very amusing people. They used to get up in the middle of the night and laugh at each other, and then go back to sleep.

When you were 18 you went to a broadcast of The Eddie Cantor Show. *I believe you were rather unimpressed with Mr. Cantor's gag writers, or with his material?*

That's what I felt at the time. I felt that I could do as well or better. And that's where I met Howard Snyder and Hugh Wedlock Jr. — as a result of that — who really gave me the first chance to show that I was not good enough to be a writer.

How did this opportunity come about?

I was living in a rooming house not far from the studio, on Waring Avenue in Hollywood. I was listening to the Cantor show, and I felt that I could do equally as well as that. And I needed a job. I thought that because of the similarity of our names, he would want to see me. I went to the stage door — this is how naive I was — and sent my name up: "I want to see Mr. Cantor after the broadcast." The stage doorman told me to wait there. And while I was waiting, there was an older gentleman, very well dressed, and he asked me what I was going to see Mr. Cantor about. And I said, "I'm a comedy writer, and I want to sell him some jokes." He said, "That's very interesting — because I happen to be a writer myself." It turned out to be Howard Snyder. He said, "What have you written?" I said, "I've written cartoons, and I've written a column for my hometown paper." Then I said I had written the senior class show, for my graduating class at NYU. Howard said, "That's interesting, because I did the same thing." He said, "Were you uptown or downtown?" And I wasn't sure that there were two NYUs, because I had never gone to NYU.

Snyder caught you bluffing.

I was caught. I said, "Downtown." He said, "I was uptown" — or whatever. The stage doorman came down at that point; he said, "Mr. Cantor will not see you. So beat it." He turned to Howard and said, "You, Howard, you better get upstairs right now." Before he did, he said, "Listen, kid, would you like to come and work for me and my partner?" He said, "We need somebody to help us out, if you really can write jokes." He gave me a telephone number to call the following morning — which I did. It was Hugh Wedlock's house. I went over to see Hugh the next day. Fortunately, it was within walking distance, again, and he was very sweet. He told me what the problem was — that they were both writing *The Eddie Cantor Show,* but they were also writing the Jack Oakie show. Oakie was on a show with Benny Goodman and his orchestra...

Yes, it was called Jack Oakie's College.

Hugh gave me an assignment to write some jokes about a prison or whatever it was, for Oakie and Stu Erwin, his sidekick. I went home, and came back later afternoon. Howard was there — he said they had bad news for me. The reason Cantor wanted to see him, was that Cantor had found out the two boys were writing for the Oakie show as well as for him. And in those days, you didn't do that, and he fired them. Because they were back to only one show, they did not need my services. So I worked with them for — probably a day. But they did say they knew another pair of writers who needed someone like me, who could type and who could spell...

Those were the job requirements?

Not necessarily did I have to write jokes, but I could type rather neatly and I could spell pretty well. So they sent me to see a man named Eddie Davis, and Eddie in turn said, "You'll go to work for us first on the Jack Haley *Log Cabin Jamboree.*" That's where I started, really.

Were you part of the whole process, starting from scratch?

Yes. There was a man named Hal Fimberg — I reported to him. He scared the jeezus out of me, telling me how to behave when I met Jack Haley. Then he took me to an apartment where they worked; they had a secretary, and she took down everything. He and I were talking back and forth about the scene, or whatever it was. Finally, Haley came in — the first time I met him. I wasn't really quite sure who he was, frankly. I was not a Jack Haley fan, in particular. Later I began to realize the value of the man as a performer.

He was rather nondescript looking.

Exactly. But that job lasted I think a week and I was fired. I wasn't able to cut it, really. So I went to work for Eddie Davis himself. He paid me out of his own pocket. I was typing, and that's how I learned the craft of writing radio jokes, really from that man, who was one of the best of the joke writers. He was a near illiterate, really — he couldn't spell very well, and words that had more than two syllables were alien to him.

He wanted you to type and spell the words.

Exactly. But he did know how to write a joke. He was great. So I spent a lot of time with him.

Did anyone in particular teach you the finer shadings of comedy writing — about writing jokes for a particular character, or how a specific person would speak?

Those things you learn from experience, really. One of the things I prided myself on at that time was that I had a very good *ear*. That I developed purposely. I was born in Savannah, Georgia, and I lived in the South until we moved — as I say, from the Deep South to the Shallow North. I was in junior high school, and the kids mercilessly teased me about my accent. So I made up my mind at that point that I was going to stop talking like a Southerner. But I damn sure as hell wasn't going to talk like a New Yorker, 'cause their accent grated on my ears. To this day, I really dislike an acute New York accent. So I deliberately began to learn why people pronounce certain words certain ways, and tried to avoid that.

A very useful tool for a writer...

As a result of that, I probably developed an ear for the speech patterns of comedians, particularly. It came in good stead later. I've found over the years — for instance, on the Bing Crosby show [*Philco Radio Time*] where we worked with practically everybody of any consequence in this business — that came in very handy, learning how to adapt to the rhythms of a Jimmy Durante one week, and a Clifton Webb the next week.

You wrote for Jack Pearl and Joe Penner early in your career.

Jack Pearl had played Baron von Münchhausen, but he wanted to be a serious actor. Long before I came on, Jack had been a star on Broadway. He was a wonderful dialectician — also, he had impeccable timing. That's another thing I learned, his timing. You learn something from everybody that you work with if...

If you're good.

I've forgotten how I met him, but Jack Pearl at that time was all but retired. And he was a very wealthy man who lived at the Warwick Hotel in New York. We had a mutual friend. I was writing a radio show very often for a man named Ted Lloyd — Ted knew Jack, and Jack wanted to be a serious actor. So he got me together with Pearl, and I did a serious piece, based on the life of [patriot] Haym Salomon. And for years I would see Pearl, and he was so delighted with that piece — "Why don't we do this as a movie?" I said, "I'm perfectly willing, but nobody wants me to write a movie." And nobody wanted him to star in a movie.

Because Pearl was so identified with Baron von Munchhausen.

Yeah. "Vas you dere, Sharlie?"

That's something Jack Pearl shared with Joe Penner, that reliance on catch phrases.

I remembered that many years later when I did *The George Gobel Show* on TV. We had a little thing — "Well, I'll be a dirty bird" — after about the third week, everybody in the country was saying it. Because the show was an instant hit. I said to George, "We're not going to do that any more." He said, "Why not?" I said, "When people stopped saying, 'Vas you dere, Sharlie?,' that's when they stopped listening to Jack Pearl. And when people stopped saying, "Wanna buy a duck?,' they stopped listening to Joe Penner. So we're not going to give them anything that they're going to stop saying." Because everything is so accelerated now, everything is so instantaneous, in three weeks it's had it. Anything has had it. So I was smart enough to stop doing that.

How did you write for somebody like Joe Penner?

For Joe Penner, again, I was like a ghost writer in a sense. Nobody got credits in those days, in radio. Very few writers ever got credit. It was Eddie Davis and Matt Brooks who were writing the show, and they had two assistants — me and Harry Crane. I never met Joe Penner. Harry and I were not allowed to come to the studio. We could come to the broadcast and sit in the audience, but we never met Penner. The way it worked was, Eddie Davis would come to our apartment, where the two of us were living in Hollywood. He would come every morning, and we would write everything except one little spot that Matt Brooks wrote. Matt wrote one spot for himself and Penner, because he was also a performer. So we did everything else. We'd start with line one and go on...

And this apprenticeship was really where you learned the basics of your craft.

In those days, you had the *thinnest* of storylines. Maybe *a* storyline. It was just a reason to do a lot of farm jokes, a reason to do a lot of carnival jokes — whatever it was. So we didn't learn very much about construction. You learned the construction of a joke, and you learned the construction of a scene — which joke is better here, and how you build up to this joke. It's the kind of comedy that they're not doing any more. They're not doing it for a couple of reasons. First of all, it's old-fashioned. And it's pretty simplistic. And I think audiences are a little bit more sophisticated. The other reason is, most people who are writing comedy today don't know how to write jokes. It's that simple. You very seldom hear jokes that you can take out of context and repeat.

Unless you're Milton Berle.

I remember, I had done a joke for Joe Penner — and three weeks later I heard it on *The Judy Canova Show*. And I was outraged that somebody had stolen my joke. I'll never forget the joke — I've forgotten in what context it was, but this guy says he takes a milk shower every morning. The other guy says, "You mean a milk bath?" He says, "No, a milk shower." "How do you take a milk shower?" He says, "I have a very tall cow." That's a pretty good joke — it popped up on *The Judy Canova Show* three weeks later and I was furious about it. And Eddie Davis said, "Don't be. Just be flattered that somebody's taken your joke." He said, "If it's the last joke you can think of — then worry."

They don't steal if it's not good.

Exactly. I said, "That's a good thing to remember." And I began stealing jokes from other people myself.

The best radio jokes are the ones that create the visual images like that. You can see a tall cow...

And someone standing under it, with soapy armpits.

How much were you making at that time, writing for someone like Joe Penner?

I was making $50 a week on *The Joe Penner Show*. Then I went to work for Olsen and Johnson, in *Hellzapoppin* — I was getting $50 a week from them. Then when I began writing their comic strip — *Hellzapoppin* was also a comic strip for King Features — I got an extra $25 a week. So I was getting $75 a week; I was in hog heaven. That was a lot of money for a kid.

You went back to radio after taking a detour to write for Hellzapoppin?

Yeah. After *The Joe Penner Show* I went back to New York, and for a while I was writing radio drama. I did a show called *Lincoln Highway*. I wrote several episodes of *Grand Central Station*. I've gotten my dates a little screwed up, but I did a show called *Command Performance*.

That would've been during the war.

No, before. It was produced by Ted Lloyd at WOR; I don't know if it was network or not. I remember supporting myself because Ted did not pay anything for scripts. But he would pay the actors. He said, "If you write a small part in, you get paid as an actor." That's how I supported myself for a while. This is before there was a Writers Guild.

How and why did you suddenly switch to writing dramatic programs?

Paul Monroe had been the producer of *The Joe Penner Show*, and he said to me once, why was I wasting time writing baggy-pants comedy when I was such an intelligent young man; I should be writing something more important. It didn't occur to me at the time to say, "Why does an intelligent man like you produce this baggy-pants comedy instead of something more important?" Anyway, he told me after the show was wrapped, he was going to New York to do another show; he said, "Look me up if you're ever there." I looked Paul Monroe up, and he was doing *Grand Central Station* — and that's when I started doing that.

Did writing these dramatic shows pose a particular challenge to you? They were so different from the kinds of programs you had written prior...

Yes. It must have. First of all, I would have no collaborators. Also, in those days, you would not go in and pitch a story, or submit a storyline. You submitted a complete script. If they liked it, they bought it; if they didn't, they rejected it. Sometimes they said, "We like this, but could you fix the last act," or something. But usually it was "yes" or "no." If it was "yes" you got $100 for all rights in perpetuity. But you did get a credit on the air; they did say "written by..."

That meant you were out if they made a movie of it, let's say.

That's right, anything. There was one script I wrote for of *Grand Central Station* that was done, to my knowledge, four times with four different casts. And I never got another penny. But they of course had to pay the actors each time, and the director — and if there was music. I guess there was an organist.

Were you under contract to the advertising agency when you were writing the show?

No, I was not. I don't think I ever worked for an agency. Very often the contract would be with the star, or the star's production entity at that point. But never for — I don't recall ever being under contract to an agency.

Was there any perceivable difference between the radio communities of Hollywood and New York, since you worked in both? Was it more easy-going out here, in Los Angeles?

I think there was considerable difference. It was more frenetic out here, it seems to me. Everybody I know in radio was always doing something else — writing pictures, or *trying* to write pictures. But they had a very active social life, a very active sports life — the writers were doing two and three shows, and making a lot of trips to Santa Anita and Hollywood Park [racetracks].

Losing the money they earned by writing. In New York they concentrated more...

In New York they seemed to be much more business-like, coats and ties and regular office hours, and then getting on a train and going to Connecticut where they lived, or out to Long Island. Whereas in Los Angeles, there wasn't that division of, now it's time for me to get out of my business suit and become a citizen.

During the war you did something called The Lowery Field Theater of the Air *on KOA, in Denver. Apparently you were stationed...*

At Lowery Field, that's right. That was one of the shows I did every week. That's probably where I learned how to write, more than any-place else. I was on my own, and I had to do a half-an-hour original

story every week. And I did various stories and various entertainments. That was in addition to doing a quiz show every week for
KMYR and a daily disc jockey show for a while, all as a soldier. So I
was very, very busy in Denver. We did a couple of programs that
went network — special events — but it was primarily local, Rocky
Mountain region.

Did you enlist in the Armed Forces?

No, I did not. I was not quite that patriotic. When I was drafted, I
went into the army here. I went in the same time as Tom D'Andrea
and Jackie Coogan. Jackie had volunteered; he was the first so-
called movie star to enlist. The three of us went up to Camp Roberts
in Monterey, Calif. When the commanding officer realized he had
Jackie Coogan there, he said, "Would you think, Pvt. Coogan, that
you could put a little show together for the boys' morale?" Jackie
said, "Yeah, I think so." We began doing camp shows at Camp
Roberts and realized, "This is great. We get out of KP, we get out of
this, we get out of that..." You just say, "The colonel wants us to do a
show."

You were doing the work that you love to do anyway.

Exactly. Once I got in the army — you look around and say, "Let's
make the best of a bad situation." We did a lot of solider shows at
Camp Roberts and then got into broadcasting. From Lowery Field, I
came out here. I trained here, and then went overseas.

You were quite active in Armed Forces Radio overseas, building stations...

Yes. Some of the AFRS stations operated out of tents, but we were
very lucky. On Enewetak the Seabees put down a big concrete slab,
and then they put up a Quonset hut and furnished it for us. And
what we did was to put in our own portable generator and control
board, the turntables, and whatever else we needed to get on the air.
When we went to Guam, we had two Quonset huts put together in
an L-shape, and had like an auditorium, so we could do live broadcasts with a soldier audience. We did a lot of that.

And you were writing and producing these shows?

Yes. I was the NCO in charge, under Jack Wormser, and we had various personnel that kept coming and going. We had our own engineers — soldier engineers — who would then take the basic equipment and do whatever they could. I remember on Guam, I was absolutely thrilled and astonished when our engineer said we could do a remote from a boxing tournament that they had somewhere else on the island. I could never figure out how they did that, but I remember going there and being the announcer. We were pretty inventive, I must say; we did a lot of original things, both on Enewetak and on Guam, particularly. We did some remarkably original things that the rest of the Armed Forces began to hear about and picked up and did their own local variations of.

So you were pretty much an autonomous unit there?

Pretty much. I was also assigned to Iwo Jima for a while; I was a combat correspondent for *Yank* magazine, and did some combat radio. I did the first fire raid over Yokohama on a wire recorder — an important documentary piece. I came back; there was a guy from WOR who said, "Let me help you with your equipment." He was going to help me do something — and fucked it up completely. Years later I realized this sonuvabitch was doing that on purpose, ruining everything I had done on tape.

Did you have any association with Jerome Lawrence and Robert E. Lee at AFRS?

Yes. They were at AFRS in Hollywood, when I was here. Jerry and Bobby were doing a radio series called *Command Performance*. We were one big happy bunch of people carrying out shows. There was another guy [comedy writer] named Al Lewis. I remember Jerry Lawrence talking to us. He says, "Now, what we've gotta get in our scripts is more guy talk." They called Al in to do a comedy spot for them. I think it was Bobby Lee who said, "Here's the idea, Al..." And he described what they wanted. When he finished, he said to Al, "Does that tweak you?" And Al Lewis said, "It tweaks the shit out of me." Bobby says, "You do it," and he walks off.

You began writing for The Danny Kaye Show *in 1945, not long after you were discharged from the army.*

That's true. I came out of the army — my first job was the Alan Young radio show, which I did for a couple of weeks and was doing rather well — then I got a call from George Rosenberg, who had been an agent in the army. He said, "How much are they paying you?" And I said, "$200 a week" — or $250. "But if I go to the Coast with them, which is where I expect to go, I'd be raised to $300 a week." Rosie said, "Jeezus, Kanter, everybody in town has been waiting for you, and you come back to New York instead of coming to California, and you take a job like that. You're out of your fuckin' mind." He said, "Have you got an agent?" I said, "No." He said, "Well, if you want an agent, I'll handle you." He said, "Now, what I'm going to do is find a show here that's going out to the [West] Coast so you don't have to pay to...

So you could go back to California at their expense.

The next day I called, and he said, "Tomorrow morning you start on the Danny Kaye radio show. You report to a guy named Goodman Ace at the Ritz Towers Hotel at 10 o'clock in the morning." Rosie said, "Be heroic. I told him you're an army hero, so be heroic." He said, "You'll work here for four weeks. Then the show is going to California and you'll come with it."

Did you find that salaries went up a lot after the war?

Rosie said, "Remember, we get 10% of your salary." I said, "Fine." He said, "Would you like to know what your salary is?" I'm just leaving this $250 a week job; I'd been laid off. He said, "You start at $750 a week." I thought I would go through the floor. I absolutely couldn't believe it. I thought he was kidding me; it turned out, he wasn't. Just a few months earlier I was sitting on an island with one of my fellow soldiers — a guy named Bob Eisenback who was also a radio writer at one time. He and I got into a big argument, because I said, "When I go home, I will have a baby I've never seen before, a wife who I barely remember..." I said, "If somebody comes along and offers me a contract for $200 a week for the rest of my life, I 'd sign it." He said, "No, you couldn't — that's too little." I said, "What are you talking about, too little? $200 a week, that's a fortune." He said, "No, you can do better than that." And we got into a big fight over this. We suddenly started to laugh — I said, "This is ridiculous, what are we fighting about? Nobody's making me the offer."

Did you work directly with Danny Kaye when you wrote for him?

Yes, quite a bit in radio. We became, I guess you would say, friends. When he finally condescended to do television — for General Motors, his first show — I wrote it, with Sylvia Fine [Mrs. Kaye] as it turned out. That was not my deal, but that's the way it turned out. Our director was a young man they brought in from Canada because he was so good with music and live television — his name was Norman Jewison.

If you wrote for Danny, you wrote with Sylvia Fine?

Yeah. She was very smart, and she was a good musician. She used to play piano for him, on the radio show. Sylvia and Herbie Baker and a girl named Lee Butler used to write the special material for Danny — the patter songs. One week Sylvia told Goody Ace, "Oh, I'm so tired, I can't — I'm just exhausted — I can't think of anything new to write. We'll have to repeat some of the old stuff." Goody said, "That's fine, we'll repeat some of our old jokes, too." Sylvia said, "You can't do that." Goody said, "Why can you and I can't?"

To what extent did Kaye participate in the writing sessions?

Danny didn't participate very much. Danny was content to come in and pick up a script and read it. One week, I'll never forget — this is when Goody was still running the show, and we'd sit around the table and read. And this one week, we finished reading the script for the first act, and everybody says. "Good, good." Except Danny. He folded his script and said, "Well, I'm the highest-paid straight man in show business." And Goody, without looking up, said, "Jack Benny makes three times the money you do."

Which was true — Benny rarely got the jokes. Benny was the only one of his stature who would do that, give the jokes to everyone else.

Jack participated in the writing. But Danny did not.

Was it a surprise to Kaye to find that he was becoming a straightman for all these foils?

He wasn't, really. First of all, Danny Kaye was not a very good radio comedian. In order to appreciate Danny fully, you had to see him. You had to see him in person. I remember when I was doing his first television show — I was talking to a colleague of ours, who had done a couple of pictures with Danny — he said, "He's not going to be a hit in television." I said, "What do you mean?" He said, "The television camera does not lie. And when the television camera is on that man's face long enough, the world is going to find out what a miserable prick he is." That was Mel Frank who said that.

Kaye turned out to be quite a success on television, nevertheless.

Yeah. But never the success that he was in pictures. Anyway, Danny could be a nasty man. My mother, who was a very tall, regal Southern lady, was in Heathrow Airport; while she was standing in line, she noticed Danny was there. She said, "Excuse me, Mr. Kaye, we met in New York you may recall — I'm Hal Kanter's mother." Danny said, "He sure got fat, didn't he?" And he turned and walked away from her. I saw him a few months later — we were during an intermission in the theater — and I said, "You were very rude to my mother." He said, "What are you talking about?" I said, "She told me you said I got fat, and you walked away." He said, "You did get fat," and he walked away from me.

Did you also write for Goodman Ace's show, Easy Aces?

No. Goody didn't have a show at that time. But I learned a great deal about comedy from him. He was an absolutely delightful man. We used to sit in his den. And he sat at the typewriter, and we'd throw lines back and forth. And there were quite a few of us in the den at that time. There was one writer named Arnold Horwith, I believe it was, who said, "How about this?" And he told a joke — a line. Goody said, "It sounds contrived." And Arnold said, "Yes, I know. I just sat here and contrived it." So what I learned from Goody is, not to sound contrived. I also learned from him the value of repetition.

The running gag?

Right. On the Kaye show, we had a running gag — he said, "My sister married an Irishman." "Oh, really?" "No, O'Reilly." We had — God knows — every week, we had at least one variation on that. Goody Ace was a wonderful comedy writer. I'd have to sit down and analyze what I know before I could extrapolate what he taught me. And it's not really worth the effort. It's not really worth the effort for me to find out what I know, because I might surprise myself and realize I don't know a whole lot.

There's a literate quality to Goodman Ace's humor, a sophistication you didn't encounter in a lot of radio comedy at the time.

Absolutely. There was a guy in Chicago named Paul Rhymer [creator of *Vic and Sade*] who also had that kind of a quality. His was more rustic and Goody's was more urban.

You wrote for Bing Crosby for four years. Was it a bit of a challenge to write comedy material for him?

No, it was not. Because Crosby, first of all, had a wonderful — a copious and facile vocabulary. He was a well-read man, he had a great sense of humor — his own personal sense of humor was sly and sophisticated and very much a musician's sense of humor. He was, by and large, for me a delight to work with.

But what would be challenging about writing for Crosby is that he had that absolutely individual way of speaking...

A lot of alliteration: "There's a lot of limber lumber on that calfskin." I think that was something he adopted after it had been established by Carroll Carroll, who wrote the first *Kraft Music Hall* shows. I have the feeling he sort of started that, the alliteration, and Bing admired that and adopted it as his own — in his own conversation.

As you said, your ear just listens very carefully, so you learn how to write for that particular personality.

I can't claim a lot of credit for that series, because I was working with an absolute master of the genre, and that was Bill Morrow. Again, no credit. *"Philco Radio Time,* produced and transcribed in Hollywood by Bill Morrow and Myrtle McKenzie." And that was it. Myrtle was the engineer.

Bill Morrow was one of the top comedy writers of that era.

Bill was good friends with Bing; they spent a lot of time socially. He had it down pat. Bill Morrow was an absolutely charming lep-rechaun. He was an Irishman from Chicago who could dazzle you with his smile — completely bald, sparkling blue eyes, great smile. Bill was one of the fastest and brightest guys with a quip. His normal conversation was pretty much like Bing's — that's why they got along so well.

Did you write for Bob Hope in pre-television days?

Bob was a frequent guest on *Philco Radio Time* — the Crosby show. I remember once, we did a show in San Francisco. Bill Morrow and I had written a thing — in the first part, [announcer] Ken Carpenter and Bing are talking about the trip up. Bing said, "It was pretty bad, because Bob broke out of his cage and was howling up and down the aisles of the train... and how he got out of the baggage car we'll never know" — those kinds of jokes. Later, he says, "We went to the zoo. I didn't have a date; Bob wanted a date, so we went to the zoo and shaved an ape." Now we come in, we're sitting around reading the script for the first time. Bob reads this, he says, "First you've got me chained up in the baggage car and acting like a wild dog, then you've got me howling up and down the train — and now you've got me shaving an ape." He looked at us; he said, "What the hell have you got against me?!" He really was disturbed by it. Bing kid-ded him out of it. We didn't change the dialogue; we did that on the air. And of course it got screams. But Bob really took it personally.

But he didn't hold a grudge...

After I did my first picture, Bob had a movie that was in trouble I guess at Paramount. They needed another writer. Bob's producer went to him on the set with a list of names, and Bob went down the list; when he saw my name, he said, "Him." I have always felt the reason that he picked me is that I worked for Bing. I was Bing's property. And anything Bing had, Bob wanted.

You were good friends with Fred Allen. How did you meet?

I think I first met him when I was very young, in New York, but I can't really pinpoint where it was. But subsequently I was at Paramount, and I was working for a producer named Harry Tugend, who had once been Fred's writer. They were very dear friends. Fred came out here and I said to Harry, "I would really love to meet him." Harry said, "Well, come have lunch." We did, and out of that came our friendship that lasted until he died. We became correspondents — he loved to write letters, and he loved to get letters. Fortunately, I liked to write letters, and I had a lot of free time inbetween assignments to write to him. It was always a challenge just to write a letter to him that he would respond to — to make him *smile*. I always thought it was like winning an award somewhere.

Fred Allen had that wonderful combination of rural lowbrow humor, along with the sophistication.

Fred, I think, was probably the most original wit in America, since Mark Twain. I was crazy about that man. I had an idea that he agreed to do — as soon as he finished his last book, *Much Ado About Me* — we were going to put together a presentation and submit to a network. The idea was to do a thing called *The Funniest Man in Town;* it would be primarily Fred, traveling around this country. Everywhere you go, people say, "You should hear my Uncle Pete, 'cause he's funny." Well, let's go see Uncle Pete, and see how funny he is — and have Fred interview these people. He would have been wonderful. Fred was getting kind of excited about it; he said, "We'll do that." Then the dirty bastard went and died. That was a very mean thing for him to do to me, and some other people too. A lot of people missed him when he left.

No one has ever filled that void.

No. There's nobody around like him. When I was doing *The George Gobel Show,* he came out here, and I asked him if he would do a walk-on for me. He said yes — he hadn't been on television in some time. After the show, we went to dinner, then we went back to NBC. It was a very windy night. Suddenly a guy loomed out of the alley and said, "Mr. Allen, may I have your autograph please?" Fred is writing, "To so and so," and the wind is blowing. The guy said, "Mr. Allen, when are you going back to New York?" And Fred said, "On the next gust." Who would think of that *word*? Only Fred.

Your stint on Amos 'n' Andy *was relatively short-lived, wasn't it?*

Yeah. I forget why I left — Freeman Gosden [Amos] and Charlie Correll [Andy] wanted to try out some other writers, and they asked me to take a vacation, or a hiatus — then they wanted me come back and I didn't go. I ran into Charlie later at a big party. He was introducing me to somebody; he said, "This is the only writer who ever fired us." They were very difficult to work for, but they were wonderful. I learned a great deal about comedy from them. I learned that if you know your characters well enough, you can write much better than if you don't know them.

How was Freeman Gosden to work with? He was the more aggressive partner of the two.

He was more taciturn, but he was the brightest of the partners. And he was the most reactionary, I guess. A real hardbound America-firster, I would imagine. But he really knew Amos 'n' Andy. Charlie was a more agreeable, blue-collar bricklayer who just got lucky — he was sweet and simple. Freeman had the feeling he was to-the-manor-born — Southern aristocracy.

There were a number of writers on Amos 'n' Andy. *Did you work in teams or...*

The way this worked was, the story had been worked out by the whole group of us, sitting around. Then I would take the first act and the third act, another writer would take the second and the first act, someone else would take the third and the second act. There was a whole group of us. We would go home and write our stuff, and then bring it in — and turn it in to Bob Ross, who was the head writer. Then we would sit around while Bob went into the big office

Charles Correll (left) and Freeman Gosden work on *Amos 'n' Andy* at their specially-designed tandem desk.

where Freeman and Charlie sat, at a sort of a tandem desk — they faced each other. A special desk, drawers on both sides. Charlie had the typewriter; he did the typing.

Then Gosden and Correll would edit the material?

Bob Ross would go in and *read* all the material to them. But he would read it in all the different voices. He could do the Kingfish, he could do Andy — and they would say, "Okay, let's take this part of that, this part of that" — and they would put together the script. Now they get to the first draft of the script, then we would all come in. They'd say, "We need something here, something there" — then we'd sit around and...

Smooth out the transitions.

Yeah. Then they would go to the first reading for the cast and every-body, and after the first rehearsal, we would all sit around in the script room at CBS and go over it and make cuts, whatever emenda-tions they felt were needed. Then Freeman and Charlie would do the show, and we never had to go down to watch the show, or listen to the show — that was great. 'Cause you could listen to it at home.

Was there much creative freedom in writing for them? I guess as long as you stayed with the characters...

If you stayed with the characters, you had all the freedom in the world. By the time I got there, they'd been doing that for so many years, they had to find new avenues to explore. By this time, Amos was hardly ever heard from.

It was Andy and the Kingfish.

Exactly. Of course, Freeman Gosden did the Kingfish too. This one time we were stuck on something. We were trying to get a line for the Kingfish — and we had a really stellar group of comedy writers seated in that room. And nobody could come up with what we wanted. Suddenly I said, "Freeman, supposing this door opened, and the Kingfish himself were to walk into this room right now, and we explained what was happening, what would he say?" Immediately his voice shifted into blackface, "Well, boys, I say..." — and whatever it was, it was absolutely the right sentence, and we all fell down laughing, and even Freeman was startled. That was the line. That's how well he knew his character.

Gosden really developed a second personality...

Exactly — like Edgar Bergen and Charlie McCarthy. It was just astonishing. That's when I realized — my God, if you know your character that well, the character can write it for you.

Who was in that "stellar group" of writers you mentioned?

John P. Medbury was probably the most famous writer on *Amos 'n' Andy*. There were others who came and went, but I don't recall them offhand. Medbury was a very amusing man. Great sense of humor.

He also could be very rude. Medbury used to smoke a Fatima ciga-rette, which had a very acrid Turkish tobacco flavor to it. A particu-larly offensive aroma. One day we were sitting around the office working, all of us, and he was smoking. This was shortly after Charlie Correll's wife had given birth to their youngest child — Charlie I guess was in his sixties at the time. Medbury started to cough. And Charlie said, "Jeezus Christ, Medbury. Those things are going to kill you. A man your age shouldn't smoke cigarettes like that." And when he finished coughing, Medbury said, "A man your age should stop fucking." I remember Charlie, with his wife there; his whole face turned purple.

Would that kind of thing get Medbury into conflict with Correll and Gosden, being so outspoken?

Constantly. With authority particularly. One day a traffic cop was giving a ticket to a car that was illegally parked. Medbury went over to the cop. He said, "Why are you giving this man a ticket?" The cop said, "Is this your car?" "That's beside the point. I asked you a question first. Why are you giving a ticket to this car?" They got into a big argument. The policeman got furious with him. After Johnny was sure that the man was furious, then he walked away satisfied.

I can imagine what Medbury would've been like in a writing session.

He looked like a very mild-mannered little Baptist minister. And he certainly was not. Medbury was an absolutely brilliant joke writer — brilliant observations of people's peccadilloes. We don't have writers like him around any more. Turn the spigot and out it would come.

Can you offer any perspective on how Gosden and Correll got along with the black performers in the cast? There are conflicting stories...

I think for all of their professional lives, they had a running gunfight with the NAACP. But they got along very well with the cast. In those days, there were very few blacks who would stand up and say, "Now, wait a minute. This is casting aspersions on the whole race." Or "This is a very bad joke to do." Very few of them would ever stand up to that. I think anyone who felt that way — like Paul Robeson — wouldn't even come on the show to start with.

When they moved into television, of course, Gosden and Correll had to cast black actors to play their parts...

A lot of their first television shows I remember watching were adaptations of the scripts that we had done in radio.

That happened a lot in early television. You didn't get paid for those, did you?

No, I didn't, and I resent it. I resented it then and now that I think about, I continue to resent it. I think every writer who worked on the show absolutely would have the same feeling now. The fact that their work was really just stolen from them. I'm sure Gosden and Correll would have a different point of view — they probably resented having to pay for it the first time.

Did you have any particular problems making the transition from radio to TV? There were things you could do on radio you couldn't do on television...

In radio, the listener was the casting director and the set designer and the cameraman and everything else. In television, it's all done for you — here it is, accept it or leave it. That's why *Fibber McGee and Molly* didn't succeed on television, because everybody had a different idea of what Fibber looked like, and what Molly looked like. And of course when they opened that closet, everybody had a different notion about what came out of that closet. And most people said, "No, that's not Fibber's closet."

Did you have to adapt your thinking much to write for a visual medium? Here you'd been writing for radio, and suddenly...

But a good radio writer, and I consider myself to be one, thought in terms of — visual terms. Not always in just audio terms. Radio was the theater of the mind — as opposed to television, the theater of the mindless. When you wrote for radio, you designed your own sets, you did your own casting. You knew exactly what people looked like in your mind's eye. There was a lot of visual going on in my

Ed Wynn gives the Perfect Fool a new look for television.

mind, and hopefully in the audience's mind too.

Again, the best jokes on radio were visual jokes.

Right. And when you were able to illustrate your jokes by means of television, it was wonderful. Also, even though I was writing radio comedy, I was interested in writing for films; I'd been a film fan ever since I was a small child. Always in the back of my mind, my goal was to write for films. And certainly in movies, you learned — if you studied them, you learned everything you had to know about how to make an audience laugh. As a child — I did not realize there were people who *wrote* comedy — I knew I wanted to be a part of it.

Your first television job was The Ed Wynn Show, *circa 1949. What made you jump into TV so quickly, when so many other people were afraid of this new medium?*

A couple of reasons. When I first came to New York, one of the first Broadway shows I ever saw was *Hooray For What?* with Ed Wynn, at the Winter Garden Theatre. And I had been *listening* to Ed on the radio, as the Fire Chief, so I had no idea — I saw him in person the first time, and I absolutely fell down. I never saw anybody that funny. And so I welcomed the opportunity to work with that great man. Again, I said, "I'm going to learn something about comedy" — and again, by God I did. So that was one of the reasons I went into television; the other was just curiosity. The feeling was, this is something for the future, and why don't I get on this wave while it's small and ride it to the beach. And fortunately I did.

You were far-sighted in that regard.

I was still doing radio at the time. When I got into television, nobody knew anything about television. They brought out a young man from New York who was an expert, named Ralph Levy. Ralph was good; no doubt about it. But nobody at the network really knew anything about it, and no writer knew anything about it. No producer, no director, nobody really. Within ten years, everybody in the world knew every fucking thing there is to know about television. I knew that we were in big trouble when our milkman came in one day and said he saw the show last night, but he really was disturbed by the mike shadows. I said, "Oh, Jeezus Christ. We're really in trouble now."

I take it Ralph Levy was more or less responsible for the technical aspect of The Ed Wynn Show, *figuring out how to put it across?*

Ralph was our director. He had already achieved some small measure of success in New York as a live TV director of variety shows. Ralph's background originally had been in ballet, I believe. But he did know music. And he did have a good sense of humor. He set up the CBS show that we did — and a lot of people learned from him, even as he himself was learning from day to day — as he admitted later.

Was Ed Wynn difficult to write for?

No. Ed Wynn was a charming delight. Sometimes irascible — but I probably learned more about the art of comedy writing from Ed Wynn than any other single person. He was a very knowledgeable man, about why people laugh, what makes them laugh, how to present comedy — he was an intelligent man. You can't say that about all comics, but he was an intelligent man.

Would Wynn participate in the writing sessions?

Well, he would participate in the editing sessions. He would not sit in the room with us while we were writing, no. After we had finished the first draft, then he would go over it and he would express his approval or his regrets or his dissatisfaction, as the case may be. Ed did know how to construct a joke. He did know how to make an entrance. He would lecture us very often why something would not work, or how something could be improved. And it was an education, just working with the man. Because Ed seemed to have total recall of every show he ever did, and he would remember details of acts he had worked with.

Did you ever disagree with him, or were you allowed to disagree with him?

You certainly could disagree with him. He welcomed disagreement. And also, if your point was well taken, he would acknowledge that too. Ed was by no means a tyrant. Once he realized that [writers] Seaman Jacobs and Leo Solomon and I were on his side, that we were there to service him, and to make him feel comfortable and to make him feel funny — once he realized that, we had nothing to worry about. He would defend us or our point of view to others, as a matter of fact.

Did Wynn seem nervous to you, as far as going into this medium?

He always seemed nervous to me, before he went on to do a show. He would try to calm his nerves by the use of alcohol. And it seems to me he would drink what looked like a tumbler full of bourbon, dab a little Seabreeze around his lips and walk out on stage.

I believe Lucille Ball made her first television appearance on Wynn's show.

That's right. And the only reason that she went on the show was that she wanted a job for Desi Arnaz. She said, "If you use Desi, I'll do the show." She wanted to keep him at home, 'cause poor Desi was wandering all over the country trying to earn a living.

How did Lucy approach TV on her first outing? Did she seem to have a interest in the technical aspect of the medium?

Did she show any signs that she was going to be a big television producer? I don't think so. Lucy approached the whole job with enthusiasm, the way she did almost everything else. Once she agreed to do something, she went all out with it. I do know that in order to lure her into doing the show, Leo Solomon and I went out to her house in the San Fernando Valley and described what we had in mind. And Lucy said, "That sounds fine. But just make sure Desi has everything possible that he can do." Once she agreed to do the show, then she showed up and picked up the script and read it and laughed, and enjoyed herself.

Lucy saw the show as sort of an audition for Desi, to show people what he could do?

I think it was really to show Desi himself what he could do. Lucy wanted him to do something musical, she wanted him to do some talk, she wanted him to get some laughs — she wanted him to look good.

You worked on three films with Dean Martin and Jerry Lewis...

Dean seemed to be all business. He had a nice sense of humor, but he'd come in and do what he was supposed to do and get out of there as soon as he possibly could, so he could go play golf. Jerry was all over the place. He wanted to do a little bit of everything — and of course, eventually he did — he did everything, including destroying his own career.

You probably weren't on the set much during the production of those films.

No, I was writing something else at the time. When I was at Paramount, you'd finish one project and go onto the next. Then, if they happened to be shooting on the lot, and they needed some-

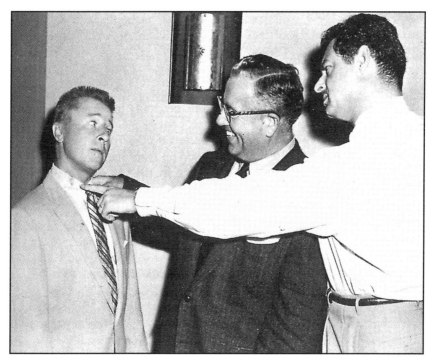

George Gobel, bandleader John Scott Trotter and Hal Kanter, during a
rehearsal for Gobel's TV show.

thing, sometimes they would call and say, "Could you fix this or do
that?" and you'd go down and do it. But that didn't happen too
often. I probably did it with George Marshall more than with other
directors. George did a couple of very good Martin and Lewis pictures.

*Steve Allen has written that "the sky was the limit" for George Gobel in
terms of the wild, offbeat material you and Jack Douglas wrote for Gobel's
TV show.*

Yeah. There was a lot of on-beat type of material too. Jack was one
of the most inventive comedy writers that we've had. In terms of
jokes and ideas. He wasn't very good at creating a storyline, but he
certainly was great at creating images and lines.

And was this something Gobel seemed to particularly appreciate?

Gobel did appreciate it. Yes, he appreciated not only Jack's sense of humor, but Jack himself as an individual. George was an offbeat person. He was an off-the-wall fellow himself. A lot of his comedy reflected that.

You yourself contributed to the zany nature of Gobel's TV show.

I like to flatter myself into thinking that I contributed everything to that show. It was my concept. I was very proud of *The George Gobel Show,* and I was very hands-on; I was all over the place. I was the head writer, I staged the show — directed the show, produced the show — it was my baby. Everything that went into that script was there because I had either written it or encouraged it or approved it. I'm very proud of that show.

In retrospect, was writing for radio more satisfying than television?

I was doing a radio show with Bob Hope [in 1965] — a big special we were doing for the USO, or something — and I'd done a spot with Bob and Connie Stevens. Afterwards he said to me, "We must have been nuts, baby. How did we let radio get away from us?" He said, "God, that was a license to steal." I said, "I guess you're right."

CREDITS

Radio: *Jack Oakie's College, Log Cabin Jamboree, The Joe Penner Show, Command Performance* (WOR), *Grand Central Station, Lincoln Highway, Lowery Field Theater of the Air* (KOA), *Command Performance* (AFRS), *The Alan Young Show, The Danny Kaye Show, Fun in Swing Time, The Don Ameche Show, Amos 'n' Andy, Philco Radio Time, The Beulah Show, The Jack Paar Show, The Academy Awards.*

TV: *The Ed Wynn Show, The George Gobel Show* (creator-producer-director), *The Chevy Show Special* (also producer-director), *Shower of Stars, An Hour With Danny Kaye* (special), *Arthur Godfrey in Hollywood* (special), *Kraft Music Hall, Three on a Island* (also executive producer), *Valentine's Day* (creator-producer), *Not Very Newsreel* (also executive producer), *Cap'n Ahab* (also executive producer), *Sally and Sam* (pilot: also producer), *Three Coins in the Fountain* (pilot: also director), *Julia* (creator-producer), *The Jimmy Stewart Show* (also producer), *Chico and the Man* (also supervising producer), *All in the Family* (also executive producer), *For the Love of It* (TV movie: director only), *Splitsville* (TV movie); *Bob Hope Presents The Chrysler Theatre* (four specials, including *The Reason Nobody Ever Saw a Fat Outlaw in the Old West Is As Follows*; also producer-director); *Just for Laughs* (series of specials: producer), *Lucy Comes to NBC* (special: producer), *The American Film Institute Tribute to Alfred Hitchcock, The Academy Awards* (1952-present), *The Roseanne Show* (talk show: comedy consultant).

Film: *My Favorite Spy* (dialogue), *Two Tickets to Broadway, Off Limits, Road to Bali, Money From Home, That's My Boy, Here Come the Girls, Casanova's Big Night, About Mrs. Leslie, The Rose Tattoo, Vera Cruz, Artists and Models, Loving You* (also director), *Mardi Gras, I Married a Woman* (director only), *Once Upon a Horse* (also producer-director), *Blue Hawaii, Bachelor in Paradise, Pocketful of Miracles, Let's Make Love; Move Over, Darling; Dear Brigitte.*

Theater: *Hellzapoppin, Does Anyone Here Do the Peabody?* (director only), *Laughing Matters* (also performer).

GEORGE BALZER

George Balzer was born in Erie, Pennsylvania, Sept. 1, 1915. When he was four he moved with his family to Los Angeles, where his father started a laundry business in 1929. The incipient Depression shaped his course. "I'm a high school graduate. In those days, even that was an achievement — instead of any of us going on to college, we all went into the family business," he observes. "But I was only in the business a short time — and that's when I started writing, or trying to write."

He began by turning out scripts as an exercise, and making a few small contributions to his local newspaper that admittedly "didn't amount to much." Before long Balzer got his first break, writing material for comedian Bob "Bazooka" Burns on *Kraft Music Hall*.

In 1941, an acquaintance with character actor Andy Devine resulted in a recommendation to Young & Rubicam, the advertising agency which handled many of radio's top shows. Balzer's first assignment lasted only 39 weeks — writing for George Burns and Gracie Allen — but had a dramatic impact on his career. His collaboration with fellow staff writer Sam Perrin outlasted most Hollywood marriages.

After a profitable detour scripting *Tommy Riggs and Betty Lou*, Balzer and Perrin found themselves living every comedy writer's dream — working for Jack Benny. It was a dream that weathered the transition to television and endured — in the here-today, gone-tomorrow world of Hollywood — over two decades. (Even after *The Jack Benny Show* was felled in a ratings war by *Gomer Pyle, USMC*, Balzer and Perrin continued writing occasional specials for the venerable comedian.)

Though Balzer spent most of his career putting words in Benny's mouth, he also wrote briefly for Lucille Ball and other comedians. His episodes for *Here's Lucy* (some written in collaboration with Phil Leslie, some with Perrin) were followed by a stint on the long-running *Red Skelton Show*. "They already had their staff; I was just filling in for someone who had been fired, or moved on," explains Balzer. "I wrote one year with Skelton, then he went off the air. Then Sam and I put in a year with Don Knotts, he had his own show for a short while; when we finished with that, he went off the air. We were doing real good."

Balzer retired in 1971 following the cancellation of *The Don Knotts Show*. "I don't know if I called it retirement at the time," he reflects. "I was probably just out of work." But before long he decided time to quit the business: "It's not easy to walk into an office for an interview, and the man behind the desk has just turned 19."

Although the record shows that Balzer earned two Emmy Awards for his work on Benny's TV show, he notes, "Make it two and a half. The reason I say that is, we won two outright — and the other one, nobody connected with the show got recognition — Jack, the producers, the writers — but the show won an Emmy. About six or eight weeks later, the Academy sent a very nice plaque, and I felt it was their explanation of what happened."

George Balzer was reluctant to be interviewed when first contacted. He had a book about his experiences with Benny in the works, he said, and didn't particularly want to talk — only to follow with several quotable remarks about his career. When the last of his comments was followed by a silence, he asked, "Did you get that all down?" "Yes," I assured him, as I finished scribbling. A few years later, by which time he had abandoned the book project — having been eclipsed by several others published on Jack Benny — he cordially agreed to an interview.

How did a good Catholic end up as a comedy writer? It seems that 95% of them are Jewish.

I'm one of those who broke the myth. I didn't know it at the time, because I was too new in the business, but I found out later that in order to write comedy, you have to come from New York, more specifically Brooklyn. I didn't know that, or maybe I'd have moved back there and come West again.

Did you intend to write for radio, or did you get into it purely by chance?

I never did any writing, actually, until I started to write comedy. That came about because I had an opportunity to listen to a lot of radio, comedy radio. I just kind of felt that maybe I could write that kind of material. So I gave it a try. And strangely enough, coming out of that period [1937] of listening a lot, I started to write my first script — which I still have somewhere. I wrote my version of *The Jack Benny Show.* The coincidence of what happened is kind of interesting. I started out of the blue to write *Jack Benny* scripts, just for my own amusement...

As a means of learning how to write — or was it just pure fantasy at this point?

This was just within my own mind. No one knew I was doing it. It was just to see whether or not I could do it. The scripts — although as I looked at them in later years, were really very bad — nevertheless they evoked a bit of interest from people who did read them. And then fate stepped in. I actually got my biggest boost from Andy Devine. His brother Tom moved to an acre of ground which butted up against our family's property out in the San Fernando Valley. They moved in, and we found out that Tom was the brother of Andy Devine...

So you naturally put that information to good use...

I made it a point to be at Tom's house a time or two when Andy came by. And I told him what my ambitions were and so forth. He encouraged me to stick with it, because they use that kind of material so rapidly. Andy at that time was on *The Jack Benny Show*, when they were doing the "Buck Benny" series.

And one thing led to another?

Several weeks after that, I get a phone call from Young & Rubicam. And I found out that Andy had put in a word, unbeknownst to me. A fellow named Tom Harrington, who was the head of the Hollywood office of Y&R, called me one day and said he would like to speak to me. So I went in and we talked for a short bit, and he said, "How would you like to come to *The Jack Benny Show* on Sunday evening, and I said, "I would be delighted." He picked up the phone and called somebody in one of the other offices. Then after a moment he put the phone down and he said, "All the tickets are gone." Here I am, as high as can be — there was a short pause, and he said, "However, would you like to come to the Artist's

Entrance at NBC and ask for me? I will see to it that you're brought around backstage." And that's what happened. I witnessed my first radio show of any kind, not just the Benny show, from the control room. You can't get started much higher than that.

No. How did things proceed from that point?

It just so happens on that particular night George Burns and Gracie Allen were there. I don't think they were on the show, I think they just came backstage to meet Jack and his wife Mary. They were going out to the Trocadero or the Mocambo or someplace after Jack's show was finished. So I got a very quick intro to them. After that kind of a beginning, I thought we were going to go very fast. But it didn't happen that way. I started doing a few other things — eventually I got another call from the agency and they said, "We're putting together Burns and Allen as a married couple." That's the first time that George and Gracie were "married" on radio. Before that time they were just a vaudeville team.

Yes, they decided to change the format of the show. Apparently Burns decided that people knew they were married in real life...

I'm not sure as to what the reason was. I really think the reason was just that Burns and Allen were more marketable and we could do more things, with them being married. The idea was Sam Perrin's. As the years go on, good ideas that writers have usually wind up being owned by somebody else. That was Sam's idea. Sam is the one that "married" George and Gracie.

It was about time.

We went on for Lever Brothers. I was with *Burns and Allen* for 39 weeks. Usually you take 13 weeks at a time. Maybe I did too, I don't recall, but the extent was that it went for 39 weeks. And in those days — a major sponsor who has a show on radio will sponsor them for 39 weeks, then comes the summer hiatus of 13 weeks in which they hold the time by putting in some other show...

They would have a summer replacement.

Sam Perrin and I moved over from *Burns and Allen* to *Tommy Riggs and Betty Lou,* which was a 13-week assignment. At the end of about 10 or 11 weeks we got word from the agency that the sponsor, Lever Brothers, wanted to keep *Tommy Riggs and Betty Lou* on the air. We had apparently done well enough rating-wise. So we didn't go back to *Burns and Allen,* we stayed with *Tommy Riggs* — and we ran that 13-week assignment into 65 weeks. On about the 62nd or 63rd week, we got word from Jack Benny that he wanted us to join his staff — and we were to meet him in New York, which we did. Jack came back from North Africa where he had spent the summer [1943] playing to the troops.

Did you write for other shows prior to Burns and Allen*? You mentioned...*

Before I got the call with *Burns and Allen,* I had a friend of mine steer me onto writing — it was an open position — for the Bing Crosby *Kraft Music Hall.* And doing the Bob Burns spot. I was writing for the writer, a fellow named Duke Atterberry. After 10 or 12 weeks there, I tried to get a $5 raise and he wouldn't give it to me, so I quit.

You were writing the spot for him*? Sort of ghost-writing?*

Duke was the writer, he was the man who talked to Bob Burns — he was the go-between. I could see what was happening. I was never going to meet anyone, because I used to write up in the attic. It was kind of semi-furnished, and it was all right, but that's where I did my writing. At his house. I can't complain, it was another step along the way — that was the first writing I had ever done professionally.

Your stint with Burns and Allen *would have been about 1941?*

It would have been 1941-42. The start of the war. I was with *Burns and Allen* at NBC when the words started coming over the teletype about the Japanese having bombed Pearl Harbor. But we went on and did our rehearsal and did our show on Tuesday evening, just as if nothing had happened. But it was not easy to get laughs from that audience.

I believe you were a protégé of Sam Perrin's?

That's correct, yes. Sam and I were partners for — oh, my gosh — probably 35 years. When I went to work on *Burns and Allen,* Sam was brought on staff at the same time. So we met, everything worked out well, and we wound up with Jack Benny.

When you started working with Perrin, did he take you under his wing, teach you the rudiments of writing or polishing your craft?

Well, I guess you could say that. I was never really aware of it. We didn't make a point of "Here's how it's done," et cetera. But there's no question I picked up a good deal from Sam.

Did you and Perrin work as a team on Burns and Allen*?*

Well, not so much because we did most of our writing in those days where all the writers were in the room together, and George was there, he worked with us. And George sort of guided things the way he wanted them to go. And we'd just all pitch ideas and lines and so, forth. So we really didn't have the partnership thing working yet. It was a group effort. When Sam and I moved over to *Tommy Riggs and Betty Lou,* then we did work as partners. We had a very unique arrangement there — we were in complete control of that script. We were strictly on our own.

How much did George Burns contribute as a writer or editor of material?

How much did he contribute? Well, George contributed quite a bit. Because George Burns was really a very funny man. He [knew] more about comedy than anyone else I can think of. George lived with this show — which showed you how smart he was — which would be a bad thing if he didn't know so much about comedy. But Jack Benny was the same way. He stayed very close to his show. However, as the years went by, it reached the point where Jack didn't have to be close any more. He knew that what we wrote — if we felt that it was right, why, he would do it.

Would Burns usually come up with a premise, or would one of the writers...

Jack Benny edits a script for his long-running radio program.

I'm sure he did. I don't recall a particular — I'm sure that George had ideas, the same as Jack had ideas. But Jack Benny never regarded himself as a writer. He would get ideas. One time I remember he came in, and he said "Fellas, last night I was watching television. And I watched the Marquis Chimps. I think it would be funny if we could somehow use them on one of our programs." And I looked at him and I said, "Yeah — then what?" He said, "Well, I don't know, that's up to you fellas." And he turned and walked out of the room.

And as he reached the door Jack turned and said, "I wouldn't have your job for a million dollars."

Pretty funny, especially considering Benny's "anything for a buck" persona.

Strangely enough, it was a good basic thought. And about an hour later — we kicked it around a little bit — an hour later, I went into Jack's office and I said, "Jack, how about this?" And I loosely outlined an idea that would hold the show together, with the Chimps.

Benny did more with absolutely nothing than anybody.

Yeah. Jack knew comedy so well that he was able to play on and extend the comedy that was there. As Jack himself used to say, "I know that when I say, 'Well...' that that's not funny unless I've got something leading up to it that's really strong." He's right. The word "Well..." without some situation or line doesn't mean a thing. And Jack appreciated that. He regarded his writers — he said to me, "I'm number one because it's my show, and I'm the star. Then after me come my four writers. After my writers come the parking lot attendant, the shoeshine boy, the janitor, my director, the producer — and you can put them in any order you want to put them. But don't put anybody between me and my writers." And for that simple philosophy, Jack Benny became known in the business as a genius.

That attitude must have endeared him to his staff.

All he did was — he hired and paid good money for what he felt was good talent *for him,* and he let us perform. All told, I was with Jack 25 years. Sam Perrin, the same thing. Milt Josefsberg was with the show 12 years, so he had a nice run, too. John Tackaberry was there 12 years. Jack never forgot he had writers. But his success was due to his own talent.

Did George Burns have that same regard for his writers?

Not to that extent. I think that George would not make a point of talking about his writers.

Jack didn't mind talking about his writers. We used to even use the writers as characters on *The Jack Benny Show* once in a while. I know in the opening show we did in New York in 1943, he used the writers — and I had a bit.

According to Milt Josefsberg, you and Sam Perrin had very different personalities. Can you describe how you collaborated?

It's really not true. We had different *philosophies*, I think, personal philosophies. We used to get into a discussion — not an argument — on religion once in a while, Sam being Jewish and I being Catholic. But nothing of any strength at all there. There were many things in Milt's book that were not really true. Milt was not the only one — Irving Fein wrote a book, Mary Benny, Joan Benny — and there was enough of that so that I couldn't publish my book about Jack. So many things were just lifted and used in the other books. I can take a very truthful stand and say I came up with "Anaheim, Azusa and Cucamonga," the "Sí... Sy" routine, and the routine in the bakery shop with Mel Blanc — the Cimarron rolls. Some pretty big things that lasted — they were written to be done on one show, and then lasted 25 years.

How did "Anaheim, Azusa and Cucamonga" develop?

Well, it just came about — we were going to go to New York, and we were going to do a scene at the railroad station. Union Station. Leaving for New York, catching the Super Chief. And we just used that as an interesting and funny thing to have happen while we were at the railway station. So just as Jack and Mary opened the doors, and you heard the crowd noises, you heard, "Train leaving on Track 5 for Anaheim, Azusa and Cuc... amonga." We did a joke or two as the show went on, and that was the end of that. We were only going to use it one show.

These were names that you picked off the map?

No. I'm almost a native here — I came out from Pennsylvania when I was four years old — I know all these towns. So when it came that we wanted to do this, I said "Use Anaheim, Azusa and..." — I think the first one was, "Anaheim, Azusa and Pomona." But at rehearsal

Jack said, "I don't know, I don't think that's quite right." I said, "How about Cucamonga?" He said, "Yeah, that'll work, we'll do that."

I believe you were also the one who dreamed up with the "I can't stand Jack Benny" contest.

We needed a show, Tuesday came along and we just couldn't get started. We didn't have anything on paper. Sunday was approaching and we didn't know what to do. We finally got a little bit of an idea where someone said, "Why don't we ask the listeners to send in lyrics, and then we'll have Mahlon Merrick, the conductor, set them to music and have a little contest..." And Jack said, "No, no, I don't want to do that." So I said, "You know, Jack, I have an idea. Nowadays all we hear on the radio is, 'I like so-and-so toothpaste because...' in 25 words or less. Why don't we do 'I can't stand Jack Benny' in 25 words or less? We'll ask people to write in letters from all over the country." Well, there was silence in the room. Dead silence. And I begin to think to myself, "Oh, oh."

"Better go look for a job."

Jack got up out of his chair and he came over to me and put his hands on my shoulder and he said, "That's it. That's what we're going to do." I said, "Jack..." He says, "No, no, we're going to do it. Only we're gonna give $10,000 as the prize." And we did. We were looking for one show; it ran for 11 consecutive weeks. We had a winner of course, who got the money — the winning letter was read by Ronald Colman. Fred Allen, Goodman Ace and Peter Lorre were the judges in the contest. And we had to hire eight girls to sort the mail. So it was very successful.

Jack Benny was probably the only star in Hollywood who would...

...have enough guts to do it.

Anyone else would have too much ego to even consider it.

That's right. I had an occasion when I first joined the show — I think I was there about three months — we were at NBC in

Hollywood, and we were doing the rewrite on a Saturday rehearsal. Just kind of cleaning it up and cutting it down to time for Sunday's show. And Jack came to a page, and he says, "Fellas, I want a new joke here." We all turned to that page. He said, "I want something stronger. Something that'll really button this whole thing up." We don't say a word. He kept talking. He said, "I want something that *really* pays this off." After a pause — I was sitting next to him — I touched his arm and I said, "Jack, we'll get you a new joke." He says, "Ohhh, you agree with me, huh?" I said, "No, but it's possible that the four of us could be wrong." He looked at me, he broke into a laugh — literally slid right off his chair and sat in the corner screaming. And he got up, and he said, "I wouldn't change that joke now for a million dollars." And he didn't. And it got its big laugh. We're all standing in the booth, and he looked up at us — as if to say, "You smart alecks." That's the kind of a man he was.

The gag about the robber confronting him — "Your money or your life?"
— has become the quintessential Jack Benny joke.

What happened was that John Tackaberry and Milt Josefsberg had been working on a script for Jack, their part of a script for Jack, and they had come to a point where they had the line, "Your money or your life?" And that stopped them. They couldn't get an answer for the question. Tack is stretched out on the couch, and Milt is pacing up and down, trying to get a follow for "Your money or your life?" And he gets a little peeved at Tack, and he says, "For God sakes, Tack, say something." Tack, maybe he was half asleep — in defense of himself, says, "I'm thinking it over." And Milt says, "Wait a minute. That's it." And that's the line that went in the script.

It's one of the classic moments in radio history.

You know, a very strange thing, most people who retell that joke tell it wrong. A lot of people who listen to comedy, when they're called upon to repeat it, they don't say it right. Most people say the punchline is: "Your money or your life?" "I'm thinking, I'm thinking." That's not the joke. The joke is, "I'm thinking it over." That's the joke. Anything else will not play as well. By the way, that was *not* the biggest laugh that Jack ever got. It has the reputation of getting the biggest laugh. But that's not true...

What would you say the biggest laugh was?

The biggest laugh? I *know* what the biggest laugh was. It was just by coincidence. It was a very short line that I threw, because the situation was building so — that was when we had [opera singer] Dorothy Kirsten on the radio show. When she came on our stage, she met the members of our cast, and she met Don Wilson. Just the night before she had given a concert here in Los Angeles. And Don being the educated one of our cast, started talking to her about music, and he said, "Miss Kirsten, I thought it was absolutely astounding when you did so-and-so" — he used all the musical terms, the *obbligato*, the *crescendo* — and she says, "Well, I don't quite agree with you in every respect. I thought the..." — and she had her string of beautiful musical terms. This went back and forth. And Jack, who's been standing there all this time, said, "Well, I thought..." And Mary said, "Oh, shut up." That's all she said. Mary delivered that line perfectly. The laugh ran 29 seconds. As long as Jack looked at that [studio] audience, they laughed. "Your money or your life?" got seven seconds — the original delivery.

"Your money or your life?" was done more than once. I believe it got a short laugh the first time and a bigger laugh on a subsequent show.

I'll tell you why it has such notoriety. John Crosby wrote a newspaper column; he visited our show on that weekend that "Your money or your life?" was going to be used. And because he spent so much time with us, and the joke played very well — he liked the joke, and he wrote about it in his column, and sort of publicized that joke in other ways for the next few weeks. It then became known as the biggest laugh Jack ever got.

Don Ameche made a guest appearance one time that Benny didn't know about...

Don Ameche happened to be in the control room once, watching our broadcast. He was on with Edgar Bergen across the hall, following our show. And we had this one situation where Jack was driving down to San Diego [California] I think, and he crossed over into Mexico, and then said something to somebody and they had a pay-off in Spanish. We're on the air, and Don walked into our control

room — we said, "You go down and get on stage, and when Jack
asks this question" — whatever it was — "you answer him with this
line." And of course Jack threw the lead and Don had the payoff,
and then at that point Jack saw who it was — it was a big laugh and
we all got a kick out of it.

Were there other times you pulled things on Benny he didn't expect?

Yeah, we did. One time when Don Wilson had a routine up front, he
had a line — Jack says, "How did you know that?" And Don says,
"I read it in Drear Pooson's column." It was supposed to be Drew
Pearson. Jack said, "What?!" Now we have a whole thing where
Jack is just kind of ad-libbing. He says, "Don, it's not Drear Pooson,
it's Drew Pearson." We fooled around with that. And then later on
in the show, we were coming to a situation with Frank Nelson. And
Jack was to say, "Are you the doorman?" I think that was the lead.
And I ran out on the stage, I said, "Frank, when he says, 'Are you
the doorman?' — you say, 'Well, who do you think I am, Drear
Pooson?' Well, Jack just about died...

Especially with Frank Nelson's delivery.

We used to do that once in a while.

Would the actors — the regulars or the guests — ad-lib very much?

Actors? No. Nobody ad-libbed.

Was that sort of an unwritten rule?

I wouldn't say it was even a rule. It was respect. Respect for Jack
and the writers. Jack used to use us, a lot of times — we went to all
rehearsals. If the guest star said, "Jack, wouldn't it be funny if I
said..." — Jack would say, "Wait a minute. Fellas, c'mere." He'd
have us all come up on the stage. "You know, he might have a funny
idea." And then we'd go up there and we'd listen to it and we'd say,
"Well, it's funny, but it interferes with something else that's following." And Jack would say, "Oh, yeah. I forgot about that. Yeah, we
just won't use it." It wasn't that great to start with, and Jack just figured, instead of saying "No, we won't do that," he'd let us play the

heavy. But that was just for fun, you know. We just had a situation between star and writers that was unheard of, and it's still unheard of.

Would guest stars like Bob Hope or Groucho Marx suggest material when they came on the show?

That becomes a whole other story. Bob had the same freedom on our show that Jack had on Bob's show. Which was that, when we gave Bob his 8 or 9 pages or whatever he was going to do on the show, he didn't change it, he did it. He also had faith in it. And when Jack would appear with Bob, he wouldn't make any changes — maybe one or two little changes.

Benny didn't feel naked without his regular writers?

No. However, we usually got to see the spot. Jack would bring it over from a rehearsal and say, "Hey fellas, take a look a this and tell me what you think." And 99 times out of 100, we'd say, "Jack, it's fine, go do it." And it was. The privilege of writing for Jack Benny for 25 years gave me very little time to write for anyone else. I did get to write for a lot of guest stars, of course.

You wrote for Fred Allen when he appeared on the show. He didn't bring his own writers.

No, no. Whenever Fred came on our show — at least once a year — we always wrote his sketch. He did whatever we gave him. Now if he had an idea and wanted to change a line, that's a different story, because he was a writer. And a very funny man. So if he changed a line, that was fine with us. And when Jack went on his show, Jack never — I should say *we* — we didn't bother to change the script because we had a lot of faith in Fred. We knew that he was funny. His staff helped him but Fred was the final word. And Jack sometimes would say, "What do you think?" and he'd show us the spot. And we'd say, "Jack, it's fine, go ahead and do it."

It's interesting that stars wouldn't bring their writers when they appeared on other shows, they just had enough faith...

...in the other star. There were certain guest stars in the business, movie actors or other radio stars, who had a reputation of being tough — when you had 'em as a guest star, beware, because they were going to pick everything apart. And yet, these same people would come on our show, and they were just as pleasant as could be, and never changed anything, did what they were given, and everything worked out fine. That tells us that on the other shows they appeared on as guest stars, so many times they were given bad material that they didn't trust anybody. But when it came to *The Jack Benny Show*, it was an entirely different story.

I understand Tallulah Bankhead was a terror.

When we got Tallulah Bankhead on a TV special at CBS, she was just terrible in rehearsal. She upset everybody. Upset Jack so much that he wanted to cancel the show. Just get it over with, just forget about it. We went on the air, and who do you think the big star was? Tallulah Bankhead. Once we got on the air, she stole the whole show. Here was a woman who kept complaining and saying she didn't like this, she didn't like that — but when you got her in front of that camera, she was the star.

Milt Josefsberg said you had a flair for wild humor. Could you elaborate on that? Or maybe you don't agree with it.

No, I do agree with it. I used to come up with things that were a little on the wild side. This isn't wild, but it might give you an idea — it's a little wild. One time Phil Harris came in and he was late for the rehearsal, and he excused himself. He says, "I'm sorry, Jackson [Jack], I couldn't get my car started, so I had to come over here on the bus." Jack says, "On the bus? Phil, you came over here on the bus, like *that*?" Phil says, "Well, how do you like that? I put on a glove that was holding a Scotch and soda."

Were there particular people on the show you enjoyed writing for moreso than others?

Well, of course it was always fun to write for Frank Nelson. And it was always fun to write for Mel Blanc, 'cause he could do whatever

Producer Hilliard Marks (left) with Benny's writing staff: George Balzer, John Tackaberry, Milt Josefsberg and Sam Perrin.

you wanted him to do.

Mel Blanc could really make Benny laugh.

It reached a point where they couldn't look at each other. If Mel looked at Jack, Jack would break up. But it was fun writing for all of them. Dennis Day was fun — I guess I can speak for the others — there was nobody that we found difficult to write for. There was no one that we shied away from.

Did you hear their voices as you wrote the scripts? You must've written specifically for them after a while.

Yeah, you'd not only hear the voices, you'd even act out the parts. I used to play different parts on the show. And usually, if Jack was going to be late for rehearsal, he'd call me late Saturday morning, and say, "George, when you get there, would you get things started?" What that meant was, he was going to be 10-15 minutes late, and when I got there I should read his part and get the reading started.

You stood in for Benny? Was there extra payment for playing bits, or being his stand-in?

Yeah, there was an AFTRA minimum at that time, not very much, a couple hundred bucks maybe.

Do you recall how much you got for writing the show?

No. But we were very well paid.

I believe Milt Josefsberg quoted you as saying, "If a writer didn't cause Jack to send his suit to the cleaners, he wasn't earning his money."

When we first went to New York and joined Jack for the very first time, we went to the Sherry-Netherland Hotel to start writing on the script, and Jack at that time was trying to get off cigars. And so he had a pipe, which he didn't put tobacco in; he just kept it in his mouth. As we worked, and the minutes and the hours went on, naturally saliva would accumulate in the bowl of that pipe. And if you came up with a real good joke, he would come over and put his left hand on your right shoulder, and with his other hand he would just kind of wave that pipe up and down and laugh. You'd begin to notice after a while that there was a stream that would run from your left shoulder down to your waist on the right. One day I said, "You know, if you leave this room looking like an ambassador, you've had a good day."

How much would the producer actually do on The Jack Benny Show? *On a lot of shows, I've been told the producer didn't do anything.*

Well, it isn't that he didn't do anything; they had their producing chores. They got the show on and off the air, and they threw the cues, and that kind of thing. But they didn't contribute much of the creative material — if any. Nobody ever sat in on our writing conferences except Jack. Hildy [Hilliard] Marks, the executive producer, was there on the final clean up.

They didn't really direct, in the sense that...

No. We were our own producers. Producers and directors. Between Jack and the writers, nobody — and I mean nobody — touched our script. Now, if they had an idea, they could come to us certainly — we'd welcome it — and say, "Would it be funny if, on this page, so-and-so said this, instead of what's on the paper." We always loved that. Once in a while we'd say, "Yeah, that is better." So we put it in. Didn't happen very often. But we never resented their being involved to that extent. But they always understood, it was Jack and the writers.

Were there any disagreements between Benny and the writers, between yourself and Benny?

No, I never had a disagreement with Jack, never. It was the smoothest operating job I can think of. Oh, we would disagree sometimes on how something should be done, but — we would just decide to go with whatever kept the most people happy.

Could you discuss your strengths and weaknesses as a comedy writer, compared to the others on Benny's staff — Sam Perrin, Milt Josefsberg, John Tackaberry? Would you each specialize in a particular type of joke or...

Well, not really. Maybe to this extent -- Milt and Tack were a little jokier than Sam and myself. They could bump into somebody on the street and literally stand there and tell five jokes. Whereas Sam and I usually wrote picture. Word picture. And got our comedy out of the situation and the questions and answers. I could do most anything. But then I guess when you come right down to it, if we had to, maybe any one of us could do the show for a week without too much difficulty.

You split the show up and wrote different sections of it.

Oh yeah, we cut the show in half. And our attitude was always with the others, we said, "Look, we don't care, take whichever half you want. The first half or second half."

The Benny show — the writers at least — really had a penchant for visual jokes.

Yeah, I guess we did — we used anything that would build the best picture. We really were bent that way. I know that when it came to doing pictures alone, with television, Sam Perrin and I moved right in, kind of headed up the television show. We just switched on over — for a while we did both the radio and television shows.

Did Benny seem to adapt to television pretty easily?

Yeah. Took about 20 minutes, I think. Sam and I made the transition to TV with Jack; we did the first several shows. Milt Josefsberg and the other guys stayed in radio — they were more prone to start something and get into a stand-up routine. But Sam and I did most of the TV work. You can't always tell this by credits, because in those days, there were no credits. The Writers Guild was not organized. A couple of the writers were unhappy with having to stay in radio, so we juggled the credits around, where everything would look better.

How did you adjust to writing for Benny in a visual medium?

I don't know, we just did. I don't recall any hurdle we had to get over. We just wrote mostly in pictures anyway. That was a little bit after we wrote the book for a Broadway show called *Are You With It?* It played the Shubert Theatre in New York for about 18 months. Universal made a picture out of it; they didn't spend enough money on it.

Did they turn the play into a film without your involvement?

I forget who wrote the screenplay — we didn't — but we got a call one day to come to the studio, if we would, because they had reached a point in the story where they were having trouble. So we went in and heard what their trouble was — in about 10 or 15 minutes, we solved their problem. And we could never understand what that big hurdle was they couldn't get over. Anyway, they went on, the picture came out — I don't know what kind of business it did; by today's standard, it probably made about 19 cents.

To return to Benny — his radio shows are funnier than his TV shows.

Jack himself was better on radio than on TV. The little faults of doing a scene on TV — you see it — whereas on radio you imagine it to be perfect. Jack had an advantage over most performers; the audience liked him as a person.

Could you assess Benny as radio comedian, as opposed to his work in other media? Why did radio capture him best?

First, he had a perfect voice. The voice was just great. And he could handle radio the best. Although I feel that on most of his television shows he was good — maybe on many he was very good — he was always better on radio.

Did you ever run into trouble with censors on the Benny show?

Never. I don't think in all my years there that we ever had — on no more than three occasions did the Continuity Acceptance Office send down their man, to ask us to take out a joke because it was too risqué.

There was one gag about a "Dr. Ballzer" that the writers...

Yeah, we did do that one. But nobody said anything.

It got past the censor, but then the writers themselves decided to cut it?

I'm not certain that we did it on the air, but I did throw it in the room. We just used good judgment, as far as what went on the air. We never had anything in there that was not proper. We didn't need it. Nowadays of course, it's a different situation — the contest seems to be, "We've got to have four sex jokes on the first page" — and from there it gets worse. There's nothing funny about young people running around doing dialogue that's based on out-and-out gratuitous sex. It's the *easiest* way to get a laugh in the world...

Most of today's comedy shows aren't funny.

They do so much today that I don't understand. I think a lot of it the performers don't understand — I think they just do it. Sometimes I'll be watching a show — I'll say to myself, "This is going to be good." Then it doesn't pay off. They have a bunch of writers sitting in a room: "Gee, that's funny, we'll put it on the air." They think because you put in a laugh at the end of a line, that makes it funny. I would dare most of those shows — if done before a studio audience, and not with any laugh track — there would not be any laughs at all.

The Benny shows still hold up remarkably well, undiminished by age.

We played to a studio audience. And any reaction we got was legit. Once in a while you fixed up a joke because the audience couldn't see the bit, or couldn't hear it or something — but when Jack came out to do a monologue or a bit or whatever, that was it. You either laughed or you didn't. And fortunately, they laughed most of the time.

CREDITS
(in collaboration with Sam Perrin, except as noted)

Radio: *Kraft Music Hall* (without Perrin), *Burns and Allen, Tommy Riggs and Betty Lou, The Jack Benny Show.*

TV: *The Jack Benny Show, Stars in the Eye* (special, without Perrin), *The Jack Benny Hour* (three specials), *Jack Benny's Birthday Special, Here's Lucy, The Red Skelton Show* (without Perrin), *The Don Knotts Show.*

Film: *Are You With It?**

Theater: *Are You With It?*

* Based on his play.

SOL SAKS

"My first ambitions as a writer were to write erudite essays and slice-of-life short stories that would appear in obscure literary magazines. I still nurture and sometimes try to gratify that ambition," reflected Sol Saks. "The trouble was that my second most important goal was to earn a living."

Sol Saks was born in New York but raised in Chicago, where he attended Northwestern University's Medill School of Journalism. He left his post as a columnist for the *Daily Northwestern* to take a job as a reporter on a weekly small town newspaper; he also began selling short stories on a sporadic basis.

He got his feet wet in radio circa 1939 by way of contributing to an anthology called *Non-Royalty Radio Plays*. "They were supposed to be plays you could you use without paying a royalty," notes Saks. "One day I heard my script on the air, on a network show — I think it was *The First Nighter Program*. Harry Ackerman said, 'Look, I liked the show and I contacted the editor; he said I could have it for $25.' I said to the editor, 'You didn't have the right to sell that.' They were paying $150-200. So I had a fight with the editor.

"Finally, I said, 'All right, give me my $25, or $22.50, if you take off your commission.' He said, 'No, you gave me trouble, now I'm not going to give you anything.' I got nothing for it, the first show on radio." However, Harry Ackerman liked Saks' writing and purchased other scripts from him. Many years later, Ackerman was the television executive who bought Saks' concept for a show called *Bewitched*, which had a magic effect on the writer's fortunes.

Long before he "went Hollywood" and earned a reputation as one of the town's top comedy creators, Saks scratched out a living in Chicago writing dramatic shows. He drew from his imagination, scripting westerns (*Thunder and Lightning*), adventure programs (*Wings of Destiny*), detective yarns and mysteries before making the transition to comedy, "where the loot was better and the competition was weaker."

An outspoken critic of the entertainment media, Saks did not hesitate to question authority in the early years of his career. As he recalled: "They created a show called *Bullet Trenton, C.D.* He was a private eye. I said, "What does C.D. mean?" They said, "Crime Detector." I said, "That doesn't mean anything." They said, "That's the whole point — they'll be thinking, 'What does C.D. mean?' "

Saks migrated to Los Angeles in 1943, joining a mass exodus of Chicago radio people. He worked briefly for Red Skelton, Dinah Shore and Danny Kaye, finding more fruitful opportunities in the employ of Ed Gardner (*Duffy's Tavern*) and Ozzie Nelson (*The Adventures of Ozzie and Harriet*). He also worked on *The Baby Snooks Show* with Fanny Brice and Danny Thomas, and *The Beulah Show* with Hattie McDaniel.

Saks made the transition to television with *My Favorite Husband,* a show he created for CBS which was picked up within 24 hours of the time the pilot was first shown. After taking time out to write a play, he developed a series called *Mr. Adams and Eve* for Howard Duff (radio's *Sam Spade*) and his wife, Ida Lupino. The show was based on an idea presented by the stars.

The pilots for *Peck's Bad Girl* and the short-lived *Eve Arden Show* followed, before Saks joined CBS as Executive Producer in charge of comedy series. Since he created the enduringly popular *Bewitched,* Saks has written screenplays (notably *Walk, Don't Run* for Cary Grant), stage plays and short stories, which have appeared in *Atlantic Monthly* and other periodicals.

In recent years the writer has found himself in demand for seminars and workshops, and has been called upon by the Denmark Television Network as a comedy consultant. Although he feels that explaining humor is "like pulling off the petals of a rose to find out what makes it beautiful," Saks has also authored a "survival kit" for aspiring scribes titled *Funny Business: The Craft of Comedy Writing.*

Radio was a unique medium...

I think it was a great training ground. The actors had it easy — they'd take the script a couple of hours beforehand — an hour beforehand — and read it through once or twice. They used to pick up these scripts — the best of them would glance at it and go right into the character. In Chicago we had people like Orson Welles. He wasn't well known then; his name meant nothing. But he had that great voice. He used to go from one show to the other. Sometimes if he had a quick transition going from one station to another, he'd get an ambulance.

You started out as a newspaper reporter. How did you get involved in radio?

Well, I wanted to be a writer, of course. As far as writers go, it used to be newspaper work, the generation before mine. But then radio was big, and used a lot of people. So that was where the jobs lie.

Had you spent a lot of time listening to radio before you began writing for it?

Yes. Everybody did, I think. Somebody once said, "What did you look at, when you listened to radio?" You don't remember. It was more compelling than TV is today — people talked about it — the next day, "Did you hear Jack Benny?" For a while, they talked about television. You don't hear people any more, saying, "Hey, did you see the show last night?" But radio was compelling...

You began your radio career in Chicago.

My first show was called a western called *Thunder and Lightning*. Then a show called *Wings of Destiny*, an adventure airplane show on which they gave away a Piper Cub every week, also out of Chicago. I'd never been out West and I'd never been up in an airplane. I was not [writing from] experience — certainly not in radio.

How did you manage to get your first job?

Well, I was writing a column for the *Northwestern Daily*, and I was trying to get a job. In those days, the advertising agencies produced practically all the radio shows. So I got a classified book of all the advertising agencies. And I only went out with girls who could type. I wrote a letter — one of the girls typed the letter to every advertising agency. I said, "I go to Northwestern University School of Journalism and I would like the opportunity to meet with you, and perhaps write for you, and I think it could be of mutual bene-fit." And some stupid producer answered my letter! And I went in, and I wrote this show — *Thunder and Lightning* — I wrote two or three of them, and finally, he bought one. I think I got $75 for it.

What stands out in your mind about that period?

One of the things that sticks out — it was a great training ground, because we appealed to only one sense — the ear. So as a writer, you had to tell that story through sound. Everybody had a sidekick, a buddy — the Lone Ranger had Tonto — and the reason you had a buddy was, you had to have somebody to tell the story to. "There's a guy now — I think what we better do is..." — because you couldn't see it. But you could certainly do action. In all of Radioland, there wasn't one carpeted floor. Somebody'd come, and you'd hear, "Clump, clump, clump..." But there were things you couldn't do — when you got in a fist fight, for instance, you'd say, "Take that." [*He punches his hand.*] "You think just because you knocked me out..."

The writer's imagination got a workout, figuring out how to tell the story.

I had a thing where my hero was alone, as I recall it. And he was locked in a cabin. And they had set fire to the cabin. He was tied up. And his sidekick was not there. Try to think for a minute how you would do that on radio. I was worrying about this and worrying about this. *The Lone Ranger* was a big show then. I guess I listened to the show — I don't know whether it was accidentally — and by golly, the Lone Ranger is tied up in a cabin. And his sidekick isn't there, and they set the cabin on fire. Exactly my situation. And I listened — how'd he do that? The bad guy said, "Now I'll set the fire, and that's the last we'll see of the Lone Ranger." And you hear the crackling of the flames, and he leaves. "Clump, clump, clump..." And by God if the narrator didn't go, "As the flames leapt higher, the Lone Ranger was able..." Use a narrator! How simple. All you had to do was have a narrator come in and say it. That was like discovering the typewriter, as far as I was concerned.

You had to do it all with sound...

We did it with sound — and I know it made me a better writer. Some fine writers came out of radio. Because you had to learn to appeal only to the ear — so when we were able to show you a picture too, it was comparatively easy. We'd done the same thing only through sound. They did these openings on *Thunder and Lightning*, you'd hear thunder... the man's name was Lightning Jim, his horse was named Thunder, and I think he'd say, "Let's go, Thunder!" The openings were big...

Was the show derivative of The Lone Ranger?

I don't think so. Except that — they did a lot of westerns and they were all about the same — there was a man, he had a sidekick, and he was either a marshal or a good guy running around doing good. So they all were approximately the same.

Was there anyone who took you under their wing, an experienced writer?

No. Nobody took me under their wing. Although you got leads from other writers. I remember the first comedy — the same advertising agency had a comedy-variety show, *Uncle Walter's Doghouse.* I guess I must've written some amusing scenes in my *Thunder and Lightning,* because he said, "Look, we have this comedy show, do you want to take a crack at it?" And I did. They had a five-minute spot, for which you got $35. Five minutes of comedy. A monologue. I wrote it and gave it to him, and he said, "This needs punching up." I went to a writer I knew, Ben Gershman, and I said, "What does he mean, 'Punching up'?" He said, "It means he wants you to make it funnier." I said, "Does he think I could have made it funnier and didn't? How do I make it funnier? I wrote this as funny as I can." Ben said, "There's a book called *10,000 Jokes for All Occasions.*" I bought the book — of course, you found nothing. Everybody thought comedy writers used gag books. None of the good ones did.

Was there a sense of community in Chicago radio among the writers, as with the actors?

The writers were different. I did not know any actors — the same was true here, until I got established and built a reputation. I worked on *Ozzie and Harriet* for two and a half years — I never was in the studio. I happened to be at a party once and met a couple of regulars on the show — they not only didn't know me, they didn't know my name. So it was different. You wrote alone.

You did a mystery show in Chicago that was relatively innovative, for its day.

I loved mysteries. I came in with the idea to CBS — I said, "Let's do a straight, clean mystery show where the clues are right there. Murder happens, we hear all the clues, and he solves it at the end. Just like the mystery books." And they gave me a chance with it. They put it on opposite Jack Benny — he was then on NBC. That was dead land.

What was the reaction to the show?

It was a good show, people liked it. That was a show that should have gone — it was well-written, and it was a new idea. To have a straight, legitimate mystery story — there were no such things on radio. Oh, there was *I Love a Mystery* by Carlton Morse. That was the only one that was on about the same time. I think I did a good job. But it was sustaining, and I gave them trouble. In those days, they took no trouble from nobody. One day they called me in the office, and they said, "On this occasion here, it was not explained why he did this." I said, "Yes, it was." The producer said, "Oh, I see. Well, I didn't hear the show. Somebody here heard it and told me about it." I said, "I don't think you should criticize a show that you haven't listened to." And he pulled the show off the air.

How did you go about finding work at that stage of your career?

What we call pilots today, they called them auditions, for new shows. The advertising agency would do it. Every agency would produce, they'd create a show. If Wrigley was looking for a new show, they'd call in five or six writers and tell them about it, and the writers would write for nothing. Then they'd take the scripts and put it together — pick what they liked out of every script, and make an audition record. And if it sold, they would not hire any of those writers — they wanted real professional writers who wouldn't work for nothing. I don't remember what agency it was — I went up there — by this time I was already selling scripts now and then. I wasn't desperate...

You didn't work on speculation.

This man took me in and sold me on this idea. I said, "Yeah, sounds good." He said, "Wonderful. Can you have it for Thursday?" "Yes." I said, "How much?" He said, "How much do you want?" I think I said $50. Or $35. He said, "Well, it isn't the money" — of course it wasn't the money — he said, "but I'm disappointed, because I felt that when you heard this idea, you'd be so enthusiastic you'd dash home to your typewriter and start writing." I said, "I am enthusiastic. And I will go home and start writing. But you know, there'll be a knock at the door and it'll be my landlord, who wants the rent. And he's not enthusiastic about this idea." I got $35 I think for it; five or six other writers did it for nothing. I don't remember whether it sold or not.

So only the writers who refused to do these freebies would be considered.

Only the successful ones. We in Chicago especially. The actors had it tough then, too — they'd come up, the producers would need a bit part, and there'd be actors in the waiting room — they'd say, "I've got a part. Will you do it for $15?" A guy would say "No." Another guy would say, "I'll do it for $15." Another would say, "I'll do it for $10."

Was there a set pay scale in radio?

No, there was no set pay scale. You negotiated, and depending on where you were you'd get different prices — whatever the guy could get. If you worked steady, you did pretty well. A 13-week contract was considered almost the ultimate. Most of us worked with no contract. Many worked week to week. Some of us had a 6-week contract — a 13-week contract, already you were in solid. Three 13-weeks made the season, 39 weeks.

We have a nostalgic picture of the old radio days. It's hard to realize how tough...

The writers were even more vulnerable. Actors, you got to know the voices. The producers were a little bit dependent on them. The writers, there were hordes of them trying to get in. No credit. Jack Benny was I think the only one who gave credit. He would give credit once a year. *Variety,* when they reviewed the show at the beginning of the season, would give the writers credit. And if you didn't happen to work on that show, you didn't get it.

What did they have against giving credit?

Ozzie Nelson told me, "I don't mind giving credit. But you see, most people think this is really happening. And if we mention writers, it ruins the illusion." Or else they'd say, "There's no time." A show like *The Bob Hope Show* had five, six, seven writers. However, they'd have a guest star. And at the end of the show they'd say, "We thank Gregory Peck, who's been loaned to us from Metro-Goldwyn-Mayer, who's just produced this picture" — and they'd name six people on the picture, but they wouldn't name writers. Until the Guild won that — there was a great fight to win it. In radio, if you heard the writer's name, it was either *The Jack Benny Show* or a sustaining show — no sponsor. Because on a sustaining show, the writer got paid very little or nothing.

Were you involved in the Radio Writers Guild when they started?

Yeah. I was one of those in the early days of the Guild. There were a couple of metamorphoses, then the radio writers combined with the screenwriters. We worked for about a year, two years — we worked for a long time on credit. I was the one who was saying, "Air credit. We should get air credit." The writers themselves would say, "We can't get air credit — how can they name six writers?" Finally, the Guild won credit.

Actors have told me, "Radio was like stealing the money."

The first time I saw a TV show — my TV show — I thought, "Finally, the actors are working." The actors were in costume and make-up, they had to learn lines. Because radio was a great thing. Marvin Miller was in Chicago then — he would make $100,000 to $150,000 a year. Nobody knew his name. He went from one show to the other, and made a lot of money. He would walk into a studio, without having any idea of what the character was, pick up a script, *glance* at it — read it twice, sometimes only once — go on the air with it and he was through. But we — the writers — we worked all week. Especially in comedy.We worked 80-hour weeks on *Duffy's Tavern*. We worked one night all night long, every week. You'd finish it just in time. The hardest work in the world.

Did you come to Hollywood because radio started drying up in Chicago?

Yeah. There was a time when Chicago, New York and Hollywood were about even. Chicago did I think all the soap operas; a lot of the drama was done in New York. And mostly comedy shows were done out here. By that time I started to do comedy. You had to make the decision, whether you were going East or West. I decided West. I was here with a new wife, on borrowed money in a borrowed car. I went to the agency I worked for then, and they were handling Red Skelton. They said, "Want to try out for *The Red Skelton Show*?" I went to work for Skelton, I think it was for $200. I said, "I expect to make more money than that." I think I asked for $250. They looked at me and said, "The head writer makes $250!" I worked on it two weeks; I got another job and I quit. I didn't like writing *The Red Skelton Show*.

You didn't like working with Skelton?

No, Red was all right. You didn't work with him; his wife Edna was then doing his writing, and it was a curious way of writing. She gave you a script, and you went home and rewrote the script with your lines — the same story with your lines — and handed it in. And then in two weeks you might hear your lines. There was no place to go with the show, anyway.

Who were the other writers on the show?

I don't know. I didn't work with any of them. I never met anybody, including Skelton's wife. I went up to the studio while Red was rehearsing. I walked in with my wife — we were the only ones in the audience, because they were doing a dress rehearsal, and Red directed everything to us — he was that kind of a guy. We were just a couple sitting there. I'm not a big laugher, but he directed every joke right to us. This was the big Red Skelton. And then later on after the show was over, I passed him in a corridor. He didn't even say hello — didn't even recognize me.

I can see why you quit.

From a writer's point of view, that show was not considered a pres-

Red Skelton rehearses for a wartime benefit with Esther Williams.

tigious writing job. Nor was *The Bob Hope Show*. Though Hope had some good writers. But it was not a prestige show. *Duffy's Tavern* was. So was *The Jack Benny Show*, so was *The Fred Allen Show*.

What did you do after you left Skelton?

I did a variety show. Joe Bigelow was the producer. And the first assignment I got was Ed Gardner. I was thrilled...

Were you a fan of his?

Before I knew I would write comedy for radio, my wife and I would listen to *Duffy's Tavern*. We thought it was the best show on the air. Ed Gardner had a guest spot on this variety show, so I wrote his spot, and Joe Bigelow — who became a friend of mine — said, "Look, Sol, you're a good writer; I like the script, but you haven't caught the flavor of Ed Gardner." Well, I heard that Gardner was looking for a writer. He wanted to see some work — I sent him that spot that they weren't going to use. He liked it better than the spot they had given him. He took my spot and used it on the variety show. He said, "I'll give you $50 to come over and work with us one afternoon."

A lot of writers started working on Duffy's Tavern *on a trial basis.*

I went out, and there's Abe Burrows, and a slew of these big shot writers — Parke Levy was there. I'd never worked with anyone. I sat there with them, and I didn't open my mouth. The reason Ed Gardner had given me this $50 was to see. At the end of the session, he said, "Look, did anybody help you write this?"

The spot you'd sent him...

I said, "Well, if they did, they're going to keep helping me." He said, "Okay, you're hired." I took a cut in pay by the way, to work for *Duffy's Tavern.*

I understand Ed Gardner was tough on writers. A lot of them didn't make the grade.

Bill Manhoff, when he was hired, said, "Look, I've been working with a partner who'd love to try out for the show." So they had the partner try out for two weeks, and Ed said, "No, he writes all right, but he writes too light." Meaning the jokes were amusing, but they weren't powerful enough to make you laugh. So they didn't give him a job. The guy stayed in New York and wrote *Paint Your Wagon* and *My Fair Lady* — it was Alan Jay Lerner. He was turned down. If Lerner hadn't written so light, he could've been a successful radio writer.

Do you recall how much you were making?

Abe Burrows was the head writer; he making $750 a week. I was getting $200 a week I think, and I was newly married — we went to New York, and we rented a furnished room. $200 a week, and I was paying my own expenses there — I didn't know any better. Although they paid my train fare out.

They took advantage of your inexperience...

The hours were terrible. And my wife would sit in the room waiting until Abe said, "Let's break for dinner." We worked at the Majestic Hotel, right across the street from the Algonquin. We had a suite there. She'd meet me, we'd go out for dinner — it was about 8 or 9 o'clock — then we'd come back. Tears rolled down, because she was going home, all alone; I was going to be gone all night. I used to lie to her sometimes — she'd say, "What time did you get in?" I'd say, "Oh, 3 or 4." She'd say, "No, you didn't. I was up at 4 o'clock, you weren't here yet." I was lying to her like a guy out with a dame. Then I complained to Abe Burrows about it; I said, "This isn't necessary that we work all night."

Did Burrows agree with you?

He said, "Sol, this is not the dress goods business." I said, "If I have to work these kind of hours, I'm going to go into the dress goods business." That was one thing different I had, because I didn't come from a poor family — and almost from the first year, I made a living writing. So therefore I was a little independent. I wasn't scared. Oh, you *were* scared. But you were scared at not being able to produce.

Duffy's Tavern *was being done in New York at this time?*

I joined the show in Los Angeles. It started in New York, then came here — that time we went to New York, we went only for three months, and came back.

How was the show written? Did you write in teams?

I didn't. Mostly they did. We had about at least four or five writers, including Burrows. They used to call me The Pigeon. I was the young one; I always worked alone. Which was very unusual for comedy writers. I shouldn't say always; there were times when I worked with a partner. But not much.

Did you find Ed Gardner difficult to work with?

Well, Ed didn't work with us when I was there — I came on the sec-

Ed Gardner (Archie) and head writer Abe Burrows take a break during rehearsals for *Duffy's Tavern*.

ond year of the show. What we would do — we would get together with Abe — and he was very difficult. One of the things I had against Abe Burrows is, he was always late. He was a socialite; he was very popular. He would do jokes very good, he would play the piano, he had these songs. He knew all these guys. He'd say, "Let's meet tomorrow at 10." And we'd go up to the Majestic Hotel and sit there, and he'd show up at 12:30.

It's almost impossible to work with someone like that.

Then we'd work on the premise — what we called the premise. Which was not much of a premise. In other words, we knew who the guest star was, and usually — Archie would be trying to get Bing Crosby to sing at the club, that was the premise. We'd have that in one day. Then we'd cut up the script, usually in halves. I would take one half and go home and write. Now, that's pretty tough. 'Cause it's jokes. And I was not trained as a joke writer. It didn't come naturally to me. So we'd work pretty hard for like two days.

It's hard enough when you're trained...

Now you'd come into the hotel room with your scripts, 'cause Abe would call the meeting for 10 o'clock, and he'd show up at 12:30 or 1:00. Then he'd read it over and usually say, "Rewrite this," and give it back to us again. Then we came back, and now it's close to the end of the week, close to show time. Now Abe sat with us. We'd go from line one — despite the fact that we had already worked practically a whole week on the scripts. Sometimes only two or three lines in the original script were left. And that's when the all-night session would come in. And part of it was because Abe *always* let it go until the last minute, and also because he was late. He'd say, "All right, we'll go out for lunch now, be back here at 2:00, and he'd come back at 4:30. And he'd have a dinner date. Terrible hours. I'd work practically all my waking hours.

But Burrows was able to produce the goods?

Yeah. Abe was a great joke writer. He was not an all-around writer for my money, a constructionist. But yes, Abe was a very witty man. For what he did for jokes, he was one of the top. Abe, for all my resentment, he took the responsibility for the show. Ed Gardner got into a fight with him once, at the end of the season. He called me and said, "How would you like to be head writer?" My first year in Hollywood. I said, "Well, look, if I had the show, I would like Abe Burrows as my head writer." And Ed made up with Abe and took him back.

Do you see any connection between Duffy's Tavern *and* Cheers?

Yeah. And James Burrows, the director of *Cheers* and one of the creators, is Abe Burrow's son. The further irony is, in a sense he wrote about a tavern, and we wrote about a tavern. First I thought, "Gee, that's little Jimmy." And after a while it occurred to me, "Hey..." It's a different kind of show, a much more sophisticated show, and more legitimate than we did. But they all are today. I'm sure the writers work hard. No one knows — because it looks easy — how many things you throw away.

Do you recall any of the jokes you wrote for the show?

I had a couple of jokes that became classics on *Duffy's*. I had one where Finnegan [Charlie Cantor] turned in his income tax. He owed $800. Archie said, "How could you owe $800?" He says, "I'll tell you the truth. I copied from the guy in front of me." Another one I wrote — Finnegan says, "I didn't hear the show. I tuned in and the show was just ending. And the announcer said, 'Tune in again next week at the same time.' So I tuned in again the next week at the same time and again it was just ending."

Writers often flew by the seat of their pants in those days...

Things were not mapped out in great detail. Miss Duffy never had a first name. You started with things like that, and you were locked in. Because we shot from the hip — everybody did.

Was Shirley Booth [Miss Duffy] still on the show when you were there?

When I came on the show, Ed Gardner had replaced her with Florence Halop. Her voice sounded exactly like Shirley Booth's. And one of my assignments was to write that Miss Duffy spot. Miss Duffy — she was the one who had a marriage license made out to "Miss Duffy and To Whom It May Concern." But I wrote the spot and it didn't work. It didn't get the laughs — Shirley Booth was a great actress — I said to Ed, "Look, she [Halop] just isn't the actress that Shirley is. I'm no genius, you know." He said, "You're not? Then why am I paying you all this money?!" $200 a week.

If you wanted respect, you didn't work for Ed Gardner.

We had to write — when I worked on *Duffy's Tavern*, they came around with a sheet to all the writers, which said in essence, "I, Sol Saks, hereby affirm that every line I have said I've written is original, and I am responsible for it, and Ed Gardner wrote it." He was

absolving himself of any responsibility if we stole a joke or there
was a libel suit. On the other hand, according to the contract, he
wrote the show. It was demeaning.

Would you attend the broadcast of the show?

On *Duffy's Tavern*, they'd have an audience come in, and all the writers except Abe Burrows had to get tickets — my wife and I got tickets, stood in line — I'd written all week, stood in line, and sat in the
audience to hear the show. Once I remember coming there, and I
asked the secretary for two tickets and she said, "Sorry, Sol, we're all
out of tickets." Ed had some sailors coming in. It was very often
demeaning.

Was Gardner a problem, in terms of his ego?

Ed Gardner was a little bit of a crazy man. He was a drinker. And
one of the things he would do — while we were writing, he'd be
down in the bar. The bartender would say a couple of funny lines,
which he probably had said to every customer for four years — and
Gardner would say, "Want to write for radio?" And he'd bring him
up.

Gardner was unpredictable, then.

When we went to New York this time, they took Ed Gardner up to
NBC — we had one of the top shows — and all the executives meet
him there in this beautiful room, with leather furniture. They're all
sitting around the table, and Ed says, "This is what I think of NBC."
And he — I know this story because one of the guys from NBC
came in to where I worked, and he said, "You may as well stop
working. I don't know if the show's going to go on the air, because
Ed Gardner opened his fly and urinated on the floor." They didn't
throw him off the air. They're not going to throw a successful show
off the air.

You also worked with Fanny Brice in radio.

Fanny Brice was a wonderful lady. Bright, talented lady. She was a
good interior decorator, by the way. She didn't do my house, but she

Fanny Brice clowns with Gracie Allen and George Burns at a
Hollywood party, 1939.

decorated some of the other writer's houses. She was an outspoken
lady, she came from New York. I remember once a Christmas show,
and we went to see her. She had a butler, a beautiful place — in Bel
Air [in West Los Angeles], as I recall. We showed her the script — it
was a very mild, warm script — and she said, "Well, it's not very
funny." We said, "Well, look, Fanny, it's Christmas, and we feel we
should get a little warmth..." She said, "Okay, if you fellas think so
— but look, not to much of this warmth shit, huh?"

She wasn't trying to be funny, either.

No, no. She was an honest lady, straightforward. We had a premise
once where you guessed how many beans there were in a jar, in a
store window. Mac Benoff was the head writer, and that was a show
that became a disaster. We did it to a live audience — and every
once in a while, a show just didn't work. At the end of the show, she
was sitting around signing autographs for the kids. The kids loved
her. And she's in her Baby Snooks voice: "Darling — you want me

to sign your book? What's your name, honey?" And Mac thought, "Hey, this is a good time to sneak out." He doesn't want to see her; he knows the show was a disaster. So he quietly goes to the door of the soundstage — as he gets to the door, he calls out, "Goodnight, Fanny." And she looks up, and she says, "You and your fucking beans." Then she went right back into Baby Snooks, with the kids: "Oh, yes, honey..."

I gather that Fanny Brice was a real no-nonsense type of person.

She was very bright — and sharp. Once she was playing with Hanley Stafford [Daddy] and she was reading, and she skipped a line. And Hanley, being a pro, picked it right up and they went on. Then she went back — you sat on stools — she went back to her stool when her scene was over. She looked at her script, and she knew something was wrong. And she saw that she had skipped that whole line. She walked back up to the mike in the next scene, and read out the line. Then went back to her place.

Danny Thomas was on Brice's show at the time.

I didn't write for Baby Snooks so much, mostly I wrote for Danny Thomas. Snooks would do a chunk, and then Danny would come in and do his spot. He was practically unknown then. As a matter of fact, I gave Danny Thomas his first radio job. He was a club performer in Chicago, the 5500 Club, and he did Jewish dialects — he did it so well, people thought he was Jewish — and I hired him, without any name recognition, for scale.

Thomas' name meant nothing when he first appeared on the Brice show, then.

Danny was a newcomer then – - Fanny Brice found him and brought him on. Danny was popular on the North Side of Chicago; he went into radio and then became nationally known. He did a spot I think was very good. He played a postman — they'd play a scene, and somebody'd get in an argument — and he was a very mild-mannered postman, very quiet. When they'd slam the door on him, he'd walk down and say, "I shoulda said... I shoulda said, 'Why don't you...' I shoulda said..." He moved up very fast.

You apparently worked on Dinah Shore's Open House *a very short time.*

Yeah. That was my first job as head writer. I had two experienced guys, Syd Zelinka and Howard Harris, and they were doing two other shows — they were doubling. I got into a thing with them and I quit the show. Although I was theoretically head writer, they were making a lot more money. But they were doubling up, which I never did. I quit the show, and I thought, I did a disservice to Dinah Shore. Because at that time she was starting, and I thought she could be a female Bing Crosby — she was. I did a couple of good shows for her, and then I quit. They let me quit, because these two guys, they thought could handle it. Well, Zelinka and Harris wrote it right into the grave. To this day I feel bad about that; I ran away.

How did you get the job on The Adventures of Ozzie and Harriet?

I wrote one script for them, and then was offered a job in New York on a show called *Hall of Fame* that was in trouble. It was a one-hour variety show by Philco. Paul Whiteman was on it. Big stars, an expensive show. They gave me a fabulous amount of money to go out there and do it. And I did it. But Ozzie Nelson liked my script very much. He kept calling me — and John Guedel, he was a friend of Ozzie's — he had some little thing to do with the show, and he would visit me in New York and say, "Why don't you come back to Hollywood, and do *Ozzie and Harriet*?" Finally they did the summer session of *Hall of Fame* — they paid me the full salary, but it was just a musical show. I used to write lines like, "We now take you down South America way while Paul Whiteman asks the musical question..." So I quit, and came back and worked for Ozzie.

How was Ozzie and Harriet *put together?*

We did a premise which was a more complicated premise, a bigger story — then we'd all go home and write a complete script. Sherwood Schwartz worked on *Ozzie and Harriet* for a couple of years. I was on the show before Sherwood, from practically its inception. Bill Manhoff also was on that show, and Jack Douglas. Hal Kanter worked on the show for a short time. We'd all write a complete script. Except Ben Gershman, who worked only on the premise.

Ben Gershman was a friend of yours from the early days in Chicago...

When Ben came out of the army, I got him a job on the show as what we call the premise writer. I said to Ben, "The new field is going to be premises, 'cause that's what everybody's looking for. That's what you ought to do." It was a half-hour comedy show, but we sat for days to get an idea. I went to Ozzie, I said, "I have this friend, he's coming out of the army, and he'd be a great premise man." Ozzie hired him; I helped him without Ozzie knowing it for a couple of years. Ben worked with Ozzie Nelson for about five years, went over to TV with him. But there was no such category as a premise man — Ben was the only one I know.

Did you work in pairs on Ozzie and Harriet?

No. I don't think anybody did. We had that one premise meeting, and Ozzie would serve ice cream at like 2 o'clock in the morning. That's all — just ice cream.

You were working at Ozzie's house?

At his home. Your stomach would be empty and that ice cream would lay down like a cold piece of ice in the pit of your stomach, and you'd come home — I'd come home 2 or 3 in the morning from the premise meeting, and then I'd have to write a complete script with jokes. And then towards the end of the deadline again, you are working practically all night. You always did. It's the gun to the head — that's what Abe Burrows used. I was fairly disciplined later, but that's the only way Abe could work. The gun was right down to his head. I think it was a standard — when you started to write, "This isn't good enough, this isn't good enough..."

You each brought in a complete script, then?

Yes. And then Ozzie would take those three scripts and put them together. He would take all the scripts himself, and pick what he liked best — and give us no credit. People didn't know there were writers on the show — they thought Ozzie — he used to tell how he would write the show. I have to take credit because credit was never given me. When I came on the show, I was very instrumental in slowly changing it from the variety — it was patterned after *Fibber McGee and Molly* — to the kind of show it became. On radio it was considered a highly rated script show; we won awards for the scripts. On TV I don't think the show was, frankly, very good. It was not near as good.

How would you assess Ozzie Nelson as an editor?

Oh, he was all right. They *were* good for themselves. Charles Correll and Freeman Gosden were not good writers, but they were great writers for *Amos 'n' Andy*. Ed Gardner — after *Duffy's Tavern* went off the air, he came to me. He wanted to become a writer. He had a great sense of humor, and he knew that show better than anyone. He was the final arbiter. And he ad-libbed fine. But when he started to write for somebody else, it was amateurish. So they learned to write for themselves. They knew their own characters so well, and the situations that were good for them. Not to write — Ozzie did not write much — but to pick what they liked.

Would Ozzie say, "I think a certain thing would work for me or..."

No. We would talk — I have to be a little bit immodest — we would talk about the premise, and he would go by what I'd say very often, 'cause the show was doing very well. Ozzie might say, "Gee, I don't think that works."

You said the show was modeled on Fibber McGee and Molly.

Yes, Ozzie patterned it after that show. The show was routines, and then he had people with funny voices. And as I say, I reshaped it entirely, from a joke-routine show, to a story show. I slowly changed it so we got rid of the people with funny voices. Bea Benaderet used to do this burlesque voice — she wanted to go to New York for three months, and Ozzie was worried sick. I said, "Ozzie, there'll be a time when you won't want Bea." 'Cause she was a funny voice. And after a while — that funny voice was off. That's where I shaped it, into more legitimate people. We had legitimate characters and a stronger story.

I understand the character of Thorny, the neighbor, was your idea.

That was my character. Ozzie named him, because he had a neighbor called Thornwell or something. But I came in with the idea of
the next door neighbor. Or course, you got no credit for it at all.
These days — especially now — you come in and do a show like
Ozzie and Harriet or *Duffy's Tavern* —- today if you do that, one show
— you go right to your own show, and if that's successful you're
doing motion pictures. In those days, you just stayed. I worked, and
I made what was considered good money, but my name was
unknown. Sherwood Schwartz, Hal Kanter, all these guys were
unknown — except to the small group of writers and employers.

You got the experience in radio and then made the money in television.

Yeah. And we knew each other. The comedy shows had a small and
incestuous group of writers. We were all about the same age, we all
knew each other, and whenever you'd see a comedy show in
Variety, you'd know all the writers. Today I don't. The big difference
is that today they don't have the same staff doing all the episodes.
They'll have a team do maybe four or five shows in a season.

*There wasn't much respect for writers in those days — especially from the
general public.*

Yeah — you never heard about the writers, they certainly were not
publicized — you heard everything about the stars, continually —
everything. But the writers, the hours we worked on the shows —
very often friends of mine would say, "Oh, you write that show.
That's a half hour show once a week, right? What do you do with
the rest of the week?"

*How did you compensate for the fact that neither Ozzie nor Harriet were
comedians? You couldn't write joke material for them.*

I preferred writing for actors. I always did. I didn't like writing for
Red Skelton. I had no desire to write for Bob Hope. I never liked
writing for comedians because that wasn't my forte. When I went
into television, I was the first one to do comedy shows [with actors],
for instance, *My Favorite Husband* with Barry Nelson and Joan
Caulfield. The first time they'd done a half hour comedy show without comedians.

Lucille Ball did a radio show with that title...

When Lucy left that show I sent her a script called *Cinderella O'Toole,* about a girl who had daydreams. Don Sharpe, who was connected with Lucy, later said to me, "You know, Lucille Ball loved your script, wanted to do it. And I talked her out of it. I talked her into *I Love Lucy."* I thought to myself, "Thanks a lot." I never heard *My Favorite Husband* on radio. I knew CBS owned the property and the title. I knew it was a husband and wife show, that's all. I went up there and I said, "Look, I'd like to do a pilot for *My Favorite Husband.* They said, "Go ahead." That was my first television show, I think.

Before you went into television, you did another radio program called The Beulah Show.

That show came from Chicago originally. And a white man [Marlin Hurt] did that. He died; they wanted to continue the show, and they were interviewing and auditioning *white men.* Then someone thought, why not do it with a black woman? And they got Hattie McDaniel. It wasn't successful until they got the idea of doing it with a black woman.

Was Hattie McDaniel a good radio actress?

Yes. She was a good comedienne. Hattie got laughs — she had that wonderful voice — she got good laughs. And she'd do it in front of a live audience. We had no tapes, no laugh machines. She was sophisticated in another sense. She wasn't so literate, but sometimes she would read a line and think it was a joke. Because she didn't know what these guys were laughing at. So when Hattie read it, she would time it like a joke. And do you know, that audience would laugh. There was nothing funny at all.

I understand she unwittingly interfered with a scheme that was rather prevalent then...

They used to do a lot of plugs on radio — Dr. Scholl's Foot Pads, Schwinn Bicycles — if you got the mention of that in, they sent you a case of any kind of booze you wanted. Schwinn Bicycles wanted a placement — all you had to do was mention their name. And Hattie couldn't say "Schwinn." She said "Swin." We could never get a Schwinn Bicycle 'cause she would say "Swin."

Did the writers try and work these plugs in?

I didn't do much of it, because I was the head writer. I didn't like it. I thought it was whorish. Once in a while I would do it, for the guys. We were paid well — and I thought, "What are you doing, for a few..." — you had to divide the booze. But the writers that worked, they'd turn in scripts to me; I'd tell 'em, "One 15-minute script, you've got four plugs in here." They'd say, "Well, what's the difference? So maybe they'll let a couple of them through." There was an agent here who placed those. They weren't supposed to be — but you did it, everybody knew it. You'd hear shows: "There's a plug, there's a plug..."

This was a surreptitious practice — did anyone crack down on it?

They tried to, yeah. If you did it, it was under the table. Sometimes you'd get away with it. And sometimes the producer would know and just let you do it. Sometimes it was a star — Dennis Day was one, I think, who would do it himself and arrange for it. It was illegal. The networks didn't like it. I imagine the agent who was doing this would get a few hundred dollars, and he'd spend $50 or $60 on a case of booze. And they'd get a plug on a network radio show.

I imagine it couldn't be anything that would present a conflict with the sponsor.

Oh, no. We'd never do conflict. Let me tell you, getting Dr. Scholl's Foot Pads into a script was pretty hard to do. And you had to do it with a joke. 'Cause otherwise it would be cut. But there were certain things that they would come and tell you — "Listen, can you get in a mention of this?" — I remember those. You mentioned "Mixmaster," you got a Mixmaster.

Did you have any trouble with sponsors in those days?

One sponsor would own the whole show, so therefore he was very powerful. He was the one who said the show was going on the air. Today it's the network — back then it was the sponsor. They were very tough. I remember once, a producer cut out the line "spaghetti and meatballs for dinner." Why? Spaghetti and meatballs is heavy — it gives the impression of a heavy stomach and gas — we don't want to do that. You couldn't say "spaghetti and meatballs." Today they talk about crotch deodorants. What happened in radio days too, letters would be — sometimes they'd say, "Look, we've had complaints — too much drinking on the show." I said, "What do you mean, too much drinking? What complaints are you getting?" They got two letters. Now, one letter, they'd consider. Two letters would scare the pants off them.

It's amazing that two letters were enough — that the public had that kind of influence.

Even today — except it's not quite so much to the powers that be, because they don't know what makes the show. They think, "Hey, this line might possibly offend two guys in Texas. Let's cut out the line." To the writer, that's a hard line to come by.

Was there a problem with censorship then?

When the censors came down — and the censors were tough on us — we always tried to get as far as we could go. As I said, I did not take to jokes naturally. When I started, very often I would take old dirty jokes and switch 'em. So I would get a double laugh — first a laugh at the joke. And then, another laugh, whoever recognized the dirty joke it came from. We would go as far as we could go — it was a continual battle between you and the continuity department. They would come down, and the old trick was — which I'm sure they were aware of — you had a line you wanted to get in, so you put in a very obviously bad line. Then you'd give in on the obvious line.

Do you miss radio?

The work was a lot harder, for less money, in radio. I miss some of the excitement. I miss the thing that I imagine an explorer on a safari down the Amazon would miss, with all the danger and the mosquitoes and the crocodiles and the heat. When he comes back years later, it was *an adventure*. Which it isn't today. You didn't know what you were going to get — the shows were live. It was closer to a World Series ballgame; you didn't always know what you had.

I imagine there were times when you wrote something where you weren't sure whether it was going to go over, and it did...

The frightening thing was when it didn't go over. We writers would make jokes — it would sometimes get a little crazy. We needed to make jokes, to keep our sanity. I remember working day after day on Vine Street in the advertising agency — I think this was *Duffy's Tavern* — and we took typewriting paper and cut it into squares and wrote "5 cents" and "10 cents." Made chips out of them. And stood there, three o'clock in the afternoon. Grown men, stupidly playing poker, just to get away from the tension. You got to hate those people in the room with you, because you looked at them all day long, their faces got so ugly — then the Dixie cups with cold coffee in the bottom and cigarettes — and them sending out the underling, for sandwiches at three o'clock in the morning...

What elements make for a great radio program?

Originality, surprise — in those days, it was jokes more than anything else. Fred Allen was jokes. I wrote with Fred Allen on *Hall of Fame*; he was a guest on it. When Fred came in, the advertising agency — all the big shots came down from Philco — "Fred Allen's going to be there." So they're all meeting Fred Allen, they're all talking, we're sitting around. And Fred leans over and says to me, "Do you have an office here?" I says, "Yeah. I've got a little cubbyhole." He says, "Can we go there?" And he and I went into this little cubbyhole. To hell with this bullshit; he wanted to talk about the script. He *knew* — Fred Allen *knew*, Jack Benny *knew*, Bob Hope *knew*— they all knew the writing is where it's at.

Did you have a favorite director in radio?

No, because the director in radio was not very important, especially on the comedy shows. Because Bob Hope, anyone — they wanted the writers there. Directors didn't do what they did in pictures, saying "I don't like the way that line is read." They wouldn't dare say that on *The Bob Hope Show*, or *Burns and Allen*. They would look to the writers. And the writer might say it, but not the director. Radio comedy was a writer's medium. Of course, we didn't get paid. We didn't get the credit. But it was a writer's medium.

Who were some of the radio writers you admired?

Herman Wouk came out of radio. The guy who wrote *The Phil Silvers Show* — who I think was one of the best in the business — Nat Hiken. He was one of the best writers who came out of radio. Artie Stander, who wrote for *Amos 'n' Andy*, and died at a young age. I thought he was one of the top writers. Those names were not known, by the way — nobody knew, except the few people who hired.

Larry Gelbart came from radio, of course.

Larry Gelbart is the kind of writer I like to think I am. He's an all-around writer. He writes musical comedy, he writes drama, he's able to write all these things. When I started, the gag writer — they called 'em gag writers, I hated that — was top. If you could write two lines that somebody could say and people would laugh, you wrote your own ticket. You got paid $1,000 a week, which was fabulous. Abe Burrows was like that. Hal Kanter was good at that, Sherwood Schwartz was good at that. I wasn't; I was not the guy. I was not a natural joke writer. But you had to do it; I learned to write jokes. However, I also wrote drama. I wrote character. I wrote plot. I wrote situation. I preferred doing that. Jack Benny was the first one in comedy who used some character and drama, and used some story — the rest were just *boom boom boom*, jokes.

For me, the jokes have to come out of the character.

I think situation comedy is a misnomer. It should be called character comedy. Those of us who learned that — and I was fortunate I did — when I went into TV, it stood me in good stead. I could start to write plot and character. Those other "gag writers," they couldn't adapt when radio comedy started to change from straight stand-up jokes...

How did the radio writers feel about TV when it came in? Did you feel threatened?

I don't think any of us felt threatened, no. The actors were probably afraid of it. The radio writers moved right into it — we knew we

were going to go into TV. But it was a different kind of writing, and
a lot of the writers fell by the wayside when they moved over.

But you had no trouble making the transition to television yourself...

No. Because I did write character. And because now, from writing
for just the ear, I could write for the eye too. It made it a lot easier for
me to write something funny. In radio and in TV, the comedy — that
scene line was all important. 'Cause we didn't have laugh tracks. It
was live. So that scene line had to get the laugh. And if it didn't —
you were left there with egg on your face — and sometimes you
were. Then when tape came in, it got easier. The laugh machine —
although every writer I know doesn't like the laugh machine, it still
made it easier.

Was it a highly competitive business in those days?

The radio writers were looked down upon. We were all young, we
were all in our early twenties, most of us were Jewish — I don't
know why that is, I think they just took to it — and there wasn't
strangely a lot of competition, because the well known writers of
comedy sneered at radio. They were doing features, or books. They
wouldn't do radio — as they eventually looked down on TV too.
Now they don't any more. But they sneered — so that when we
came in, we did not have to buck big names. If you could learn your
trade, and learn to write an amusing scene, and could produce a
script a week, you worked. I never had trouble.

You never had trouble finding jobs?

I was one of the guys who had quit a job — I didn't like it — and then
I was out of work. I turned down jobs like *I Married Joan*. I didn't like
that kind of show. They were comedians — I didn't like comedians,
I didn't like broad comedy. Eventually I took it because Artie
Stander asked me to do it, and I wanted a swimming pool. I figured
I needed four weeks to pay for the pool. Then my wife said to me,
"What about income tax?" I said, "Oh, my God, I didn't think of
income tax." I called them, I said, "I'll make it six weeks." It was
such hard work — and also, it was skilled. So if you were skilled

enough to do it and had the intestinal fortitude to come up every week with a script, you found a job. And there weren't a lot of us.

CREDITS

Radio: *The First Nighter Program, Grand Central Station, Thunder and Lightning, Wings of Destiny, While America Sleeps, Uncle Walter's Doghouse; Bullet Trenton, C.D.; The Red Skelton Show, Duffy's Tavern, Toasties Time (The Baby Snooks Show), Dinah Shore's Open House, The Danny Kaye Show, Hall of Fame, The Adventures of Ozzie and Harriet, The Beulah Show.*

TV: *My Favorite Husband, I Married Joan, Mr. Adams And Eve, Peck's Bad Girl, The Eve Arden Show, Bewitched, Norman Corwin Presents.*

Film: *Walk, Don't Run.*

Theater: *Balloon Going Up; The Beginning, Middle And End; Soft Remembrance, Faces of Love.*

LARRY GELBART

One of Larry Gelbart's distinctions among those writing for radio in the 1940s was his youth. He was all of 16 when he turned professional. "I think Larry was younger than any of the really working writers," asserted Charles Isaacs. "He was possibly the youngest of that era."

The wunderkind was still a student at Fairfax High School when he made his debut with a sketch for comedian Danny Thomas, in which Thomas' Walter Mitty-type character fantasized about being a barber, like Gelbart's father. His apprenticeship in deadline-oriented radio taught him discipline, above all else. "It was a gift to be given that training," he stressed, "and it never leaves me."

Gelbart was born February 25, 1928, in Chicago, where he was raised, moving with his parents to Los Angeles in his mid-teens. He had dreams of becoming the next Fred Astaire — or Benny Goodman — before he fell into writing. "There were no books in my house when I was a child," he recalled. "My folks were immigrants and they didn't read. So I think maybe the word became this Holy Grail."

He got his "higher education" on the staff of *Duffy's Tavern*, writing for mercurial star-producer Ed Gardner. He wasn't so much writing at this stage, he later noted, as exercising a knack for coming up with funny lines — a talent he continued to hone in radio days on behalf of Joan Davis, Jack Paar, Jack Carson and Bob Hope. He also learned how to play with language; turn off the picture on his *M*A*S*H* episodes, Gelbart recently asserted, "and they would make pretty good radio shows."

While he has lambasted television at every opportunity, both as an entertainment medium and as a market for writers — "that's really just putting your brain in a meat grinder" — TV paid the mortgage for many years. It also gave Gelbart the opportunity to write for one of the icons of the medium's Golden Age, Sid Caesar, as part of a "dream team" of comedy writers (including Neil Simon and Mel Brooks) which has become near-legend in itself.

Gelbart has carved out a formidable reputation in the years that followed that experience, moving back and forth between TV, film and theater. After writing a pair of television specials for Art Carney which netted a Sylvania Award, he collaborated with Burt Shevelove on the book for *A Funny Thing Happened on the Way to the Forum*, a raucous musical comedy that won him a Tony Award. In 1963 he went to England to open the London production of the show and ended up staying for nine years.

He returned to the U.S. after a stint writing for Marty Feldman, when CBS agreed to finance a pilot for *M*A*S*H*. Gelbart and his old friend Gene Reynolds adapted the hit Robert Altman film to fit the small screen, not knowing it would become a landmark in TV history. The show — for which he co-wrote, co-produced and/or directed the first 97 episodes (1972-1976) — won him an Emmy, a Peabody and a Humanitas Award, to name a few. "I never dreamed it would turn out to be the mother lode it has," observed Gelbart. "You never know when your work is going to impress people. You do the best you can. I think if you know you're working on a masterpiece, you surely aren't."

While he has written a number of unproduced screenplays — and doctored several others he prefers not to acknowledge — Gelbart's name appears on the cult film, *The Wrong Box*, and two comedy classics, *Oh, God!* and *Tootsie* — both of which garnered Oscar nominations. More recently, two movies for cable television, *Barbarians at the Gate* and *Weapons of Mass Distraction*, proved that he has lost none of his satiric bite. If Gelbart has weathered his share of misfires, notably the TV series *United States*, his work is of a consistently high caliber. "I am very tough on myself; consequently I approve of very little that I do."

He has labored hard for his success, particularly in theater where the financial rewards are comparatively small — *Funny Thing* took five years to write; the Tony Award-winning book for the musical *City of Angels* took eight. "People are chipping away at writers' rights; in theater, there remains the appeal of not having to write for corporate entities... I like writing for live audiences with no agenda at all except to enjoy the work."

A writer as much in demand as Gelbart was not easy to pin down, as one might expect. But once I set up the interview — long-distance by telephone, from his home in Palm Springs — he was more than generous with his time. He was warm, good-humored, modest and unassuming. Better yet, he was patient with my approach — it was soon apparent that I wasn't after a mere "sound bite" — and wonderfully articulate. As he told another interviewer: "I get longer and longer winded as I get thicker and thicker waisted."

Radio really laid the foundation for your success.

Well, it was certainly the school I attended.

You began in 1944?

God, sounds a century ago, doesn't it?

I believe your father was a barber...

Yeah. My father used to look after Danny Thomas, and he began to tell him — he thought I could write for him, could write comedy professionally. I had written on a strictly amateur basis at school. I was acting in plays, writing school revues or sketches. And Thomas gave me the chance to write for him — he was a regular on the Fanny Brice program, *Maxwell House Coffee Time*. And that's the long and short of it.

Thomas reportedly told your father that if you were so funny, to have you come up to the barber shop and make him laugh.

No, no. He asked me to write something, so he could see if he could help me. It wasn't a question of making him laugh.

Was radio a medium you specifically wanted to break into?

No, not really. I didn't have any thought to do that at all. My dad's part was strictly his own idea. I didn't know what I was going to do — I hoped it would be something in entertainment.

Did you aspire to a career as a writer at that time or...

No, that was too — too exalted a position, and a presumption.

But your father evidently saw something there.

Yeah. Or didn't see, but thought maybe he would just troll a little, to see what he could catch.

Did anyone teach you the craft of writing for radio, or take you under their wing?

Well, that happened once I was exposed to it. Nobody took time — no one had the time to give anybody lessons, but you learned by observing, as you did it right along with them.

Alongside writers like Abe Burrows?

Well, Abe was on *Duffy's Tavern*. Actually, he left the show the day I came on — there was no connection. But I later worked with him on Joan Davis' radio show. I never got to work with Abe at the very beginning — but I did work with a fellow named Bill Manhoff, who became the head writer on *Duffy's Tavern* after Abe left, and he was very generous with his time. He was really the first — of course, Mac Benoff on *Baby Snooks* — but over a longer run it was Bill, and a good many other older men whose work I was influenced by.

In what way?

When I say influence, it's not as though one tried to write the kind of joke they did, but began to know the shape of a joke, or the application of a joke to a situation in a script. I don't think any of them were influential in terms of, "I want to be funny *that* way."

Were you a big fan of radio prior to this?

Oh sure, like all the kids in my generation.

Any particular shows that you would single out as a favorite?

Well, first of all were the shows you could hear all week long, the serials. *Don Winslow of the Navy, Little Orphan Annie* and all of that, *Captain Midnight* — the stuff you listened to every day after school. But then of course the special programs, those high-powered comedians' shows — Jack Benny, Bob Hope, Fred Allen, *Duffy's Tavern*. Edgar Bergen had a wonderful program...

On The Baby Snooks Show, *did Fanny Brice work with her writers?*

I don't think so. In any case, I wasn't at that level. I never got near those people. I would just work with Mac Benoff. That was the extent of my — I had trouble getting in backstage at CBS, even though I was connected with the show. They thought I was there for an autograph.

Were you just writing Danny Thomas' spots?

Yeah. I would go over to Mac's house when he worked on that spot, and the pitch, during that period. But that was not a long period — that was maybe six or seven weeks. As a matter of fact, after that period the show was going on hiatus, so there was no opportunity to continue with it. A fellow from the William Morris Agency named George Gruskin said that if I wanted to do more, he thought I had a future. He arranged for Ed Gardner to take a chance. He signed me, and got me a position on *Duffy's Tavern* at $50 a week.

Rudy Vallee said once that Gardner had a strange streak of irrationality.

It wasn't strange to Ed at all. I saw him once reading some material that one of the people he'd hired had written, and he read the first page and said, "This stinks, this is really terrible." And he called the guy up and fired him on the phone. And then read the next page and liked that, called him back and rehired him. Ed Gardner was a wild man, he really was, especially when it came to hiring and firing writers.

I think there were over 100 writers who worked on the show, during its run. According to actress Sandra Gould, there were a couple of guys in Sing Sing or San Quentin who sent in jokes that were used...

I have no doubt. Ed paid nothing, absolutely nothing. I remember his brother sent him a letter saying, would he please contribute $100 toward the purchase of a headstone, for one of their parents? Ed said, "A hundred dollars is a lot of money. I'll send it, but you gotta send me a monologue." The guy did, and Ed said, "Jesus, he calls this a monologue?"

Sol Saks recalled being in a bar with Gardner, and Gardner thought the barman was so funny he asked him if he wanted to write for the show.

Yeah, Gardner did that a lot. He would hire people that way. Gardner was a wonderful editor of material — and the best Archie there ever was, or could be. And the only one. But he did drink in those days, and he did some pretty irrational things. I once kept a list of people who came and went during a certain period of my employment — I quit after about six years. He was just wild in that way.

Would the writers work in teams on the show?

Yeah, I was teamed — well, for a long time, I just reported to Bill Manhoff's house after school. Then somewhere along the line, Ed teamed me up with Sid Dorfman. And Sid and I really liked working together; we stayed together for a couple of years, going on beyond that as a team. A lot of the time — after a certain time — Sid and Vinnie Bogert and I were the people who put the show together, took all the rough drafts and put them together — so that was sort of a three-way team, although it was really Sid and me who functioned as partners.

Any other recollections of Gardner?

There was a marvelous time once when he and Monty Woolley — this was in pre-tape days, when you did the show live — in between the East and the West Coast broadcasts, he and Woolley went out for a light dinner or supper. Or neither — they just had a ton of martinis and came back. And during the broadcast, Monty Woolley fell on the floor he was so out of it, and Ed got down on the floor with him. And they just finished the program lying on their side — reading the script of course, into the microphone.

The stories I've heard about Gardner...

He was a piece of work. I remember the day Bob Schiller came on the show, when Ed signed him — he sent him over to Sid Dorfman's house to work with us. Ed called and said, "Just answer yes or no, is this Schiller guy any good?" "Uh, yeah, Ed. Uh huh." It was a little early to know, because he called about a half an hour after Schiller checked in for work. Ed was always— sort of checking on his writers. Once he was trying to cut down on the budget, and he said to me, "Tell me the truth, are you any good?" I said, "You want me to rat on myself, so you can fire me?"

Would you do anything as drastic as rewrites on the day of the broadcast, due to Gardner's eccentricities?

I will say this — his eccentricities didn't get in the way of his selectivity. He was, as I said, the best editor for that show, of anybody around. He really knew the characters.

Did his drinking impair his abilities as an editor?

No, I don't think so. Or maybe I was too young to realize that was a fact, but it seemed to me — he knew his stuff. I don't think I've ever worked for a very successful comedian who wasn't a wonderful editor — in terms of himself. I would say "herself," but I think the only comedienne I worked for was Joan Davis, and she sort of left all that to others.

Was Duffy's Tavern the show where the writers had to stand in line with the public, to get into the show?

You may be right. There wasn't room for everybody backstage. There were weeks when there were might've been 10 or 12 guys hanging around. Each guy did — I don't know whether we wrote an act or whether we did a guest spot. The show got divided and you would do write different parts of it.

The workload would be divided up among the different writers.

Right. And then Ed would take the work and read it out loud, so in a sense you were being asked to judge your co-worker's work. And it was very awkward — to laugh, not to laugh — to hear very clearly that someone had really written some very poor material that week. It was not a good way to do it.

There were shows where the writers were asked to sit in the audience and laugh.

It wouldn't surprise me about other shows; I don't remember that being the case there. I can't do that, anyway. I do remember asking Ed for a raise just before I went into the army when I was 18. I was drafted — I think by then I had worked my way up to $75 a week, after two years. And I said, "Look, for the last couple of weeks — I would just love to be able to say I made $100 a week before I went in the army, if you could just do that for two weeks." And Gardner said, "No, kid, I'd love to do it, but the budget won't allow it." He said, "Tell you what, don't ask me again, and when you go in I'll give you a nice set of military hair brushes." That was Ed's idea of a raise.

So you were drafted at 18 and assigned to Armed Forces Radio?

Yeah. After a couple of weeks in Marysville, California, at the induction center, they brought me back and I went with AFRS.

Do you recall who else was there at the time — probably Sherwood Schwartz?

No. Being younger than everybody — the real heavyweights had gone home, been discharged — none of those guys were there. There was a fellow named Hal Goldman, who went on to work for George Burns. [He was] a civilian — for all intents and purposes, so was I. I think I was there five minutes and they made me a PFC, and then two days later they made me a sergeant.

Was this after the war?

The war was over; I got to live at home with my folks. I was able to do civilian jobs as well, because I was in Hollywood — so I was hardly in the army then. But happily, I was hardly in the army for a year and eleven days, and that eleven days saved me from being drafted again when the Korean action started.

How did this work, with Armed Forces Radio? You were able to do civilian jobs three days a week or...?

Writer Hal Goldman, George Murphy, Connie Moore, producer Clare Weidenauer, actor Hal Peary, writers Bill Norman, Jack Douglas and Larry Gelbart, and announcer Ken Niles gather for *Command Performance*, 1946.

Command Performance didn't take up all the time. And as luck would have it, Armed Forces Radio was on Santa Monica Boulevard, quite close to Sid Dorfman's house, very close — he and I were still a team — and so it was just a short hop for me to go to his place, or him to come to my office at AFRS.

Do you recall writing for particular guest stars on Command Performance?

They all came through there, they really did. Frank Sinatra, Judy Garland, Bob Hope, Groucho Marx, Phil Silvers. Jack Benny certainly; probably Fred Allen. I know I did some stuff for Allen when he came on *Duffy's Tavern,* or Ed Gardner was on *The Fred Allen Show.*

Jack Benny said he "lived and died" by his writers. But when he appeared on other shows, he depended on their writers?

Yes, he did. He was smart, you know; he'd so established his character, he knew that people would write pretty close to it. I remember once writing a sketch for George Burns and Gracie Allen — and being told that Burns wouldn't do anything unless his own writers did it, because only they knew how to write for them. So I just put Paul Henning's name on it when I sent it over, and George said, "Fine. Good. I'll do it." It was a funny period, and a fun period in my life.

From AFRS you went on to Bob Hope, or Eddie Cantor?

It might've been Cantor first. Cantor was a very abortive and unpleasant situation. Sid Dorfman and I were there just a very short time. It was not a good experience — but happily a short one. And then I think we wrote for Joan Davis — that was 13 weeks, we worked with Abe Burrows. Aside from the unhappy fact that Abe used almost nothing that we wrote, he was brilliant. He really wasn't a great admirer of other people's efforts — comedy writers, anyway. But it was wonderful being with him. He was incredibly entertaining, and instructive, just being in his company while he wrote — or rewrote your stuff. After that, I guess, Sid and I split up and I went to work for Bob Hope, with Larry Marks.

Working for Cantor was unpleasant? In what way?

We just didn't really hit it off well. And I don't know what we were doing there. Sid Dorfman and I had asked Ed for a raise — I think we wanted $500 a week each.

Ed Gardner?!

Gardner, yeah — shows you how unrealistic we were. He said, "No, no, I can't do that." We said, "Then we have to quit, Ed." He said, "I understand. That's okay, good luck." Then he went to the reading of the show later that morning, and when we weren't there, he said, "Where the hell are those guys?" Somebody said, "We don't know, Ed." He said, "Fuck 'em, they're fired if they can't show up on time."

So you ended up on The Eddie Cantor Show — *briefly, at least.*

Sid and I were just looking for a job that we thought would give us what we thought we were worth, and Cantor did. I remember Sid got hepatitis, and our work suffered as a result. I think our first assignment was to write a guest spot on the next week's Cantor show for Al Jolson. And Cantor didn't like it much. I had to go to the meeting alone; Sid was too sick to get out of the house. It was awkward and clumsy, and in truth I think maybe lasted two weeks. And that was it, over and out.

I've heard a lot of horror stories about Cantor.

We weren't around long enough to know that, but we knew it wasn't going to be good. We didn't really have anything to do with him. Abe Burrows was our guide; Abe had the chief responsibility for the script. Sid and I were there for rehearsals, and we were there for the broadcast. Si Wills still got credit as a writer, although I don't know that he wrote anything — he was Joan Davis' husband. There was another show in between there — Jack Paar.

That was at the outset of Paar's career.

That was his first shot, yeah. He went on as Jack Benny's summer replacement.

What was Paar like then, at the very beginning?

Not nice. It was a tough spot to be in, for a young man. And he didn't handle it especially well, at least in terms of the writers — Artie Stander, Larry Marks and Sid Dorfman and I. Three of us wound up quitting *The Jack Paar Show* several weeks into the season. Larry Marks didn't quit because he had a personal contract with Jack — or he had a percentage deal with Jack, a percentage of his earnings. Jack, to get someone of Larry's caliber that early in his career, made that sort of arrangement. So some lawyering had to go on before Larry was able to get off the show too.

"Fat" Larry Marks who worked on Duffy's Tavern?

Yes. His first day on *Duffy's* — we were all sitting in the conference room at NBC, and Ed Gardner was in there with all the writers, as usual. And Ed said, "There's a new guy coming on the show." Of course, everything was colored — not just by his New York accent but his nasal, herky-jerky delivery — and he said, "This guy weighs about 400 pounds. He's a terrific writer, but he's very, very sensitive about his weight, so don't nobody get out of line with him." With that, Larry Marks comes in the room, and Ed says, "Sit down, you fat fuck." Vintage Gardner. I don't know what it did to Larry, who was a tower of insecurity anyway.

You wrote for Jack Carson after you left Jack Paar...

That was fun. What he did, it was kind of a faux *Jack Benny Show*. He was very much influenced by Benny. It was Jack Carson and Dave Willock, Arthur Treacher, Eve Arden. Carson had a middling career; he wasn't considered one of the major — it was just an okay show. For Sid Dorfman and I, it was a step up. As we went from show to show, we were able to get a better price each time.

Were you getting your $500 a week by then?

I think by the time we did *The Jack Carson Show* we were up to $750.

Quite a jump from $50 a week with Ed Gardner and Duffy's *Tavern.*

Yes, I was able to buy my own hairbrushes.

Did you work with Sid Dorfman on The Bob Hope Show*?*

No, we had split up by then. I just went from one partner to another. I didn't feel I *could* work alone. I felt I needed a partner.

It helps to be able to bounce the jokes off someone else.

I thought that. There were people who didn't, but I was not one of them. And I thought other people would supply whatever it was I didn't have in the way of — equipment.

Bob Hope in the early days had 8 or 10 writers.

The year that I began working with him was considered kind of a —
well, Hope was trying something new. He wasn't going to have 8 or
9 or 10 writers. He had Larry Marks and I, and then he had Marvin
Fisher and Al Schwartz, Sherwood's brother. And we were supposed to be *the* staff. And he paid us extremely well — instead of
spreading out all that money over that many people, he'd be paying
a few people all of that money. That prevailed for the four years I
was with him.

This was quite a departure for Hope, in terms of the writing process.

It never ever got to be the mob scene again — which was kind of
nice — it makes you feel a little special. Because there's something
demeaning about being a member of a platoon. Norman Sullivan
was another writer — I guess he wound up working for Hope
maybe for 40 years. But at that time I believe Norm just did monologues. He would go by Hope's house, open the Monologue Night
Deposit Box, and put it in.

So there were two teams, and each team would work on a part of the script?

Everybody would do monologues. And we'd agree on how many
we would write — we didn't want to start a monlogue war where
we wound up writing hundreds of jokes every week. There would
be four or five topics that would be the subjects for the monologue
that week, so each team would do maybe 20 jokes on each subject.
Then somebody would write the guest spot, but not in competition
so to speak. Then we'd get together at Hope's and he would put the
monologue together. I guess we would kind of punch up each
other's spot there and then if they needed punching up. But it was
the monologue — Hope is first and foremost a monologist — that
was *always* the center of his focus.

In terms of putting the script together, Hope would supply the glue?

No, it would be a stapler really. You just stitched it — there was not
a great deal of artfulness required, you're just going joke to joke to
joke.

Was Hope a good editor? Did he know what worked for him?

Hope knew what worked for him; he knew what worked with an audience. A good deal of the time Hope's written material was inferior to his own sense of humor. He's a very bright, witty guy — but he knows the audience expects a certain thing from him, and that's what he gives them.

Would he contribute much as a writer himself?

No. He didn't have to. If you have say 20 jokes per subject, and you've got two teams writing 'em, you've got 200 jokes to pick from.

Even when he had the script in hand, would you find Hope ad-libbing?

No, no. He wouldn't do that. If something went wrong, yeah, he might ad-lib. But there was no need to. Why do that, when you've spent all this time getting the material? Also, in pre-tape days, you knew you had a time span within which to do the show, and you weren't about to start pushing the envelope.

Hope was pretty generous to his writers — but not as generous as Jack Benny, giving his writers credit on the air...

Benny *was* really terribly kind to his writers, in terms of how he behaved. Hope's point of view was always, "I can't give you credit because my fans think I make this up, I don't want to spoil the illusion." And he genuinely believed that.

I think you made the transition into television with Hope.

Yeah. Because he eventually dropped radio altogether and we were all in TV together.

At that point, I guess television pretty much took over.

The picture got louder than the words.

How did that change what you were writing? You now had to start writing visual jokes for him?

At first we weren't really writing television at all; we were writing radio shows with funny costumes. We didn't appreciate — we didn't *know* what to do. We were just taking pictures of jokes — of Hope telling jokes — whether in a monologue, which never did change, or in a cowboy suit or whatever. Radio was so purely and undeniably a unique medium — there was never anything like radio before. In the beginning, middle and end there's the word, and that's it. Television is far more theater than it is broadcasting.

So the transition was quite difficult. How did you finally adapt to writing for a visual medium?

I never did do that on the Hope show, I don't think. I don't know how you learn, you just — do it. Who knows? It turns out you don't have to be all that visual anyway, if the particular piece of material doesn't require it — if you're doing a scene with two people doing absolutely brilliant dialogue on a divan, then what the hell do you have to be visual about? But there was an awful lot of costume comedy then. The nature of what we did made it visual. It was only later when I began working for other people — in which you had to do character comedy — that you began writing more in the theater sense rather than in the broadcasting sense.

Because the medium was so new nobody knew what to do with it? Or because of Hope's inability to adapt?

I think Hope was very comfortable in television — he was back in vaudeville, in a sense. He never did sketches when he was in vaudeville but he sang and danced, which he never did in television or radio.

I think it was Morey Amsterdam who said TV stood for "tired vaudeville."

Fair enough. I said when vaudeville died, TV was the box they put it in. Hope was very much at home in it. It was a throwback to that — for which he was well prepared.

Could you give me an example of a gag you would write for radio that might not work on television?

In radio, you could tell a joke that had a $20 million budget. You could describe — any one of the Professor [Jerry] Colonna jokes, about being on top of a skyscraper that's being built from the top down. Imagine the production required to film something like that, where it would be enacted as opposed to just being told.

So you went from a big budget show to a low budget show when you switched over to TV — in a sense.

That's right. Bigger budget, but smaller in that way.

Which medium was more difficult to write for? Or should I say, more stressful?

Well, the truth is — that neither was either for me. It was only because I was young and dumb — and having a very good time. So I didn't feel that kind of stress. I was neither the owner nor the producer nor the packager, or any of that. I was just really happy go lucky. I didn't feel the pressure that a lot of people did.

I've been told that doing radio was a lot less pressure than TV...

No, it wasn't. No. Pressure's pressure. There were different pressures on *The Bob Hope Show*, or any radio show. There was no scenery to be built — there were a lot fewer production requirements. You just had to have the pages, that's all...

What were some of the special challenges of writing for radio that were unique to that medium?

Well, first of all you had to be fast, because that broadcast time came around awfully fast. There was no lead time ever; you finished one show and would maybe have a day off, and would go right back to work on the next. You also learned to write for different kinds of people very quickly, if you were doing the kind of show which — well, you learned two things: you learned to write for continuing characters, and you learned to write for new characters. On *Duffy's Tavern*, you would have the ensemble that was there every week, and then you would have — anyone from Tallulah Bankhead to Leo

Gorcey — so you had to be pretty good about picking up on characteristics an audience would recognize immediately, the stuff you put in the guest stars' mouths. I guess what I'm talking about is just being very facile.

Would representatives from the agency or the sponsor generally be present during rehearsals?

I don't think in rehearsal — well, maybe. They were certainly there at the broadcast, and they might have been there if you had a rehearsal *with* an audience. On *The Jack Carson Show*, I remember — the show was sponsored by Sealtest Ice Cream and Dairy Products. There was an advertising agency man — he used to pride himself that he wrote the copy for the commercials. And one day, when we were doing a rehearsal with an audience — to see where to cut, and what worked and so forth — it came time for the first commercial, and the announcer said through the mike, "Hi, I'm the schmuck who drives the truck for Sealtest." We couldn't believe our ears. We said, "What do you think you're doing?! You can't say 'schmuck' on the air. You know what it means?" He said, "Yeah, it means I'm kind of a wise guy." We said, "No, it means you're a prick."

Did you ever run into any trouble with censors?

It probably came to me from the top. I remember we were in New York doing *Duffy's Tavern*, and Fred Allen was the guest, and he just — it wasn't funny to him, he just really hated those guys. He was really tough on them...

Fred Allen certainly gave the censors a bad time.

Yeah. He did so much writing himself, and he was imaginative. Fred really wrote, and encouraged people to write, in a way that probably challenged those guys a great deal more than those of us really doing "cookie cutter" humor — turning the same thing out, week in and week out. I'm not sure "humor" is the word. They were canned witticisms.

Writing for Fred Allen would certainly inspire you.

Dean Martin and Jerry Lewis clown it up on air.

Being in the same room with him did that.

Did you ever have any say in casting in radio?

In the early days? No, not at my level. We just were told who had been booked. I don't remember anybody ever saying, "Who do you think would be a good guest?" That was not something we had to bother with — and just as well. There were times — I remember saying to Bob Hope, "There are two young guys I just saw at Slapsy Maxie's [restaurant], you really ought to use them." They were Dean Martin and Jerry Lewis. But that was not in an official capacity, that was just — sort of a social recommendation.

It couldn't have been too long after that that Martin and Lewis got their own radio show.

They did get their own show. I remember that because, when they came on our show, they literally could barely read. They'd never had a script in their hands. All their stuff was put together — stuff they made up on their feet. They were very green. I remember a few months later being in the Brown Derby and Jerry Lewis came in. Several of us were sitting there. "God," he said, "I'm beat. I was up all night with the writers — they just don't know how to write. They just don't get us." He went from semi-illiteracy to a professorship in about three months.

It was a pretty sudden rise for them...

Martin and Lewis had an incredible rise, yeah. And they deserved it, they were hysterical. But they were hardly a radio act.

Was there something you learned in radio that you were able to use later on, in TV or theater or film?

I don't know. The first phrase that comes to mind is, "to deliver" — just to get it there, just to do it. Just to sit down and do it, because there was no not doing it then. There was no such thing as *not* finishing a script in those days — no "Can we have five minutes more?" or "We'll fix that on a dub." We had to have those pages.

The pressure was really on you to perform.

To get on with it, to come up with it. And everybody was working without a net, the writers and the actors — the actors went out there and faced a live audience. The stuff had to succeed, through a combination of material and delivery. If something really was terrible — there wasn't a lot of time to fix it between say, five o'clock and eight o'clock, and that stuff would have been untested as well. That's the one thing I think I learned, that works in whatever medium you're in, and whatever business you're in. Just to do your job in the time and the limitations that come with the job.

As tough as your job was under those circumstances, you were probably glad that you weren't the actor in front of the live mike.

I've always been glad not to be the actor — although I did act in some of the Bob Hope radio shows — when we were in some of the more remote parts of the world, and there weren't actors you could have sent over from Central Casting, or from AFRA. I would do the occasional bit, the quasi-Sheldon Leonard role.

You say the more remote parts of the world — Korea, for example?

Korea's sort of big time. Some of the military bases that Hope would play — there was a place called Johnson Island, which is about a half a mile wide, and about two miles long.

It must've been extraordinarily difficult doing a radio show under those circumstances.

Difficult, and exciting. Hope would go for a jet fighter ride with a guy and come down — "Let's use this guy on the show" — so you'd go to your Quonset hut or whatever, and you'd write a new spot and work it in. It was fun in a way — I mean, I probably bitched about it then — it probably wasn't that much fun then, but it sure seems like it now. Flying in the Berlin Airlift, all that stuff.

Radio provided the grounding for your career.

Yeah — and not just professionally. I think the discipline that comes from having to perform often in very difficult circumstances — I have to believe spills over into other parts of your life. I don't think we're one kind of worker and another kind of person. I don't feel that compartmentalized. So I think radio was good preparation — probably better preparation than formal schooling.

After you moved into television with Bob Hope, you went on to Red Buttons' show. He had a huge success at first, then just plummeted in popularity...

Yes. We had a wonderful first year.

Do you have any idea what happened?

My crystal ball is clouded. It also requires a rear-vision mirror. It's a little hard — I don't really remember.

But you were there the first season when he was having some success.

Yes. I will say rather immodestly — I was responsible for the scripts. I worked with the late Hal Collins on that show, and a team called Buddy Arnold and Woody Kling.

I understand Buttons was hiring and firing writers furiously.

There was a bit of traffic just when I started to work for him. There was a lot of coming and going. Before me there was Will Glickman and Joe Stein. I came on as they were going off, then I stayed with Red for the first season and some part of the second. I left the show — my replacements were Neil and Danny Simon.

Did Buttons participate much as an editor of material?

To some degree. We were using a lot of characters that he had created himself in nightclubs and personal appearances. They were variations on something he had done before.

In television, were the comedians as autonomous as they had been in radio where they more or less acted as their own editors and producers?

It would depend on the stature of the comic. Somebody like Hope who was just entering a new medium but carrying the weight of his previous successes with him, continued to function very much in that manner, whereas someone like Red Buttons — who was really being exposed to the mass audience [for the first time] through television — didn't have yet that kind of clout. But make no mistake — it was his show. He was the star; he was the guy who got out there and faced the bull every week. He had a lot to say about what he did. But he had a lot of faith in what I was doing for him, however immodest that may sound. We were a very good combination for a very long time.

Did he put a lot of faith in his writers?
He did in me.

Steve Allen quoted a writer as saying Buttons was unable to resist redoing the script his way. I take it there was a lot of conflict.

As I recall, he was getting a lot of pressure from the network. I don't think it was so much a matter of Red wanting to impose himself on

The Red Buttons Show enjoyed a knockout first season, then quickly faltered.

the script, as it was wanting to please the powers that were. I don't think it was ego so much as survival.

After you left The Red Buttons Show...

I had a stint at CBS as sort of a staff person. I worked on an ill-fated series called *Honestly, Celeste,* starring Celeste Holm. I was replaced on that by Norman Lear. I did a season on *The Patrice Munsel Show,* which wasn't a comedy show but which paid the rent. She was an opera star who had her own half-hour variety series. Then I did 13 weeks on *The Pat Boone Show.* Then I think came *Caesar's Hour.*

It's a little-known fact that you did not *write for* Your Show of Shows — *virtually every published reference states that you did.*

I did not. It's ridiculous — it's not fair to the original guys. I think the people who did do it were very unique, and it was a much smaller group. I hate to see them robbed of the distinctive quality of that credit.

You were undoubtedly familiar with Your Show of Shows *when you began writing for Sid Caesar.*

Well, I first saw Sid — as a lot of people did — in *Tars and Spars.* The movie. And of course *Your Show of Shows* was — it was a religious experience every week. You just went to the set and watched that.

In The Funny Men, *Steve Allen states, "Where others are at the mercy of their material, Sid Caesar seems to affect a supreme indifference to material. He is amusing no matter what he's doing or saying."*

That's not true. To take nothing away from Sid, but let's not give him something that's not his. I can appreciate the folly of that statement — of Steve's.

Caesar needed good material.

Oh, yeah. It's not so much a question of being "at the mercy of the material," it's a question of having the material at your service.

How much of what people saw was written and how much was Sid Caesar?

Oh, it was all written.

I've heard he was quite a genius at improv. And ad-lib.

Yes, he was. But there was no need to be. Sid would take advantage of moments. But I mean moments, I'm not talking about whole riffs or suddenly working without a net. Don't forget, these people were on live TV. On radio, Jackie Gleason would throw away the pages and just talk, and drag the other actors along with him, or inspire the other actors.

Was Gleason more often inspiring them or more often dragging them along?

Well, first it scared the shit out of them. He'd say during the commercial break — which would've been live too — "Listen, forget about the third act. We'll just wing it. Follow me." And they would. Gleason did that a lot. But Sid did not. Sid was not called upon to

Sid Caesar's garrulous Professor is interviewed by Carl Reiner's roving reporter.

improvise. He might improvise during the rehearsals of a routine, and that would get padded — and if something went wrong he would have to improvise to bridge, somebody going up [blank] in their lines — or taking advantage of a mistake. But there was not a lot of that.

Would Caesar have a tendency to ad-lib moreso during rehearsal than when he was on the air live?

I believe so, yeah. 'Cause there were other performers, there were all kinds of other things going on. You couldn't just go into business for yourself. And an actor has great comfort and security. The show was very well rehearsed, very well organized, and you can't get too far off, you can't jump the tracks.

Was Caesar easy to work with, or was he fairly demanding?

We were all demanding. We all wanted the best for him. For us. For the show. By the time I went to work for Sid, I had worked for a lot of comics, and if he was difficult I just took it in my stride. But I don't remember him as being difficult.

Could you briefly describe the process of writing a Caesar's Hour?

The work started on a Monday morning, the program having been done on Saturday evening. We'd sit down and say, "Well, what'll we do? We have an hour show." Mostly comedy — by and large. Comedy and variety, but even comedy in the variety. Sometimes. We would have odd things. We would have an actor; we'd have a concert pianist. Sid had a taste for some finer moments in the show, which I think he picked up from Max Liebman. And so we would think, we'll do a Hinkenlooper sketch — which was sort of a domestic comedy sketch — we'll do a movie takeoff, we'll do a pantomime, a rock 'n' roll thing like "The Haircuts," an interview with a jazz musician.

Pretty similar to what he had done on Your Show of Shows.

Oh, yeah. They were just a carry-over from that, absolutely. It was a continuation. He did what he did. It was just a question of now doing it under his own auspices.

And working with Nanette Fabray instead of Imogene Coca.

Exactly. And so we'd spend the next three days writing, and then by Thursday they were on their feet in a rehearsal room. Sid had a floor of a building on 57th Street which he rented, and which housed the whole production entity. There was the writer's room, there was the rehearsal hall, there were offices, various little cubbyholes. So he would go into rehearsal, and we would be available to make changes. We would then try to come up with ideas. Around Friday I guess we would see a rehearsal of the material we had written – make notes, make changes and so forth. Then Saturday it all went in front of the cameras, and we watched, made changes. There was a complete run-through a couple of hours before air time. We would make notes and give them to the cast. There might be some cutting necessary. And then they did it.

How many writers were working on the show?

There could be five, six, seven. Neil Simon, Mel Brooks, Mel Tolkin, Sheldon Keller, Michael Stewart. One year Selma Diamond was there. Sid, unlike a lot of comedians in those days, worked with the writers. He was in conference all the time; so was Carl Reiner. The way it worked is, we would all sit in a large room — two rooms actually — and Michael Stewart sat at the typewriter, and somehow did a very good job of putting down the stuff. Mel Tolkin was the head writer, but I take nothing away from him when I say it was a very democratic organization. There was no such thing as Mel saying, "That's in, that's out." It was all done by mutual agreement. But mostly Sid called the shots: "That's wonderful, that's good..."

So the various writers didn't pair off in teams?

We did that now and then. As I said, maybe in twos — write a sketch, come back, and sort of put that into the mosaic of the show. And someone else might be doing that too. But mostly just kind of gang-bang. It was really kind of organized chaos in a way. We were just all there together, punching away, from I think 11 o'clock till 6 every evening. I was determined that we didn't work beyond 6, but it didn't always work out that way. But there were no all-nighters. There were enough of us that we didn't all have to be good all the time. And it got done.

Lucille Kallen, who wrote for Your Show of Shows, *said "Coming up with an idea in that group was throwing a magnetized piece of a jigsaw puzzle into the middle of a room — all the other pieces would come racing toward it." Would that pertain to* Caesar's Hour?

That's right. That's very apropos. It did work that way. Very much so. Neil Simon's play, *Laughter on the 23rd Floor,* is remarkably accurate. He captures the mood. I was very impressed with his ability to get it down on paper.

Apparently the writing sessions were just frenetic. Mel Tolkin said, "We were too young to know it was impossible."

Yeah, exactly. We all were. On every show. You know something? They were probably more frenetic than I remember them. On the other hand, I have been in some pretty frenetic situations, so I just sort of took it in my stride.

For the record, Woody Allen did not work on Your Show of Shows *or* Caesar's Hour.

Woody actually worked on a Sid Caesar series on ABC, a half-hour series I believe it was. And I did not work with Woody when he was on that series. The first time Woody worked for Sid was — after *Caesar's Hour* went off the air — on two specials, for Chevrolet. I wrote one with Woody.

Did Caesar use much of Allen's material?

Woody would've worked in committee, in the room with the guys — I'm sure with everybody pitching, he got his share of stuff done. I don't think they did it any differently than we did it. Occasionally we would go off in ones or twos or threes and write a section of the show and bring it in. But then all the hands got laid on.

Among all the comedy writers you worked with or associated with in those days, are there any whose work you particularly admired?

Abe Burrows, certainly. He had an imagination that was uniquely his, and a manner of expressing it. Just a flair. It's like watching me swing a golf club and watching Jack Nicklaus do it. You just know — he's doing something pretty wonderful. Artie Stander was another guy who was very special, I think; a brilliant, funny guy. He had a fresh comedy mind. We often didn't — we weren't allowed to do whatever might have been our best. We did our best for Bob Hope, we did our best for Jack Carson — but as I said, that was really kind of writing for order.

Would you say you had a particular style in those days?

I had the style of whoever I worked for. If I wrote for Hope, I wrote Hope jokes. They took on that flavor.

Much of your work in film, theater and television has a kind of zany irreverence to it. Did that sort of develop along the way?

That probably came from admiring but not necessarily working for Groucho Marx — just by osmosis, as a member of the audience. Although I wrote the odd guest shot for him.

CREDITS

Radio: *Maxwell House Coffee Time, Duffy's Tavern, Command Performance, The Eddie Cantor Show, The Sealtest Village Store, The Jack Paar Show, The Jack Carson Show, The Bob Hope Show, Mastergate* (NPR).

TV: *Star-Spangled Revue, Chesterfield Sound Off Time, All Star Revue, The Colgate Comedy Hour, The Red Buttons Show; Honestly, Celeste!, The Patrice Munsel Show, The Pat Boone-Chevy Showroom, Caesar's Hour, The Chevy Show* (Sid Caesar special), *Hooray for Love* (Art Carney special), *The Danny Kaye Show* (developer and consultant), *The Marty Feldman Comedy Machine* (also producer), *M*A*S*H* (creator, also co-producer and occasional director), *Roll Out, Karen, Aftermash* (also supervisor), *United States* (creator, also executive producer), *V.I.P.* (special), *The Academy Awards* (1985-1986: also co-producer), *Mastergate* (TV movie), *Barbarians at the Gate* (TV movie), *Weapons of Mass Distraction* (TV movie; also executive producer).

Film: *The Notorious Landlady, The Thrill of it All, The Wrong Box* (also associate producer), *Not With My Wife, You Don't!, On My Way to the Crusades, I Met a Girl Who...* (aka *The Chastity Belt*), *A Fine Pair; Oh, God!, Movie Movie, Neighbors, Tootsie, Rough Cut*, Blame it On Rio* (also executive producer), *Bedazzled, Chicago.*

Theater: *The Conquering Hero, My L.A.* (revue), *Gulliver* (unproduced**), *A Funny Thing Happened on the Way to the Forum•, Jump, Sly Fox, One Two Three Four Five, City of Angels, Feats of Clay, Mastergate, Power Failure, Peter and the Wolf, A Star Is Born.*

* Gelbart used pseudonym of Francis Burns due to a dispute.
** Later used as the basis for a recording.
• Gelbart had no involvement in the film version of this show.

Russell Pratt (left) and Ransom Sherman perform surgery on a sick script.

Appendix

More Laugh Crafters

"Comedians, even the best ones, are often poor judges of material. They buy their comedy from known writers to make sure they aren't buying tragedy instead!"
— *David Freedman*

Ace, Goodman (1905-1974) was best known for radio's *Easy Aces*, in which he co-starred with his wife, Jane. The newspaperman-turned-comedy writer also wrote for Danny Kaye, Milton Berle, Tallulah Bankhead, Sid Caesar and Bob Newhart.

Adams, Stanley wrote for radio's *The Mel Blanc Show* and *My Friend Irma*.

Allen, Woody started by writing one-liners for Earl Wilson and other columnists, then provided material for radio comedians Peter Lind Hayes and Herb Shriner. His big break came in 1955 with TV's *Colgate Comedy Hour*, where he was mentored by head writer Danny Simon; Allen worked on a series and two specials for Sid Caesar, a short-lived Buddy Hackett sitcom and *The Garry Moore Show* before he began performing his own work.

Arnold, Bernard "Buddy" co-wrote the opening theme for *The Texaco Star Theater* ("We're the men of Texaco...") and scripted *The Red Buttons Show* with partner Woody Kling. He wrote special material for Ray Bolger and worked as a staff writer on *The Ed Sullivan Show*.

Atterberry, Duke wrote for radio's *Kraft Music Hall* and *The Bob Burns Show*. A longtime writer for Burns, he was a comedian himself; as half of a team he appeared on *Komedy Kapers, The Mirth Parade* and his own series, *The Two Daffodils*.

Baker, Herbie wrote special material for Danny Kaye, Lena Horne, Ethel Merman and Beatrice Lillie. He won an Emmy for *The Flip Wilson Show*.

Beloin, Edmund (1910-1992) co-wrote *The Jack Benny Show* (on which he was heard as Mr. Billingsly) and the comedian's films *Buck Benny Rides Again* and *Love Thy Neighbor*, with longtime partner Bill Morrow. He also wrote for Eddie Cantor's radio show and scripted several films for Bob Hope and Jerry Lewis.

Benoff, Mac wrote for such radio shows as *The Texaco Star Theater* with Ken Murray, *Duffy's Tavern, The Jack Paar Show, The Mel Blanc Show* and *Life With Luigi* (which he also directed). He wrote and starred in an unsold pilot, *The Adventures of a New York Taxi Driver*; he also co-scripted the Marx Brothers film *Love Happy.*

Bigelow, Joe wrote for Edgar Bergen and Milton Berle, and produced radio's *The Spike Jones Show.*

Boasberg, Al (1892-1937) contributed material to *The Ziegfeld Follies,* George White's *Scandals* and other revues. The legendary gag writer's clients included Buster Keaton, Burns and Allen, Wheeler and Woolsey, Eddie Cantor, Bob Hope and Jack Benny — who paid him $1,000 a week to polish his early radio scripts. Boasberg also dreamed up the famous "stateroom scene" in *A Night at the Opera* for the Marx Brothers.

Bogert, Vinnie wrote for such radio shows as *The Zany Family, Free For All Revue, The Singing Druggist, Laugh with Zeke Manners* and *Duffy's Tavern.* He later won an Emmy for his work on *The Phil Silvers Show* and also wrote for *The Garry Moore Show.*

Brooks, Matt wrote for *The Joe Penner Show* (on which he also performed) and *The Eddie Cantor Show.*

Brooks, Mel co-scripted the Broadway revue, *New Faces,* and wrote for several Sid Caesar TV series — *Admiral Broadway Revue, Your Show of Shows, Caesar's Hour* and *As Caesar Sees It* — before venturing into films.

Burrows, Abraham S. "Abe" (1910-1985) was head writer and co-creator of *Duffy's Tavern.* Other radio credits included *This Is New York, The Rudy Vallee Show, The Dinah Shore Show, The Eddie Cantor Show* and his own award-winning but short-lived program. He went on to write and direct such Broadway shows as *Guys and Dolls, Silk Stockings* and *How to Succeed in Business Without Really Trying,* for which he won a Pulitzer.

Carroll, Bob Jr. and longtime collaborator Madelyn Pugh Davis were CBS staff writers who co-scripted radio's *It's a Great Life* with Steve Allen and *My Favorite Husband* with Lucille Ball. They moved into TV with *I Love Lucy.* Carroll and Davis also worked on *The Lucy-Desi Comedy Hour, The Lucy Show* and *Here's Lucy.* They later wrote for *The Mothers-In-Law* and served as producers for TV's *Alice* series.

Carroll, Carroll (1902-1991) started out as a movie critic, before joining the radio department of the J. Walter Thompson advertising agency. The celebrated writer worked for Burns and Allen, Bob Crosby, Rudy Vallee, Guy Lombardo, Milton Berle, Joe Penner and *Kraft Music Hall* with Bing Crosby.

Chevillat, Dick wrote for radio's *The Rudy Vallee Show, The Phil Harris-Alice Faye Show* and *The Sealtest Village Store*. His film credits include *Neptune's Daughter.*

Collins, Hal wrote for Milton Berle for many years, notably on *The Texaco Star Theater*. Other TV credits include *The Red Buttons Show.*

Conn, Harry began his writing career by supplying gags to Burns and Allen. He served as Jack Benny's principal writer from 1932-1936, then sued the comedian for breach of contract. (Conn was best known for the line, "Jack Benny couldn't ad-lib a belch after a Hungarian dinner.") The tap dancer-turned-comedy writer went on to work for Eddie Cantor, Mae West and Al Jolson.

Davenport, Bill wrote for radio's *The Adventures of Ozzie and Harriet* and *A Day in the Life of Dennis Day* with partner Frank Fox.

Davis, Eddie wrote for *The Eddie Cantor Show, Log Cabin Jamboree* and *The Joe Penner Show* on radio.

Davis, Madelyn Pugh was one of the first female comedy writers, along with Selma Diamond. (See the entry on her longtime collaborator, Bob Carroll Jr., for credits).

Diamond, Selma (1920-1985) began her career by writing for Groucho Marx, and helped script such radio shows as *Duffy's Tavern, The Adventures of Ozzie and Harriet* and *The Big Show*. The writer-actress then wrote for TV's *Caesar's Hour, The Perry Como Show* and Como's *Kraft Music Hall* series; she performed on *The Jack Paar Show* and *Night Court*, among others. The character of Sally (played by Rose Marie) on *The Dick Van Dyke Show* was based on Diamond.

Dorfman, Sid wrote for *Maxwell House Coffee Time* before collaborating with Larry Gelbart on *Duffy's Tavern, The Eddie Cantor Show, The Jack Paar Show* and *The Sealtest Village Store*. Later TV credits include *M*A*S*H, Three's Company* and *Alice.*

Douglas, Jack (1908-1989) began his career as a drummer. His radio credits include *The Bob Hope Show* (Hope dubbed him the "mad dog" of his writing staff), *The Red Skelton Show, The Adventures of Ozzie and Harriet,*

The Jack Benny Show, The Durante-Moore Show, The Jack Carson Show and *The Martin and Lewis Show.* He continued writing for Skelton in TV, as well as Johnny Carson and *Rowan and Martin's Laugh-In.* He won an Emmy for his work on *The George Gobel Show* and authored several books, but is best remembered today for his guest appearances with Jack Paar.

Elinson, Irving "Izzy" and his brother, Jack, both began their careers writing for Walter Winchell. He wrote for radio's *The Eddie Cantor Show* and TV's *The Many Loves of Dobie Gillis.*

Elinson, Jack wrote for *Double or Nothing, The Eddie Cantor Show* and *The Durante- Moore Show* before moving into television. His TV credits include *All Star Revue, Make Room for Daddy, The Andy Griffith Show, The Real McCoys* and *The Facts of Life.*

Fimberg, Hal wrote for radio's *Log Cabin Jamboree, The Joe Penner Show* and *The Abbott and Costello Show.* He also produced *The Spotlight Revue* for Spike Jones.

Fine, Sylvia wrote special material for husband Danny Kaye's nightclub act, radio shows and films, including such trademark patter songs as "The Lobby Number" and "Anatole of Paris."

Fisher, Marvin wrote material for Bob Hope, Jack Oakie, Phil Harris and Jack Carson. He was also a songwriter.

Foster, Royal wrote for *The Chase and Sanborn Hour* with Edgar Bergen and Charlie McCarthy, and radio's *The Texaco Star Theater* with Ken Murray.

Fowler, Keith wrote for *Fibber McGee and Molly, Burns and Allen* and radio's *The Texaco Star Theater.* His TV credits include *The Addams Family.*

Fox, Frank wrote for radio's *The Adventures of Ozzie and Harriet, The Judy Canova Show* and *A Day in the Life of Dennis Day.* He later created TV's *My Little Margie.*

Frank, Melvin (1913-1988) was Norman Panama's longtime collaborator in radio and movies (see Panama chapter for joint credits). He wrote and directed several films after the team split up, notably *A Touch of Class,* which garnered Oscar nominations for Best Picture and Original Screenplay. Frank also directed *The Facts of Life* (co-written with Panama), *The Prisoner of Second Avenue* and *The Duchess and the Dirtwater Fox.*

Freedman, David (1898-1936) was the Rumanian-born son of a newspaperman who became the dean of radio and revue comedy writers in the 1930s. He created a virtual joke factory to satisfy his customers, who included Eddie Cantor, Fanny Brice, Fred Allen, Jack Benny, Bert Lahr and Willie Howard. ("He supplied material to five or six shows at a time, maybe the same jokes," noted Irving Brecher.) His play *Mendel, Inc.* was filmed as *Heart of New York* with Smith and Dale. At his peak Freedman brought a $250,000 suit against Cantor, his longtime client and friend, for breach of contract; the writer died tragically of a heart attack at 38, the day after the trial began in Supreme Court.

Freeman, Everett was co-creator of TV's *Bachelor Father*. Radio credits include *The Baby Snooks Show* and *The Eddie Cantor Show;* he also co-scripted films for W.C. Fields (*You Can't Cheat an Honest Man*), Bob Hope (*The Princess and the Pirate*), Danny Kaye and others.

Galen, Frank was the creator of radio and TV's *Meet Millie*. He began his career as Abe Burrows' collaborator on radio's *This Is New York, The Rudy Vallee Show* and *The Texaco Star Theater*. Galen also wrote for *Burns and Allen* and *A Day in the Life of Dennis Day,* and provided material for Henny Youngman.

Gershman, Ben wrote for radio's *The Adventures of Ozzie and Harriet*. His TV credits included *The Many Loves of Dobie Gillis, The Andy Griffith Show, Here's Lucy, The Addams Family, The Brady Bunch* and *Diff'rent Strokes*.

Glickman, Will got his start in radio as an assistant to Billy K. Wells. He wrote for Abbott and Costello (on *The Kate Smith Hour*), *Gang Busters* and *The Alan Young Show,* collaborating with Joe Stein on radio's *The Ethel Merman Show* and TV's *The Red Buttons Show*. He also wrote for *U.S. Steel Hour* and *The Keefe Brasselle Show*.

Goldman, Hal wrote for Armed Forces Radio and Jimmy Durante's radio show. Goldman won three Emmies with longtime partner Al Gordon; two for *The Jack Benny Show,* and a third for *An Evening with Carol Channing*. He wrote for George Burns for 17 years, until the comedian's death.

Gosch, Martin was Abbott and Costello's longtime radio producer and writer. He also produced radio's *Melody and Madness* and with Howard Harris co-wrote *The Amazing Mr. Smith*.

Harris, Howard wrote for *The Abbott and Costello Show* and *The Amazing Mr. Smith*. With partner Syd Zelinka he worked on radio's *Dinah Shore's Open House* and TV's *The Honeymooners;* he later wrote for *Here's Lucy*.

Hiken, Nat (1914-1968) created and produced *The Phil Silvers Show* (originally titled *You'll Never Get Rich;* syndicated as *Sgt. Bilko*), which won him three Emmy Awards. A legend among his fellow comedy writers, Hiken cut his teeth in radio on *The Grouch Club, The Fred Allen Show, The Texaco Star Theater* with Milton Berle and *The Magnificent Montague* with Monty Woolley. He also created TV's *Car 54, Where Are You?*

Jacobs, Seaman "Si" wrote for radio's *Jack Paar Show*. TV credits include numerous specials for George Burns and Bob Hope, *The Ed Wynn Show, Here's Lucy, The Addams Family* and *The Jeffersons*.

Josefsberg, Milt (1911-1987) began his career supplying gags to newspaper columnists. Josefsberg was a longtime member of Jack Benny's writing staff on radio and TV; he also worked for Bob Hope, Milton Berle, Lucille Ball (*Here's Lucy*) and Danny Thomas. He later served as writer, producer and script supervisor on *All in the Family*, for which he won an Emmy.

Kallen, Lucille collaborated with Mel Tolkin on TV's *Your Show of Shows* and its predecessor, *Admiral Broadway Revue*. She also wrote for *U.S. Steel Hour*.

Keller, Sheldon wrote for *Caesar's Hour, An Evening with Carol Channing, The Spike Jones Show, The Steve Allen Comedy Hour, The Bing Crosby Show, Ensign O'Toole* and other TV programs.

Kling, Heywood "Woody" wrote for *The Texaco Star Theater* with Milton Berle, *The Red Buttons Show* and *The Carol Burnett Show*, for which he won two Emmies. He served as executive producer on *All in the Family*.

Klinker, Zeno was a longtime writer for Edgar Bergen and provided the namesake for the ventriloquist's female dummy, Effie Klinker.

Knight ,Vick (1908-1984) made his radio debut as a singer in 1935. He wrote for Willie Howard, *Stoopnagle and Budd, Columbia Workshop* and other programs, and adapted over two dozen Broadway plays for radio. He became better known for his work as a producer-director on *The Eddie Cantor Show, The Fred Allen Show, The Kate Smith A&P Bandwagon* and *Command Performance*. Knight wrote additional dialogue for *It Happened On Fifth Avenue* and other films; he was also a prolific composer.

Lear, Norman collaborated with Ed Simmons on *The Martin and Lewis Show* for radio and the teams' appearances on NBC TV's *The Colgate Comedy Hour;* they also scripted *Four Star Revue* for Danny Thomas and *The Martha Raye Show.* Lear wrote for George Gobel before turning producer.

Lewis, Al wrote for *The Fred Allen Show, The Rudy Vallee Show,* Milton Berle's *Gillette Original Community Sing,* Bob Hope's *Rippling Rhythm Revue, Stoopnagle and Budd* and *Command Performance* on radio; he later wrote and directed *Our Miss Brooks.* (Lewis is not to be confused with the TV character actor of the same name).

Lipscott, Alan (1898-1961) began writing for radio in 1933. He provided material for Ben Bernie, Bert Lahr (*Manhattan Merry-Go-Round*), Willie and Eugene Howard (*Folies de Paris*), Milton Berle (*Royal Gelatin Hour*), *The Eddie Cantor Show* and *The Life of Riley.* Lipscott frequently collaborated with Parke Levy on Broadway shows (see the chapter on Levy for joint credits).

Manhoff, Bill worked on *Duffy's Tavern, The Adventures of Ozzie and Harriet* and *Meet Millie* for radio. He later wrote the stage revue *My L.A.* (with Larry Gelbart) and the play, *The Owl and the Pussycat.*

Mannheim, Manny wrote for such radio programs as *Kraft Music Hall* with Bing Crosby and *The Rudy Vallee Show;* he also wrote and produced *Sweeney and March* and directed *The Andrews Sisters Eight-to-the-Bar Ranch.*

Marks, Laurence "Fat Larry" wrote for *Duffy's Tavern, The Fred Allen Show, The Jack Carson Show* and *The Jack Paar Show,* all on radio. He was partnered with Larry Gelbart on *The Bob Hope Show* and later wrote for *M*A*S*H.*

Medbury, John P (1893?-1947) was a syndicated humor columnist before he contributed to Burns and Allen's vaudeville act and radio show; he wrote additional dialogue for the team's films, including *Here Comes Cookie* and *Love in Bloom.* His radio credits included *The Adventures of Ozzie and Harriet, Amos 'n' Andy* and *Captain Flagg and Sergeant Quirt.* Medbury wrote dialogue for Columbia short subjects, *Hold 'Em Jail* with Wheeler and Woolsey, *Country Gentlemen* with Olsen and Johnson and other films; he also wrote and narrated travelogues.

Morrow, Bill (1907-1971) began writing for radio circa 1929. He collaborated with Ed Beloin on Jack Benny's radio show and feature films. The one-time cartoonist also wrote for W.C. Fields and worked on Armed Forces Radio programs like *Command Performance;* he enjoyed a lengthy association with Bing Crosby on the singer's radio and TV shows.

Oppenheimer, Jess (1913-1988) is best known for creating *I Love Lucy.* The prolific writer-producer began his career in radio scripting *The Packard Hour* with Fred Astaire. He also wrote for Jack Benny, Edgar Bergen and Fanny Brice before becoming head writer and producer for radio's *My Favorite Husband* with Lucille Ball. Following his five-year tenure with *I Love Lucy,* he created *Glynis* and *The Debbie Reynolds Show* for TV.

Packard, Elon wrote for radio's *Kraft Music Hall* with Bing Crosby and *Three Ring Time* with Milton Berle. His TV credits include *The Roy Rogers & Dale Evans Show.*

Perrin, Sam (1902-1998) began in vaudeville as a drummer. The venerated comedy writer scripted such radio programs as *Show Boat, Maxwell House Coffee Time, The Texaco Star Theater, The Screen Guild Theater* and *The Phil Baker Show* early in his career. He collaborated with Arthur Phillips before teaming with George Balzer on *Burns and Allen* and *The Jack Benny Show* (see the chapter on Balzer for additional joint credits). Perrin won two Emmies for his work on Benny's TV program; his other credits include the film *The Goldwyn Follies.*

Pierson, Buddy wrote for *The Eddie Cantor Show* and Tim and Irene Ryan *(The Royal Crown Revue).*

Quillan, Joe wrote for *The Eddie Cantor Show* and *Our Miss Brooks.*

Quinn, Don (1900-1967) was an unemployed cartoonist and gag writer when he began his long association with Jim and Marian Jordan in 1931 on *Smackout.* He went on to create *Fibber McGee and Molly* for them, and became the highest paid writer in radio at the show's peak. Quinn quit the show to create *The Halls of Ivy* for Ronald Colman, which won him a Peabody Medal. He also wrote for *Olsen and Johnson's Swift Revue* in the early '30s and created two *Fibber* spin-offs, *The Great Gildersleeve* and *The Beulah Show.*

Rapp, John wrote for Rudy Vallee's *Royal Gelatin Hour, The Eddie Cantor Show* and *Jack Oakie's College* on radio. He later worked on several of Bob Hope's TV specials.

Rapp, Phil (1907-1996) scripted Eddie Cantor's first radio show and *The Baby Snooks Show* for Fanny Brice, but he was best known for creating *The Bickersons*, immortalized by Don Ameche and Frances Langford. ("Phil Rapp was, to me, a genius," said Langford. "I would pick up the script, and I'd say, 'I swear you've been listening at my bedroom door.' He said, 'No, all I have to do is do something that my wife doesn't like, and I get *two* scripts.' ") Rapp wrote several films for Danny Kaye, including *The Inspector General*. He also adapted *Topper* for television and supplied material to George Burns.

Rhine, Larry began his career as an announcer, and went on to write for singer-comedian Frank Crumit, Rube Goldberg, Ben Bernie and radio's *Duffy's Tavern*. His TV credits include *Here's Lucy, The Red Skelton Show, All in the Family* and *Love, Sidney*.

Schwartz, Al (1911-1989) wrote jokes for Walter Winchell's column and Milton Berle's vaudeville act before completing law school — then joined *The Bob Hope Show* in its first season on radio. He wrote for *The Eddie Cantor Show* and *The Kate Smith A&P Bandwagon* before working with younger brother Sherwood Schwartz on various radio and TV shows (see the chapter on Schwartz for joint credits); he subsequently provided scripts for *Here's Lucy* and *The Brady Bunch*.

Shavelson, Melville worked on Bob Hope's radio show and later wrote the screenplays for several of the comedian's films, including *The Seven Little Foys* and *Beau James* (both of which he directed). He also created the Danny Thomas TV series, *Make Room for Daddy*.

Simmons, Ed was Norman Lear's writing partner in the early days of television (see the entry on Lear for joint credits). Simmons directed radio's *Quiz Kids* and served as a front for other writers during the black-list; he later co-wrote and produced *The Carol Burnett Show*, for which he won five Emmies, and worked on *The Red Skelton Show*.

Simon, Danny collaborated with brother Neil on the radio version of *The Texaco Star Theater* with Milton Berle and TV's *The Red Buttons Show*. Other television credits include *The Colgate Comedy Hour, Kraft Music Hall* and *Diff'rent Strokes*.

Simon, Neil wrote for Milton Berle, Sid Caesar (*Your Show of Shows, Caesar's Hour*), Phil Silvers (*Sgt. Bilko*), Jackie Gleason, Jerry Lewis, Red Buttons and Garry Moore before concentrating on the theater.

Singer, Ray wrote for radio's *Three Ring Time* with Milton Berle, *The Fitch Bandwagon* and *The Rudy Vallee Show*. His TV credits include *The Donna Reed Show, The Danny Thomas Show* and *The Lucy Show*.

Snyder, Howard (1909-1963) scripted *The Eddie Cantor Show, The Jack Benny Show, Show Boat* and *Lum and Abner* in collaboration with his partner, Hugh Wedlock Jr. They also provided special material for Ben Bernie, Bert Wheeler and Jack Haley; their film credits included *George White's Scandals, It Happened Tomorrow* and *Abbott and Costello Meet the Killer, Boris Karloff*.

Solomon, Leo wrote for TV's *The Alan Young Show* and *The Andy Griffith Show*.

Stander, Arthur "Artie" wrote for radio's *Amos 'n' Andy, The Baby Snooks Show, Life With Luigi, The Jack Paar Show* and *The Sad Sack*. His TV credits included *I Married Joan* and *The Andy Griffith Show*.

Stein, Joe scripted *The Ethel Merman Show* and *The Henry Morgan Show* for radio, and TV's *The Red Buttons Show*, before finding success as a playwright with the book for *Fiddler on the Roof*.

Stewart, Michael worked on *Caesar's Hour* before he wrote the book for such Broadway musicals as *Bye Bye Birdie* and *Hello, Dolly!*

Stillwell, Edna wrote much of husband Red Skelton's vaudeville and radio material in the '30s and '40s, including the celebrated donut-dunking routine. The comedian later denied her influence after they divorced.

Sullivan, Norman wrote for Bob Hope for decades in radio and TV, and acted as a consultant on several of the comedian's television specials.

Tackaberry, John "Tack" was Milt Josefsberg's longtime collaborator on *The Jack Benny Show*, often writing for Eddie "Rochester" Anderson. He wrote special material for Horace Heidt early in his career, but was a relative novice when hired by Benny.

Tolkin, Mel wrote for TV's *Admiral Broadway Revue* and the programs that grew out of it, *Your Show of Shows* and *Caesar's Hour*. He also wrote for Danny Kaye, Bob Hope and Spike Jones; later TV credits include *All in the Family, Diff'rent Strokes* and *Gimme a Break*.

Tugend, Harry (1898?-1989) got his start in vaudeville as a singer-actor, and wrote many sketches for *The Ziegfeld Follies*. He co-wrote and directed Fred Allen's radio show in the '30s and wrote a number of films for Shirley Temple, including *Poor Little Rich Girl*. Later screenwriting credits include *Caught in the Draft*, *A Song is Born* and *Take Me Out to the Ballgame*. He also produced films (*Road to Bali*) and TV series (*General Electric Theater*), and was one of the founding members of the Screen Writers Guild.

Wedlock, Hugh Jr. (1908-1993) was Howard Snyder's longtime collaborator (see the entry on Snyder for their joint credits). Wedlock wrote TV material for Sid Caesar, Edgar Bergen and Red Skelton, and won an Emmy for *Rowan and Martin's Laugh-In*.

Wells, Billy K. (1883-1956) began his career as an actor, appearing in minstrel shows. He was best known for creating the character of Baron von Münchhausen, which he originally conceived as "a lazy blackface teller of tales" and reworked for Jack Pearl at the behest of an ad agency (based on the tales of the 18th century German soldier-raconteur). Wells was working as a monologist in burlesque when he discovered Bert Lahr and launched him on the road to stardom; he also wrote for Weber and Fields, Lou Holtz, Willie and Eugene Howard, Clark and McCullough, and Jack Benny. His credits included 12 editions of George White's *Scandals*, in addition to books for Broadway musicals and dialogue for movies (*The Cock-Eyed World*), radio shows (*Amos 'n' Andy*) and television sketches.

Wouk, Herman wrote for *The Fred Allen Show* for five years before authoring novels like *The Caine Mutiny* and *The Winds of War*.

Zelinka, Syd collaborated with Howard Harris on *The Honeymooners*. He also worked on *The Rudy Vallee Show* and *Dinah Shore's Open House* on radio, and TV's *Keefe Brasselle Show*.

This list includes only the writers mentioned in this book, representing but a few of the unknown soldiers who did battle in radio and early television.

Notes

PARKE LEVY
Levy was interviewed Apr. 4, 1992; May 27, 1992; and Jul. 28, 1992.

3   *Jack Pearl:* The burlesque comic-turned-vaudevillian (1895-1982) introduced the Baron — who told tall tales of wild exploits in a thick German-Yiddish dialect — on radio's *Ziegfeld Follies of the Air.* His own show debuted on September 8, 1932.

5   *Dennis Day:* The singer starred in *The RCA Victor Show* (aka *The Dennis Day Show*) for NBC TV for two seasons, 1952-54.

5   *Joe Penner:* The Hungarian-born comedian (1904-1941) was a one-time female impersonator who made his radio debut on *The Rudy Vallee Show.* Penner's own show, also known as *The Baker's Broadcast,* debuted on CBS October 8, 1933.

8   *Ben Bernie:* The bandleader (1891-1943) made his network debut on CBS in 1931. Bernie's famous "feud" with Broadway columnist Walter Winchell resulted in much publicity for the show.

13   *Ed Gardner:* The co-creator and star (1901-1963) of *Duffy's Tavern* was a theatrical jack-of-all-trades before he joined J. Walter Thompson advertising agency and directed *The Rudy Vallee Show, Kraft Music Hall, Burns and Allen* and *Good News of 1938.* Radio historian John Dunning called him "one of the great maligners of the King's English."

13   *This is New York:* A short-lived sustaining (unsponsored) show that aired on CBS in 1939. Gardner's Archie was then heard on the audition series, *Forecast,* in mid-1940; *Duffy's Tavern* became part of the regular CBS schedule March 1, 1941.

16   *My Friend Irma:* The popular series starred Marie Wilson as Irma, and premiered on CBS in 1947. Cy Howard created *Life with Luigi* the following year.

16   *The guy that created:* Ruth McKenney wrote the book that served as the basis for the stage and film versions of *My Sister Eileen* and the Broadway musical *Wonderful Town.*

17   *Harry Ackerman:* The producer known as "Sire of the Sitcom" joined CBS in 1948, where he oversaw the development of *Studio One, Suspense, I Love Lucy, Gunsmoke* and other programs at the network.

19   *December Bride:* This series began on radio, making its debut June 8, 1952. It made its way to TV in 1954, with Spring Byington reprising her role as Lily Ruskin.

19   *Harry Morgan:* The actor inherited Hans Conried's role, Pete Porter, when the show moved from radio to TV. Morgan got his own show when Levy created the spin-off, *Pete and Gladys,* in 1960.

PAUL HENNING
Henning was interviewed May 15, 1991.

22   *when she ran for President:* Gracie Allen campaigned for office in 1940 and again in 1944. (*How to Become President,* a joke book bearing her byline, was ghosted by several writers and press agents.)

23   *Gene Austin:* The singer was renowned for his 1927 rendition of "My Blue Heaven," perhaps the best-selling record of its era.

25   *Hugh Studebaker:* The actor, who worked with the Hennings on *Happy Hollow,* was heard regularly on such Chicago-based soap operas as *The Romance of Helen Trent* and *The Guiding Light.*

25   *Fibber McGee and Molly:* The popular comedy series premiered April 16, 1935, starring Jim and Marian Jordan.

29   *The Joe E. Brown Show:* This 1938-39 CBS series starred the broad-mouthed stage and film clown as a frustrated talent agent.

29   *I had never even heard of a file:* "The producer said, 'You call yourself a comedy writer and you don't have a joke file?'" Henning later recalled. "Writing in those days was a matter of wrestling with a filing cabinet. I have to lock myself up in a room with a typewriter. I haven't had a file to this day." (*TV Guide,* April 24, 1971).

30   *The Rudy Vallee Show:* The singer's half-hour NBC series — which made its debut March 7, 1940 — was a "striking departure" from his long-running *Fleishmann Yeast Hour.*

32   *John Barrymore:* The actor died during the run of the show in 1942. Two episodes from this tragicomic last act of Barrymore's career, including one with John and Lionel reading scenes from *Richard III,* have been released on compact disc.

34 *George Burns and Gracie Allen:* The comedians enjoyed an 18-year run on radio beginning February 15, 1932 on *The Guy Lombardo Show,* on which they shared airtime with the bandleader. (The official title of their show varied largely according to the sponsor.)

34 *He absolutely left the writing of the radio show:* Carroll Carroll asserted that Burns "was numero uno in thinking up what Gracie would say, *should* say and could *not* say" in his autobiography, *None of Your Business.*

37 *Bea Benaderet:* In addition to her radio and TV role as Gracie Allen's neighbor, Blanche Morton, the popular character actress (1906-1968) was heard as telephone operator Gertrude Gearshift on Jack Benny's radio show, and the original voice of Betty Rubble on TV's *The Flintstones.*

37 *Hans Conried:* One of the busiest character actors in radio, Conried was heard regularly on *My Friend Irma* (as Professor Kropotkin), *The Mercury Theatre on the Air, Escape, The Whistler* and other shows. He was seen as Uncle Tonoose on TV's *The Danny Thomas Show.*

39 *George would let off steam to Willy:* Burns paid appreciative tribute to his youngest brother in *Living It Up, or They Still Love Me in Altoona* (Putnam's, 1976). "Besides contributing to the scripts, Willy also handled all my business activities..." he noted. "To sum it up, Willy ran interference for me so I didn't have to worry about anything except writing and performing." Burns also acknowledged using Willy as a scapegoat.

40 *Ralph Levy:* The Yale graduate began his apprenticeship in network television with CBS in 1946 and soon became the most sought-after director in the new medium. Veterans Ed Wynn and Jack Benny entrusted their reputations to him, despite his youth; he also directed the pilot of *I Love Lucy.* A decade after Levy guided Burns and Allen to TV, Henning hired him to direct the pilots of *The Beverly Hillbillies* and *Green Acres.*

42 *Elvia Allman:* The veteran character actress was featured on radio as Cobina on *The Bob Hope Show* and Miss Rhoda Dendron on *Fibber McGee and Molly.* She appeared in both the radio and TV versions of *Blondie* and *Burns and Allen,* and was also seen on *I Love Lucy.*

CHARLES ISAACS

Isaacs was interviewed Feb. 22, 1993; and Feb. 19, 1995.

46   *Pat Weaver:* The brother of Doodles Weaver — and the father of actress Sigourney Weaver — went on to create television's *The Today Show* and *The Tonight Show,* and became president of NBC. Isaacs produced a number of Weaver's *Wide, Wide World* TV specials.

47   *Alan Reed:* The actor (1907-1977) best remembered as Falstaff Openshaw on *The Fred Allen Show* became the voice of Fred Flintstone on TV. He made his radio debut in 1929 and was featured on such shows as *The Baby Snooks Show, Life with Luigi* and *Duffy's Tavern;* he played the title role on *Joe Palooka.*

47   *Leon Schlesinger:* The producer of Merrie Melodies and Looney Tunes cartoons for Warner Bros.

48   *The Jack Haley Show:* Debuted Oct. 8, 1937 on NBC, two years before Haley portrayed the Tin Man in *The Wizard of Oz.*

48   *Al Pearce and His Gang:* The show debuted as *The Happy Go Lucky Hour* in 1929. Comstock (Lish) worked as a drummer in vaudeville before joining the cast.

49   *Al Jolson-Oscar Levant Kraft Music Hall:* This edition of the NBC variety show aired from 1947 to 1949. Jolson first hosted the program in 1933-34, prior to Bing Crosby's tenure; Levant was heard on *Information Please* a decade before the *Kraft* show.

49   *The Chase and Sanborn Hour:* Edgar Bergen's appearance on Rudy Vallee's show in 1936 proved an unexpected hit, despite the absurdity of a ventriloquist act on radio. Edgar and Charlie got their own program May 9, 1937 on NBC.

50   *Mae West:* The salacious "Adam and Eve" sketch — in which West conversed with a "palpitatin' python" in the Garden of Eden — resulted in over 1,000 letters of protest, FCC reprisals and a 15-year network ban against West. The sketch was written by Arch Oboler, best known for the horror anthology *Lights Out.*

53   *Jerry Lester:* A nightclub comic, later prominent in early television (*Broadway Open House*).

53   *Fleischmann Yeast Hour:* The NBC program premiered in 1929 and became "the most important show on the air in the early to mid-1930s," according to radio historian John Dunning. It was known as *The Royal Gelatin Hour* in the late '30s, when Isaacs apparently contributed to it.

53   *Sid Fields*: The actor who played the landlord on *The Abbott and Costello Show* was also a regular on CBS TV's *The Frank Sinatra Show* and *The Jackie Gleason Show*.

54   *Jimmy Saphier*: Also producer of radio's *The Saint* with Vincent Price.

54   *Bing Crosby Kraft Music Hall*: Crosby emceed the popular NBC variety show from 1935 to 1946.

55   *Three Ring Time*: This comedy-variety series premiered on Mutual in 1941 and moved to the Blue Network after Charles Laughton jumped ship. Milton Berle had several unsuccessful radio shows between 1936 and 1949.

57   *Herb Shriner*: A homespun humorist in the vein of Will Rogers, he headlined the 1942 CBS edition of *The Camel Caravan*.

58   *Elliott Lewis*: One of the busiest actors in radio (1917-1990) was also a prolific writer, producer and director. Lewis was identified with such shows as *Suspense, Broadway's My Beat, On Stage, Big Town* and *Crime Classics*; he also produced CBS TV's *Climax*.

58   *Doris Singleton*: Heard as Miss Duffy on *Duffy's Tavern*. Other radio credits include *Burns and Allen, December Bride* and *The Alan Young Show*.

58   *Command Performance*: The show debuted in 1942, sponsored by the Special Services Division of the War Department; the following year it was transferred to the newly created AFRS and moved from New York to Hollywood.

58   *Amos 'n' Andy*: The broadcasting phenomenon aired from 1928-1955 on radio, changing format several times during its run.

59   *I probably killed the show*: Fanny Brice's character got her own half-hour series in 1944. Contrary to Isaac's assertion, *The Baby Snooks Show* aired on NBC until 1948, then switched to CBS; it ran until Brice's death in 1951.

59   *Spike Jones*: The unsuccessful pilot consisted of three "audition shows." The bandleader had more success with *The Spotlight Revue*, which debuted in 1947 on CBS.

60   *Billie Burke*: Best known for her role in *The Wizard of Oz* as Glinda, the Good Witch of the North.

62   *John Guedel:* A one-time writer for Hal Roach Studios, he produced
      People Are Funny and *House Party* with Art Linkletter before creating
      You Bet Your Life in 1947.

64   *Bob "Bazooka" Burns:* The star of *The Arkansas Traveler*, a humorist
      whose name was synonymous with the instrument he crafted from a
      whiskey funnel and a gas pipe.

64   *Dean Martin and Jerry Lewis:* The team's radio show premiered Apr. 3,
      1949 on NBC.

67   *Jeff Chandler:* Best known for his roles as Mr. Boynton on radio's *Our
      Miss Brooks*, and Cochise in the movie *Broken Arrow*.

69   *Jimmy Durante:* The comedian appeared as an alternating host on
      TV's *All Star Revue* and *The Colgate Comedy Hour* for four years
      before he got his own television show in 1954.

69   *Joe Santley:* A prominent child actor, Santley co-directed the Marx
      Brothers' 1929 film debut, *The Cocoanuts;* he was among the first film
      directors to work in television.

7?   *Red Skelton:* The comedian's radio show (*The Raleigh Cigarette
      Program*) aired from 1941-1953, introducing many of his familiar
      characterizations; his TV show enjoyed a 20-year run from 1951-1971.

      IRVING BRECHER
      Brecher was interviewed January 29, 1992.

75   *sole credit on a Marx Brothers film:* Harpo and Buster Keaton con-
      tributed visual gags to both *At the Circus* and *Go West*. According to
      author Joe Adamson, Harry Ruby and Bert Kalmar wrote a screen-
      play for *Go West*, which was replaced by a new Irving Brecher-Dore
      Schary script — which was in turn discarded in favor of a third
      script by Brecher. Groucho and Nat Perrin contributed to *Go West*
      during live appearance road tryouts of the script.

80   *Willie Howard:* The comedian (1886-1949) was a mainstay of
      Broadway revues and musicals for four decades, notably Shubert's
      The Passing Show and George White's *Scandals*, with brother Eugene
      (1881-1965) generally acting as his straightman.

81   *I was the only writer:* "I was writing it by myself... I didn't realize that
      was impossible," Brecher recalled. "When you're young, nothing's
      impossible."

82   *Bert Gordon:* The dialect comic (1895-1974), who first gained notice in George White's *Scandals,* made the Mad Russian ("How dooo you dooo?") one of radio's most memorable second bananas. In addition to the Cantor and Berle shows, Gordon appeared on *Duffy's Tavern* and was seen in several films.

84   *Frank Morgan:* The veteran character actor began his career in silent films, eventually becoming a familiar face in supporting roles at MGM. In addition to his memorable turn in *The Wizard of Oz,* he was seen in such films *as Naughty Marietta, The Great Ziegfeld, Tortilla Flat* and *The Human Comedy.*

84   *Fanny Brice... as Baby Snooks:* "Everybody said that I originated the character, but I didn't really, because it came out of her mouth. Fanny started talking like a baby when I handed her a script," recalled Phil Rapp. "Word went out that I invented the name Snooks. I didn't. I must have seen it somewhere; I guess it was in some literary piece." (Interview with the author, Jan. 9, 1992).

86   *that happened with two films:* Brecher turned down the assignment for the Marx Brothers' next picture, *The Big Store.*

87   *William Bendix:* Best known for his role as Riley, the actor enjoyed a busy movie career. Among his films were *The Blue Dahlia, The Hairy Ape, The Babe Ruth Story* and *Wake Island,* which brought him an Oscar nomination.

87   *it had been used on other vehicles:* Lionel Stander played J. Riley Farnsworth in a earlier CBS series called *The Life of Riley.*

89   *John Brown:* The English-born actor's characterization of Digger was so popular that Brown (1904-1957) played the role in the radio, film and TV versions of *The Life of Riley.* He was also heard regularly on such radio shows as *The Adventures of Ozzie and Harriet, The Fred Allen Show* and *The Saint.*

91   *Phil Rapp sued Gleason:* "We closed the show for a while and Gleason picked it right up, using my scripts," asserted Rapp. "Right in the same theater, on the same stage. There were *Bickersons* scripts lying everywhere. As soon as I left New York — bingo, he went right into it. I had to sue to stop him. But I later became friendly with him." (Interview with the author).

NORMAN PANAMA
Panama was interviewed October 9, 1991.

94   *Bob Hope: The Pepsodent Show* was first heard Sept. 28, 1938 on NBC.
      "I hired eight of the best comedy minds I could find and generously
      paid them whatever I could get away with," Hope recalled in his
      book, *Don't Shoot, It's Only Me.*

95   *The Glass Bed:* written in collaboration with comedy writer Albert E.
      Lewin; published by Morrow.

96   *his first radio show:* According to John Dunning, Hope actually had
      four short-lived programs prior to *The Pepsodent Show*, beginning in
      1935 with *The Intimate Revue.*

103   *Phil Baker:* The comedian (1896-1963) teamed with Ben Bernie early
      in his career in a violin-accordion act "which started as a serious per-
      formance and gradually developed into a comedy routine," accord-
      ing to historian Anthony Slide. *The Phil Baker Show* began in 1933;
      Panama and Frank wrote for the Dole Pineapple-sponsored edition
      of the show, *Honolulu Bound,* in 1939.

      SHERWOOD SCHWARTZ
      Schwartz was interviewed Sept. 26, 1991.

113   *Norman Corwin:* The preeminent writer of radio's heyday, best
      known for such dramas as *On a Note of Triumph, We Hold These Truths*
      and *The Plot to Overthrow Christmas.*

117   *Jack Benny had two writers originally:* Al Boasberg and Harry Conn.

124   *Jerry Colonna:* The pop-eyed comedian with the walrus moustache
      played trombone for Hal Kemp and other big bands before lending
      his talents to *The Bob Hope Show.* He appeared in several of the *Road*
      movies and was a regular on Hope's overseas trips to entertain the
      troops.

126   *Jerome Lawrence and Robert E. Lee:* Radio paid the bills for years before
      they wrote successful plays like *Inherit the Wind* and *Auntie Mame.*

127   *Jubilee*: This show, a morale booster for black service personnel host-
      ed by Ernie "Bubbles" Whitman, debuted in 1942.

131   *Ozzie and Harriet:* The long-running sitcom premiered Oct. 8, 1944, a
      decade after the couple made their radio debut on *The Baker's
      Broadcast* with Joe Penner.

133   *The Alan Young Show:* This edition of the sitcom aired on NBC in 1946-1947. The British-born comic is best known for the 1961-1965 TV series *Mr. Ed.*

133   *Wally Cox:* Bespectacled comedian best known as TV's *Mr. Peepers* and the voice of cartoon superhero Underdog.

133   *Jim Backus:* The actor, to his dismay, was best known as the voice of the nearsighted cartoon character, Mr. Magoo. Early in his career, he appeared uncredited on such radio programs as *The Danny Kaye Show.*

135   *The Beulah Show:* This 15-minute version of the show aired on CBS from 1947-1953. The sitcom was also a television series on ABC from 1950-1953.

135   *Hattie McDaniel:* The actress also appeared regularly on radio's *Show Boat* and *The Eddie Cantor Show.*

135   *Marlin Hurt:* The actor — who once sang with Vincent Lopez's band — originated the character on *Fibber McGee and Molly.* Beulah was later played on radio by Bob Corley, Louise Beavers and Lillian Randolph, in addition to Hattie McDaniel; Beavers and Ethel Waters essayed the role on TV.

138   *I Married Joan:* The series aired on NBC TV from 1952 to 1955.

BOB WEISKOPF
Weiskopf was interviewed February 4, 1992.

141   *A lot of shows originated from Chicago:* The Windy City was the hub of radio prior to World War II. Among the comedy shows based in Chicago were *Amos 'n' Andy, Fibber McGee and Molly* and *Vic and Sade.*

142   *Eddie Cantor:* The comedian's top-rated radio show began in 1931; though he changed time slots, sponsors and formats several times, Cantor lasted nearly two decades on the air.

147   *Joan Davis:* The star (1890-1958) of TV's *I Married Joan,* who began her career in vaudeville, played a supporting role on Vallee's program before inheriting the show from him in 1943. Davis headlined *The Sealtest Village Store* and other radio series, paving the way for Lucille Ball with her broad slapstick.

147   *Fred Allen:* The vaudevillian made his radio bow with CBS' *The Linit Bath Club Revue,* October 23, 1932. His program ran for 17 years under various sponsors.

148   *Portland Hoffa:* The actress was a chorus girl when she first met Allen in *The Passing Show of 1922.*

151   *relocation camp* : Between 1942 and 1945, the U.S. Government — fueled by wartime hysteria — uprooted over 110,000 Japanese-Americans from Western states and herded them into detention camps in desolate areas.

153   *Charlie Cantor:* The veteran character actor (1898-1966) provided the voice of Clifton Finnegan on *Duffy's Tavern* and Socrates Mulligan on *The Fred Allen Show.* He was also heard on such radio shows as *The Life of Riley, Flash Gordon, Dick Tracy* and *Terry and the Pirates,* and seen on TV's *The Ray Bolger Show.*

154   *Minerva Pious:* The dialect comedienne (1903-1979) made her radio debut with Fred Allen on *The Linit Bath Club Revue,* and remained with his show for 16 years. Other radio appearances include *Columbia Workshop, Columbia Presents Corwin, The Henry Morgan Show* and *The Kate Smith Hour.* Pious replaced Fanny Brice in the 1936 edition of *The Ziegfeld Follies,* and also appeared in films.

155   *Kenny Delmar:* The actor (1910-1984) best known for playing Senator Beauregard Claghorn ("That's a joke, son!") began his career in vaudeville at age 8. He was also heard on radio as Commissioner Weston on *The Shadow,* and such shows as *The March of Time, Columbia Workshop* and *The Mercury Theatre on the Air.* He reprised Claghorn for TV's *Jackie Gleason Show* and provided voices for a number of animated cartoon shows.

155   *Lionel Stander:* The gravel-voiced character actor (1908-1994) made his first radio appearance in 1932 with Fred Allen. He was heard on *The Baby Snooks Show* and other programs. Stander was one of the highest paid supporting players in Hollywood when he was black-listed in 1939, after Columbia Pictures chieftain Harry Cohn branded him "a red sonuvabitch" for supporting unpopular liberal causes. He worked abroad for many years; his best known post-blacklist role was Max on TV's *Hart to Hart.*

156   *Orson Welles:* The actor-director first performed the *Les Miserables* spoof with Allen in 1942, recreating it four years later.

157   *George Jessel:* The vaudevillian who starred in the stage production of *The Jazz Singer* — but lost the role in the film version to Al Jolson — had several short-lived radio series.

158   *Beatrice Lillie:* The Canadian-born comedienne was best known for her London and New York stage revues and cabaret entertainments.

158   *Tallulah Bankhead*: The stage and film actress was heard as mistress of ceremonies on NBC's *The Big Show*, and was much in demand for guest appearances.

159   *Jimmy Wallington:* The announcer's other programs included *The Eddie Cantor Show* and *The Big Show*. He was preceded on Fred Allen's show by Harry Von Zell and Arthur Godfrey.

163   *Fred really did ad-lib:* "Fred with his writers furnished most of the material although now and then we of the Alley might ad-lib," recalled Parker Fennelly, who played the laconic New England farmer, Titus Moody. "Generally we stuck to what the writers furnished us. There was never any objection to these ab-libs as long as they fitted." (Letter to the author, Apr. 29, 1979). "One of the reasons Fred liked me was because I was able to ad-lib *with* him and get him back to the script," observed Lionel Stander. "You stick to the script in radio. If the star ad-libs, you ad-lib." (Interview with the author, Oct. 15, 1989.)

164   *Fred Allen-Jack Benny rivalry:* This long-running gimmick began in 1936 when Allen played host to a 10-year-old boy who, he claimed, could play the violin better than Benny.

169   *LSMFT:* "Lucky Strike [Benny's longtime sponsor] Means Fine Tobacco." The 1946 show described here — and the "King for a Day" sketch which ended with the comedian losing his pants — represented the culmination of the celebrated Allen-Benny feud.

171   *Our Miss Brooks:* The CBS sitcom starring Eve Arden aired on radio from 1947-1956; the TV version premiered in 1952.

172   *I Love Lucy:* Lucille Ball and Desi Arnaz made their television debut on *The Ed Wynn Show*. Their own show premiered October 15, 1951.

BOB SCHILLER
Schiller was interviewed February 4, 1992; and Feb. 23, 1995.

179   *measuring contest*: "It's an apocryphal story — a penile myth," noted Larry Gelbart. "There's an alternate version, where Milton Berle said, 'I'll take out just enough to beat you.' "

184   *He and his wife*: Gardner married New York stage and radio actress Simone Hegeman after his divorce from Shirley Booth.

185   *Stoopnagle and Budd*: The 1930s comedy team of Frederick Chase Taylor and Budd Hulick, who anticipated the oddball satire of Bob and Ray by two decades.

188   *Phil Cohan*: Also helped create *The Saturday Night Swing Club*.

189   *Danny Thomas*: The comedian supported Fanny Brice on *Maxwell House Coffee Time* before getting his own radio show circa 1944.

191   *Ezra Stone*: Best known for the role of Henry Aldrich in radio's *The Aldrich Family*.

191   *Ed Wynn*: The *Ziegfeld Follies* headliner was first lured to radio in 1922, a decade before his *Texaco Fire Chief* show premiered on NBC. He brought his buffoonery to live TV in 1949.

191   *Graham McNamee*: The one-time singer, who became a pioneer in sportscasting, was the most influential radio announcer of the 1920s.

192   *Dick Mack*: Directed *The Rudy Vallee Show*, *The Danny Kaye Show* and *The Martin and Lewis Show* for radio. His TV credits include *The Red Buttons Show*.

192   *The Red Buttons Show*: The comedy-variety series premiered Oct. 14, 1952 on CBS, changing time slots three times the first season.

194   *According to Steve Allen: The Funny Men* (Simon & Schuster, 1956).

196   *My Favorite Husband*: The CBS radio show, which made its debut in 1948, was based on characters in Isabel Rorick's novel, *Mr. and Mrs. Cugat*. The TV version premiered in 1953 on the same network.

196   *There were never any other writers*: Eddie Maxwell, longtime staff writer for Spike Jones, wrote songs for *I Love Lucy*.

198   *rewriting and rewriting*: "It's really fear, or hope, that you can get something better. We blame Norman Lear for that," says Schiller. "In later years, we talked to Norman, blamed him for rewriting all the

time. He said, 'We made it better, didn't we?' I said, 'No, we didn't. We just made it different. I don't know whether it was better or not, because we always did it your way.' "

201   *Cara Williams:* The comedienne had her own sitcom on CBS for one season, 1964-1965.

202   Seymour Berns: Directed *Art Linkletter's House Party* on radio and television. Other TV credits include *The Jack Benny Show* and *Gunsmoke.*

HAL KANTER
Kanter was interviewed by Randy Skretvedt and the author on December 5, 1990; and by the author April 20, 1995.

204   *Hellzapoppin:* Historian Anthony Slide has described the Olsen and Johnson show as "the ultimate in comic, low-brow vaudeville revues." Recalled Kanter: "I contributed a few topical jokes for each show. The other stuff I wrote, well, that didn't show up until they did their other shows and didn't tell me about it." (Christon, Lawrence, "Kanter's Life Is Still Full of Chuckles," *Los Angeles Times,* Mar. 15, 1994).

204   *Grand Central Station:* This dramatic anthology series premiered in 1937 on the Blue Network.

207   *I had never gone to NYU:* Kanter received his higher education at the Art Students League of New York, the Federal Art Project and the University of Kansas.

209   *Ted Lloyd*: Also produced *My True Story* and *Whispering Streets* for radio.

209   *Haym Salomon*: A Polish-born businessman who was one of the financiers of the American Revolutionary war.

210   *The George Gobel Show*: The comedy-variety show premiered Oct. 2, 1954 on CBS. The comic began his career as a boy singer on radio's *National Barn Dance.*

212   *Paul Monroe*: Also directed radio's *Crime Doctor.*

214   *Tom D'Andrea*: Best known as Gillis on TV's *Life of Riley.*

224   *others who came and went*: Joe Connolly and Bob Mosher, who went on to write *Leave It to Beaver,* were among the other writers on *Amos 'n' Andy.*

GEORGE BALZER

Balzer was interviewed February 12, 1992; and October 24, 1995.

235   *Balzer retired in 1971:* Since giving up golf he claims to have no particular hobbies, apart from overseeing his investments. He takes pride in the fact that his three children are all university graduates, and not one is a comedy writer.

236   *The Jack Benny Show:* Benny made his radio debut on *The Ed Sullivan Show* shortly before own show premiered on CBS, May 2, 1932; it ran for 23 years on radio, ending May 22, 1955.

236   *Andy Devine:* Best remembered for TV's *Wild Bill Hickok* and his own show, *Andy's Gang.*

237   *his wife Mary:* Mary Livingstone, *nee* Sadye Marks, played Benny's girlfriend on his radio show.

238   *Tommy Riggs and Betty Lou:* Riggs, whose impersonation of a little girl was often mistaken for a ventriloquism act, was a regular on Rudy Vallee's show before his own series began in 1938.

241   *Jack never forgot he had writers:* Hal Goldman and Al Gordon wrote in tandem for Benny for over 20 years, alongside Balzer and others, beginning in 1950.

242   *Irving Fein:* Personal manager for Benny and George Burns.

242   *Mel Blanc:* The inimitable voice of Bugs Bunny, Porky Pig and Daffy Duck was almost equally revered as the train conductor and other characters on Benny's radio and TV series. Other radio credits included *Burns and Allen, The Cisco Kid, The Abbott and Costello Show* and *Fibber McGee and Molly.*

243   *Mahlon Merrick:* Also supplied the music for such films as *The Girl From Monterey* and *Red Planet Mars.*

245   *The laugh ran 29 seconds:* Benny wrote a guest column for Hank Grant in *The Hollywood Reporter* (June 16, 1969), in which he observed there were at least 10 jokes that got bigger laughs than "Your money or your life?'" Recalls Balzer: "He proceeded to name the 10 jokes. Then he said, 'The biggest laugh my show ever got on radio, stage, screen or anywhere was...' — and he described the situation with Dorothy Kirsten, where Mary says, 'Oh, shut up.' He said, 'Now *that* is the biggest laugh I ever got.' "

245   *Your money or your life?:* The gag was first heard Mar. 28, 1948, then repeated the following week. It was later reprised on Benny's TV show.

245   *John Crosby:* The writer's highly complimentary review in the *New York Herald Tribune* was followed by a column which reprinted two pages from the show's script — "two of the funniest pages we had ever written," noted Milt Josefsberg — and described it as flat and contrived.

245   *Don Ameche:* Radio credits included *The First Nighter Program* (1930-1936), *The Edgar Bergen-Charlie McCarthy Show* and his own series.

246   *Don Wilson:* Benny's announcer and foil for 30 years also handled announcing duties for *The Baby Snooks Show, The Victor Borge Show* and *Kraft Music Hall;* his film credits included *Million Dollar Legs, Thank Your Lucky Stars* and *Niagara.*

246   *Frank Nelson:* The character actor (1911-1986) regularly antagonized Benny on radio and TV, often in the role of a salesman ("Yeeeeees?") He was also heard on *Blondie, The Eddie Cantor Show, Fibber McGee and Molly, Burns and Allen* and *Flywheel, Shyster and Flywheel.* TV credits included *I Love Lucy.*

248   *Phil Harris:* The singer-bandleader made his debut on the Benny show in 1936. He co-starred with wife, Alice Faye, on *The Fitch Bandwagon* (aka *The Phil Harris-Alice Faye Show),* which ran from 1948-1954.

250   *AFTRA:* American Federation of Television and Radio Artists, formerly AFRA in pre-TV days.

251   *I never had a disagreement:* "I heard rumors... Both Perrin and Balzer had increasingly frequent flare-ups with Jack that led to periods of open hostility where they didn't talk to each other," Milt Josefsberg asserted in *The Jack Benny Show* (Arlington House, 1977). He also claimed that Perrin and Balzer eventually confirmed the rumors.

252   *both the radio and television shows:* Benny appeared concurrently in both mediums for five years after making his TV debut on Oct. 28, 1950. His weekly television show was canceled by NBC in 1965.

252   *Are You With It?:* The 1948 film version of Perrin and Balzer's musical comedy starred Donald O'Connor. "We started a couple of other plays," recalls Balzer, "but we were very busy with Benny."

253   *one gag about a Dr. Ballzer:* As Milt Josefsberg recalled: "We had Jack going for a medical examination and walking down a long hallway in a building... as he passed each doorway he read off the medical men's names and specialties: 'Let's see... Dr. Eyman, Eye Doctor... Dr. Earlich, Ear Doctor... Dr. Footer, Foot Doctor... Dr. *Ballzer*????' "

       SOL SAKS
       Saks was interviewed January 29, 1992.

256   *Mr. Adams and Eve:* The series ran from 1957-1958 on CBS. Many episodes were reportedly based on situations in the stars' lives.

257   *Wings of Destiny:* The adventure drama was broadcast on NBC from 1940-1942 and sponsored by Wings Cigarettes.

259   *Uncle Walter's Doghouse:* The show aired on NBC from 1939-1942.

       Radio Writers Guild: The union was formed in 1947 — the year the blacklist began. It was dissolved when the Writers Guild of America was created in 1954 as a collective bargaining force for radio, TV and film writers.

262   *Marvin Miller:* The actor-announcer (1913-1985) appeared on *The Romance of Helen Trent, The First Nighter Program, The Whistler, Duffy's Tavern* and countless other radio shows — as many as 40 a week at one point. He was later seen on TV's *The Millionaire.*

269   *Florence Halop:* The actress (1923-1986) appeared on *Coast-to-Coast on a Bus,* at the age of five, alongside her brother Billy. In addition to Miss Duffy, she was heard as Hotbreath Houlihan on *The Jimmy Durante Show.* Decades later she had regular roles on TV's *St. Elsewhere* and *Night Court* (replacing Selma Diamond).

272   *Hanley Stafford:* The English-born actor (1900-1968) was also heard as Mr. Dithers on *Blondie.* Other radio credits included *Fu Manchu, Tarzan, John's Other Wife* and *The Cinnamon Bear.*

277   *Don Sharpe:* Lucille Ball's agent was also producer of radio's *Richard Diamond, Private Detective* and creator of *The Screen Director's Playhouse.*

       LARRY GELBART
       Gelbart was interviewed Mar. 26, 1992; and Mar. 1, 1995.

285   *Burt Shevelove*: Long before he recruited Gelbart to co-author a musical comedy based on the work on Plautus, Shevelove directed *The Red Buttons Show*, where they first met.

285   *M*A*S*H*: The show premiered September 17, 1972, and ran 11 seasons; Gelbart departed after the first four.

285   *Tootsie:* Don McGuire and Murray Schisgal, earlier writers on the project, shared credit with Gelbart; Elaine May was one of several uncredited writers.

285   *United States:* This show, based largely on Gelbart's enduring marriage to former actress Pat Marshall, has been described as "Ingmar Bergman with laughs." It premiered March 11, 1980; despite a cult following, NBC pulled the plug in a matter of weeks.

288   *Sandra Gould*: Best known as Miss Duffy on *Duffy's Tavern* and Mrs. Kravitz on *Bewitched* (replacing Alice Pearce). Also heard on radio's *A Date With Judy, The Sad Sack* and *The Life of Riley*. Film credits include *June Bride, The Clown* with Red Skelton, *Teacher's Pet* and *The Ghost and Mr. Chicken*.

294   *The Jack Paar Show:* Debuted June 1, 1947. John Dunning described the show as "a high-class, first-rate production that went absolutely nowhere."

295   *The Jack Carson Show:* The film comedian's 1943-1947 CBS show evolved from an earlier program he hosted called *The Signal Carnival.*

305   *Caesar's Hour:* The successor to *Your Show of Shows* — TV's most influential comedy-variety program — premiered September 27, 1954 on NBC, and ran three seasons.

308   *Max Liebman*: The Austrian-born writer-producer (1902-1981) began his career in American vaudeville. Liebman helped launch the careers of Danny Kaye and Imogene Coca with *The Straw Hat Revue,* and contributed to Kaye's early films. He put together *Tars and Spars,* the wartime Coast Guard revue that introduced Sid Caesar, before producing *Your Show of Shows.*

Bibliography

Adamson, Joe. *Groucho, Harpo, Chico and Sometimes Zeppo.* New York: Simon & Schuster, 1973.

Allen, Fred. *Treadmill to Oblivion.* Boston: Little Brown & Co., 1954.

Allen, Steve. *The Funny Men.* New York: Simon & Schuster, 1956.

Brooks, Tim, and Earle Marsh. *The Complete Directory to Prime Time Network TV Shows, 1946-Present.* New York: Ballantine, 1985.

Burns, George. *Living It Up.* New York: Putnam, 1976.

Burns, George, with David Fisher. *All My Best Friends.* New York: Putnam, 1989.

Burrows, Abe. *Honest, Abe.* Boston: Little, Brown & Co., 1980.

Buxton, Frank, and Bill Owen. *The Big Broadcast 1920-1950.* New York: Viking Press, 1972.

Carroll, Carroll. *None of Your Business.* New York: Cowles, 1970.

Carskadon, Tom. "Gagging Their Way Through Life." *Radioland,* Sept. 1933.

Christon, Lawrence. "Hal Kanter's Life Is Still Full of Chuckles." *The Los Angeles Times,* Mar. 15, 1994.

DeLong, Thomas A. *Radio Stars.* Jefferson, NC: McFarland & Co., 1996.

Dunning, John. *On the Air: The Encyclopedia of Old Time Radio.* New York: Oxford University Press, 1998.

Feld, Bruce, "Larry Gelbart: A Lot of Funny Things Happened After the Forum." *Drama-Logue,* Jun. 22, 1989.

Gallo, Clifford. "Larry Gelbart: The Entertainer." *Los Angeles Reader,* Feb. 28, 1992.

Gelbart, Larry. *Laughing Matters.* New York: Random House, 1998.

Goldman, Herbert G. *Fanny Brice: The Original Funny Girl.* New York: Oxford University Press, 1992.

Hope, Bob, and Melville Shavelson. *Don't Shoot, It's Only Me.* New York: Putnam, 1990.

Isaacs, Charles. "Jimmy Durante: The Man Behind the Schnozz." *Remember,* Dec. 1994-Jan. 1995.

Josefsberg, Milt. *The Jack Benny Show.* New Rochelle, N.Y.: Arlington House, 1977.

Josefsberg, Milt. *Comedy Writing for Television and Hollywood.* New York: Harper & Row, 1987.

Klein, Woody, "Parke Levy: He Made a Saint Out of Mother-in-Law," *World Telegram and Sun,* June 8, 1957.

Kuntz, Jonathan. "Norman Panama and Melvin Frank." In *American Screenwriters.* Ed. Robert E. Morsberger, et. al. Detroit: Gale Research Co., 1984.

Maltin, Leonard. *The Great American Broadcast: A Celebration of Radio's Golden Age.* New York: Dutton, 1997.

Marx, Arthur. *Red Skelton.* New York: Dutton, 1979.

Oppenheimer, Jess, with Gregg Oppenheimer. *Laughs, Luck... and Lucy.* Syracuse, N.Y.: Syracuse University Press, 1996.

Panama, Norman, and Melvin Frank. "25 Years of Togetherness," *The Los Angeles Times,* Jul. 26, 1964.

Saks, Sol. *Funny Business: The Craft of Comedy Writing.* Los Angeles: Lone Eagle Publishing Co., 1991.

Sennett, Ted. *Your Show of Shows.* New York: Macmillan, 1977.

Server, Lee. "Irving Brecher." In his *Screenwriter: Words Become Pictures.* Pittstown, NJ: Main Street Press, 1987.

Slide, Anthony. *The Encyclopedia of Vaudeville.* Westport, CT: Greenwood Press, 1994.

Stumpf, Charles, and Tom Price, *Heavenly Days! The Story of Fibber McGee and Molly.* Waynesville, NC: World of Yesterday, 1987.

Wertheim, Arthur Frank. *Radio Comedy.* New York: Oxford University Press, 1979.

Whitney, Dwight. "Paul Henning: For Him... The Corn is Golden," *TV Guide,* May 1963.

Wilde, Larry. *How the Great Comedy Writers Create Laughter.* Chicago: Nelson-Hall, 1976.

Wilk, Max. *The Golden Age of Television: Notes from the Survivors.* New York: Delta, 1977.

Winer, Laurie, "Larry Gelbart: A Lot of Funny Things Have Happened." *The Los Angeles Times,* Jan. 1, 1997.

Index